THE PACATNAMU PAPERS

THE PACATNAMU PAPERS
Volume 1

Edited by
Christopher B. Donnan
Guillermo A. Cock

Museum of Cultural History
University of California, Los Angeles

This publication was supported by funding from the
National Endowment for the Humanities, The Ahmanson
Foundation, The Ethnic Arts Council of Los Angeles, and
Manus, the support group of the Museum of Cultural
History.

International Standard Book Number 0-930741-14-5 (Hardcover)
0-930741-11-0 (Softcover)
Library of Congress Catalog Card Number: 86-061112

Museum of Cultural History
University of California, Los Angeles
405 Hilgard Avenue
Los Angeles, California 90024

Printed in the United States of America.

Table of Contents

Preface

In 1983, the Museum of Cultural History at the University of California, Los Angeles, signed a formal agreement with the Instituto Nacional de Cultura in Peru to develop a five-year, archaeological research project at Pacatnamu, a spectacular ancient city located on the North Coast of Peru. As part of the Museum of Cultural History's commitment to the Pacatnamu Project, a series of publications was planned to provide a means of disseminating the results of the research in a timely fashion. This volume is the first publication in that series, which is titled *The Pacatnamu Papers*. The first volume is dedicated to Don Oscar Lostaunau in recognition of his efforts to preserve the archaeological and historical monuments of the Jequetepeque Valley, his invaluable assistance to archaeologists and historians who have worked on the North Coast of Peru, and his fondness for the site of Pacatnamu.

Publishing findings while research is still under way has certain inherent limitations. Foremost among these is the fact that the reports must be seen as preliminary—subject to changing interpretations as more data become available. Nevertheless, we feel that the advantages of publishing a series in this manner far outweigh the disadvantages. First, the long delay that normally occurs between the end of a multiyear research program and the systematic publication of its results is avoided. Also, there is the opportunity for the project to receive feedback from readers concerning aspects of the research that may need further investigation, or ideas for entirely new avenues of research that would be particularly enlightening. With the project still underway, it is possible to implement these suggestions. It is also anticipated that this series of publications will illustrate the evolution of the research and its interpretation. This in itself may be of value to future scholars who wish to understand how the final synthesis was achieved—a synthesis that as of this date is still unformulated. Having the opportunity to examine the evidence and interpretations as well as to follow the sequence in which they were achieved should enable future researchers to more accurately evaluate the results.

Publishing the results of the Pacatnamu research together rather than having it disseminated in diverse professional journals should make it much easier for readers to get access to the information. It should also demonstrate how various aspects of the research are interrelated and underscore the advantages of the project's multidisciplinary approach.

From the outset *The Pacatnamu Papers* was conceived as a bilingual publication series, with reports in both English and Spanish, each accompanied by a summary in the other language. The Museum of Cultural History feels strongly that the results of the Pacatnamu Project must be made readily available to the people of Latin America, for it is their cultural heritage that is the focus of the research.

The Museum takes pride in its role in the Pacatnamu Project, and is pleased to inaugurate the *The Pacatnamu Papers* with the publication of this volume.

Acknowledgments

The Pacatnamu Project is made possible by the generous support of various institutions and individuals, and it is a pleasure to have this opportunity to acknowledge their assistance.

Primary funding for the project is provided by the National Geographic Society and the National Endowment for the Humanities. This has been generously augmented by support from the Ahmanson Foundation and the Ethnic Arts Council of Los Angeles.

Of critical importance at the inception of the Pacatnamu Project, and continuously through the last three years, has been the support, both financial and spiritual, of ten very special people: Wendy and Ross Cabeen, Geraldine Clift, Lloyd Cotzen, Joan and Jack Hoch, Debbie and Jay Last, and Ann and Bill Lucas.

The Pacatnamu Project involves a formal convenio between the Instituto Nacional de Cultura in Lima and the Museum of Cultural History at the University of California, Los Angeles. We are very grateful to Lila de Cueto Fernandini and Jose Antonio del Busto, former directors of the Instituto Nacional de Cultura, and Elwin Svenson on behalf of the University of California, for their support in making the convenio possible.

The office of the Instituto Nacional de Cultura in Trujillo has been very helpful in supervising the field excavation and providing facilities for the permanent storage of the Pacatnamu collections. We are particulary grateful for the assistance of Cristobal Campana, Ricardo Morales, Ana Maria Hoyle, Daisy Barreto, and Carlos Deza.

The project has benefited in many ways by the hospitality and friendship of the people in the town of Guadalupe. In particular, we are grateful for the assistance of Oscar Lostaunau and his brother Luis Lostaunau.

Ramiro Matos, Amalia Castelli, Franklin Pease, and Maria Rostworowski have been very supportive of the Pacatnamu Project since its initial planning and have continued to provide advice and assistance. The same is true of Werner Haeberle, Donna McClelland, Betty Meggers, Franklin Murphy, and Gene Sterud, each of whom has taken a personal interest in the development and continuation of the research.

The staff of the UCLA Museum of Cultural History has been very supportive of the Pacatnamu Project. Of particular importance was the assistance of Doran H. Ross, Millicent Besser, Barbara Underwood, and Benita Johnson.

Preparation of this publication has been assisted by Robert Woolard, Irina Averkieff, Mary E. Doyle, Richard Todd, Phillip M. Douglas, and Giselle Flores. Particular recognition must be made of the contribution of Geraldine Clift. She patiently edited multiple versions of each of the individual papers. Her skill, her commitment, her wise counsel, and her charm have been critical in the production of this volume.

Christopher B. Donnan
Guillermo A. Cock

Dedicated to Don Oscar Lostaunau.

Pacatnamu, July, 1984.

Don Oscar Lostaunau

Duccio Bonavia

I met Oscar Lostaunau nearly thirty years ago, in 1958. I was still a student then, and as part of my first archaeological field experience, I was traveling to Piura with David Kelley. Oscar was waiting for us in Guadalupe's Lafora Hospital, where he worked, and he gave us a very warm and friendly reception. I clearly recall his diminutive stature, plump shape, his round face, lively eyes, curly white hair, and his happy smile.

We stayed in Guadalupe several days, visiting the ruins of the region. Pacatnamu impressed me. It was the second time I had been to that monumental complex. I had been there in 1953, and I was surprised that in the five years that had passed, there had apparently been no clandestine excavations. The same was true at the other archaeological sites in the region. For us, this different situation seemed incredible.

We had been traveling by land from Lima, visiting the principal archaeological sites. The abandoned state of the sites and depredation by the looters had not only affected the remote sites and cemeteries, but also the important and famous archaeological monuments. We had been in Paramonga and Chan Chan, and found that not even those sites had escaped the looters' activities. In contrast, this was not the case in the Pacasmayo area. At night, under the trees of the Plaza de Armas in Guadalupe or in Oscar's house, we spoke at length about the problem of looting and general disregard for the preservation of Peru's archaeological sites. It was then that I learned the truth. Oscar Lostaunau had created a system of keeping the archaeological patrimony of his area protected by educating the authorities and the local communities. Surprised and full of admiration, that same year I published an article in Lima's newspaper, *El Comercio*, dedicated to Lostaunau and his work (Bonavia 1958). This was my first newspaper article.

More than a quarter of a century has passed since then and the great admiration of 1958 has turned into an unbreakable friendship. Now, I have been asked to write a few lines in honor of this old and dear friend. The task is difficult. When friendship of this nature is involved, there is always the fear that the praise will be misunderstood and that the pen might get carried away with those feelings. Besides, the memories resurface and one does not know where to begin. Thousands of images are brought to mind and each one has its story to tell. There is Morrope with its shell mounds, Nanchoc which today is becoming famous and that Oscar showed us in great detail back then. Then there is La Calera de Talambo, Moro, and the other sites in the Jequetepeque Valley, and Zana with its Colonial ruins. There are so many memories. . . . But I think that all things considered, anything that is said about Oscar will always be too little in comparison with what he has done.

Oscar Lostaunau is not a professional archaeologist. His French ancestry goes back to the beginning of the Colonial Period, and he dedicated a large part of his life to hospital work. But he dedicated his free time to other activities, primarily archaeology, which was always his great love. Actually, for a long time he has been inspector ad honorem of the different bureaucratic organizations that over time have been in charge of preserving Peru's patrimony.

This not only led him to survey carefully all of the archaeological sites, but also to register them on a map and establish their boundaries. In that way he has become the person who best knows the archaeology of the Jequetepeque region. While he has not published extensively, without hesitation or egoism he has shared this knowledge with everyone who has needed it. There is not an archaeologist who has worked on the North Coast who doesn't know Oscar and who doesn't owe some debt of gratitude to him.

He can be proud of having guided and worked with the most famous archaeologists who have had interest in Peruvian archaeology: from Kosok, Schaedel, Ubbelohde-Doering, Disselhoff, Izumi, and Muelle to the younger generations of Hecker, Keatinge, Conrad, Donnan, and many others.

His help has always been in many forms— from finding housing and workers, to organization, equipment, the location of sites, and even physical help. His jovial nature is always present, always ready to raise everyone's spirits, faced with any difficulty. I've never seen him pessimistic. His altruistic spirit is admirable.

He has never been reluctant to share his notes and photographs when someone has needed them and he offers them with the same naturalness and happiness with which he toasts his good Guadalupe clarito on the long nights of talks and discussions about subjects of mutual interest.

I am one of the people who has had the good fortune of knowing Oscar closely. Together we have walked a lot under the hot northern sun, in the desert, in the cotton fields, in the wet soil of the rice fields, on hard rocks and soft sand. I've learned a lot from him about archaeology and about life. My books about mural paintings (1974, 1985) owe a lot to him because he was able to save evidence that otherwise would have been lost.

Oscar Lostaunau forms part of that category of individuals that unfortunately is disappearing: those who feel that life is a task but that the result belongs to everyone. Of those people who make Peru, in shadows and in silence, without asking anything and who feel satisfied with having given everything. Of those self-educated people, who without ever having set foot in a university, do science in a serious and honest form, without calling attention to themselves, without pretensions, without looking for publicity, with affection and great humility.

Today, retired from public life and with the constant danger of a heart attack, Don Oscar, as he is affectionately called in the North, continues to help and cooperate. He is the supervisor, advisor, and friend of the project that Donnan and Cock direct at Pacatnamu. Work is his philosophy and that work is probably what has permitted him to continue living. But Oscar must also feel a great spiritual tranquility, knowing that the job that life gave him has been satisfactorily accomplished and in the best of ways. For me it is an honor to express these feelings in a public form, because friendships like that with Oscar can only make one proud. They give us a purpose to life and in the moments of crisis, make us continue the marked path, even when great doubts arise along the way.

After more than thirty years dedicated to Peruvian archaeology, I think I have the right to speak for all of us and in everyone's name say: Thank you very much, Oscar. You have our profound gratitude, our affection, our admiration and our desire that the pre-Hispanic gods keep you for a long time so that your wise advice will continue to enrich us.

RESUMEN:
Don Oscar Lostaunau

Conocí hace muchos años a Oscar Lostaunau. Corría el año 1958. Yo era aun estudiante y esa era mi primera práctica de campo. Viajaba con David Kelly rumbo a Piura.

Oscar nos esperaba en el hospital Lafora de Guadalupe, donde trabajaba, y nos acogió afablemente. Recuerdo claramente su figura baja y regordeta, su cara redonda, sus ojos vivos, el pelo blanco ensortijado y una sonrisa alegre en su boca.

Nos quedamos en Guadalupe varios días recorriendo las ruinas de la región. Me impresionó Pacatnamú. Era la segunda vez que llegaba a ese conjunto monumental, había estado allí en 1953. Me quedé asombrado cuando pude comprobar que en los cinco años que habían transcurrido, no se veían huellas de excavaciones clandestinas. Y lo mismo pude comprobar en los otros sitios arqueológicos de la comarca.

Para nosotros, que veníamos viajando por tierra desde Lima, visitando los principales sitios arqueológicos, esta realidad tan diversa parecía increíble. El abandono y la depredación de los huaqueros no habían afectado solo los sitios alejados o los cementerios perdidos, sino también a los yacimientos importantes y famosos. Habíamos estado en Paramonga, en Chan Chan, donde comprobamos que ni siquiera esos conjuntos se habían librado de la acción vandálica. Eso no se veía en el área de Pacasmayo. En las noches, bajo los árboles de la Plaza de Armas de Guadalupe, o en la casa de Oscar, conversamos largamente sobre este asunto y allí conocí la verdad. Oscar Lostaunau había ideado un sistema, basado en la educación de las autoridades y de las comunidades indígenas, por medio del cual era posible mantener protegido el patrimonio arqueológico. Asombrado y lleno de admiración, publiqué ese mismo año un artículo en El Comercio de Lima *dedicado a Lostaunau y a su obra (1958). Fue mi primer artículo periodístico.*

Ha pasado más de un cuarto de siglo, desde entonces, y la gran admiración de 1958 se ha convertido en una inquebrantable amistad. Hoy se me pide escribir unas líneas en honor de este viejo y querido amigo. La tarea es difícil. Cuando hay de por medio una amistad de esta naturaleza, existe siempre el temor que el elogio sea mal interpretado y que la pluma se deje llevar por los sentimientos. Además, renacen los recuerdos y no se sabe por donde empezar. Regresan a mi memoria miles de imágenes y cada cual tiene su historia que contar. Están allí Mórrope con sus conchales, Nanchoc, que hoy se está volviendo famoso y que Oscar nos enseñó palmo a palmo en aquel entonces, La Calera de Talambo donde, sin quererlo y en forma totalmente inesperada, nos vimos envueltos en una asonada campesina y solo el prestigio de Oscar nos salvó de una situación difícil, y Moro y los tantos sitios del valle del Jequetepeque y el de Zaña con sus ruinas coloniales. En fin, son tantos los recuerdos . . . Pero pienso que, a pesar de todo, cualquier cosa que se diga de Oscar será siempre poco en comparación con lo que ha hecho.

Oscar Lostaunau no es un arqueólogo profesional. Su origen francés se pierde en los albores de la colonia, y gran parte de su vida la dedicó a la práctica hospitalaria. Pero sus horas libres las empleaba en otras actividades, fundamentalmente a la arqueología, de la que ha sido siempre un enamorado. En efecto, durante mucho tiempo ha sido inspector ad-honorem de los diferentes organismos burocráticos que, con el pasar del tiempo, han tenido a su cargo la defensa del patrimonio monumental.

Esto lo llevó no sólo a reconocer cuidadosamente todos los conjuntos arqueológicos, sino a ubicarlos en el mapa y delimitarlos. De modo que él se ha convertido en la persona que más conoce esa región, desde el punto de vista arqueológico, y si bien ha publicado poco, él ha entregado su conocimiento sin reticencias ni egoismo a cuantos lo han necesitado. No hay arqueólogo que haya trabajado en la Costa Norte que no conozca a Oscar y no tenga alguna deuda de gratitud con él.

El puede estar orgulloso de haber guiado y haber trabajado con los más renombrados arqueólogos que han tenido interés en la arqueología peruana. Desde Kosok, Schaedel, Ubbelohde-Doering, Disselhoff, Izumi y Muelle, hasta las jovenes generaciones de los Hecker, Keatinge, Conrad, Donnan y tantos otros.

Y su ayuda ha sido siempre multiple. Desde conseguir facilidades de alojamiento, hasta la mano de obra, la organización, el equipo, la ubicación de los sitios, e inclusive, la ayuda física. Su carácter jovial estaba siempre presente, siempre presto a levantar el ánimo frente a cualquier dificultad. Nunca lo he conocido pesimista. Su espíritu altruista es de un desprendimiento admirable. Nunca ha escatimado sus notas y sus fotografías cuando alguien las ha necesitado, y las ofrece con la misma naturalidad y alegría con la que brinda su buen clarito guadalupano en las largas noches de charlas y discusiones sobre temas de interés común.

Soy uno de los que han tenido la suerte de conocer muy de cerca a Oscar. Juntos hemos caminado mucho bajo el sol abrasador norteño, en el desierto, entre los algodonales, o en las tierras húmedas de los arrozales. Sobre la dura piedra o la arena blanca. Puedo decir que mucho he aprendido de él. Sobre la arqueología y sobre la vida. Mi libro sobre pinturas murales (1974 y 1985) le debe mucho, pues él llegó a salvar evidencias que de otra manera se hubieran perdido.

Puedo afirmar que Oscar Lostaunau forma parte de esa categoría de hombres que desafortunadamente se está perdiendo. De aquellos que sienten que la vida es una tarea, pero que el resultado es de todos. De aquellos hombres que hacen Patria a la sombra y en el silencio, sin pedir nada, y que se sienten satisfechos con haber entregado todo. De aquellos autodidactas que sin haber pisado nunca una universidad, hacen ciencia en forma seria y honesta. Sin alborotos, sin pretensiones, sin buscar publicidad, con cariño y con gran humildad.

Hoy, retirado de la vida pública, con el constante peligro de un infarto, Don Oscar, como se le llama cariñosamente en el Norte, sigue ayudando y cooperando. Es el supervisor, asesor y el amigo del proyecto que dirigen Donnan y Cock en Pacatnamú. Y es que su filosofía es el trabajo, y es éste, probablemente, el que le ha permitido seguir viviendo. Pero también porque Oscar debe sentir una gran tranquilidad espiritual, al saber que la tarea que le encargó la vida ha sido cumplida satisfactoriamente y en la mejor de las maneras.

Es, para mí, un honor poder dejar expresados estos sentimientos en forma pública, porque amistades como la de Oscar solo pueden enorgullecer. Ellas le dan un sentido a la vida y, en los momentos de crisis, nos hacen seguir el camino trazado, incluso cuando surgen grandes dudas en el camino.

Después de más de treinta años dedicados plenamente a la arqueología peruana, pienso que tengo el derecho de tomar su palabra y, en su nombre, decir: muchas gracias Oscar. *Y en ello va incluido todo nuestro agradecimiento, nuestro afecto, nuestra admiración y nuestro deseo que los dioses prehispánicos te conserven por mucho tiempo, para que sigas brindando consejos llenos de sabiduría.*

Vita of Don Oscar Lostaunau
Luis Lostaunau

—Born in Guadalupe (Pacasmayo Province) February 15, 1922.

—Primary and secondary schooling in Guadalupe (1931-1942).

—Pharmacy technician, chemical-bacteriological laboratory technician, X-ray technician, Lafora Hospital, Guadalupe. Administrative Director of the same hospital (1942-1965).

—Founder of the Sociedad Amantes del Progreso Cultural.

—Founder of the Francisco Pérez de Lescano Library in Guadalupe.

—President of the Junta Administrativa de Ejecución de Obras del IV Centenario de la Fundación de Guadalupe (1964-1969).

—Mayor of the town of Guadalupe (1973-1977).

—Inspector "ad honorem" of Archaeology, Jequetepeque Valley (1952).

—Member of the Patronato Departamental de Arqueología de la Libertad (1953).

—Member, acting as Archaeological Inspector, of the Dirección de Cultura, Arqueología e Historia of the Ministry of Public Education (1958).

—Inspector of Archaeological Monuments of the Departments of Piura, Tumbes, and Amazonas, Ministry of Education (1963).

—Inspector "ad honorem" in Archaeological Affairs for the 2nd Jusgado de Instrucción of Pacasmayo Province (1967).

—Delegate of the Consejo Superior de Cultura before the Patronato de Ciencias Sociales of the University of Trujillo (1967).

—Inspector of Archaeological Monuments of the Jequetepeque Valley for the National Institute of Culture (INC) (1969-present).

—Executive President of the Committee for Restoration of the Colonial Architectural Complex (Monastery) of San Agustín in Guadalupe (1970).

—Conservator of the Centro Zonal de Pacatnamú y Jequetepeque for the National Institute of Culture (1972-present).

—Member of the Centro de Estudios Arqueológicos of Lambayeque (Chiclayo).

—Member of the Centro de Estudios Históricos y Sociales "Baltazar Jaime Martínez de Compañón y Bujanda" (Trujillo).

Participation in Professional Meetings

—II Congreso Nacional de Historia del Perú (Lima, 1958).

—Congreso Nor-peruano de Arqueología (Chiclayo, 1963).

—Simposio de Arqueología de Lambayeque (Chiclayo, 1967).

—II Congreso de Hombre y la Cultura Andina (Trujillo, 1974).

—Mesa Redonda sobre la problemática Arqueológica del Norte del Perú (Chiquitoy, 1975).

—Seminario del Patrimonio Arqueológico (Huampani, 1974).

—Simposio Algodón del Perú y artesanía textil: un esfuerzo de recompensación de tecnología nativa (Lima, 1985).

Advisor

1949	Paul Kosok (Long Island University, New York).
1951	Richard P. Schaedel (Universidad de Trujillo).
1953	Berlin Museum.
1954-58	Berlin Museum, Tokyo University.
1958	Munich Ethnographic Museum.
1959	Expedición Arqueológica Italo-Peruana.
1962	Munich Ethnographic Museum.
1968-69	Universidad de Trujillo.
1973-74	Richard P. Schaedel (University of Texas).
1975	Richard Keatinge (Columbia University, New York).
1977	Herbert Eling (University of Texas).
1978	David Chodoff (Columbia University, New York).
1979	John Hyslop (Institute of Andean Research, New York).
1980	Richard Keatinge (Columbia University, New York), Geoffrey W. Conrad (Harvard University).
1980	University of Munich.
1981	Instituto Arqueológico Aleman (Bonn).
1982-83	James M. Vreeland (University of Texas)
1983-85	Christopher B. Donnan (University of California, Los Angeles), Guillermo A. Cock (Universidad Catolica, Lima).

Unpublished Manuscripts

Proyecto de defensa de monumentos arqueológicos.

Campos funerarios, tumbas y posiciones cadavéricas en las épocas prehispánicas, en el valle de Jequetepeque.

Mapa arqueológico del Valle de Jequetepeque.

Apuntes sobre sistemas de riego y almacenamiento y uso de tierra en la época prehispánica.

Análisis descriptivo del material del Museo de Arte Religioso de Nuestra Señora de Guadalupe en el Antiguo Convento de San Agustín.

Observaciones y Estudios Arqueológicos en torno al Cultivo y Manejo de Plaga Algodonera en la Epoca Prehispánca Tardía del Valle de Jequetepeque.

Publications

1952a	"Seis puntos sobre pre-historia de la Provincia de Pacasmayo." *La Unión*, Pacasmayo 12 abril, No. 11, 6 III.
1952b	"Antigua red de irrigación en la Provincia de Pacasmayo." *La Unión*, Pacasmayo, 28 de julio.
1955	"La Zona arqueológica de Jequetepeque," *Chimor* (Boletin del Museo de Arqueología de la Universidad de Trujillo), Año III, No. 1, pp 4-9.
1982a	"Por que se destruyen los monumentos arqueológicos." *Ultimas Noticias*, Pacasmayo, 6 de agosto.
1982b	"El distrito arqueológico de Chepén." *La Palabra*, Chepén 28 diciembre, Nos. 2 y 4.

The Pacatnamu Papers
Volume 1

Introduction

Christopher B. Donnan

Pacatnamu is a uniquely important archaeological site, located at the mouth of the Jequetepeque Valley on the North Coast of Peru (Figs. 1,2). Ringed by precipitous cliffs on two sides and guarded by high city walls on the third, it is one of ancient Peru's most spectacular yet least explored archaeological sites (Fig. 3). The core of the sprawling architectural complex has an area of approximately one square kilometer. It is dominated by more than fifty truncated pyramids that support elaborate summit structures and sanctuaries. Flanking the mud brick pyramids are attendant complexes of spacious courts, corridors, and elite quarters, and cemeteries are scattered inside and outside the city's perimeter walls. Because of the arid climate and Pacatnamu's location high above the valley floor, archaeological preservation is extraordinary. Walls often stand to nearly their original height, painted facades survive, and elaborate tombs preserve their full contents—coffins of cane, gourd and ceramic vessels, jewelry, and exquisitely woven garments, which comprise the largest collection of ornate textiles ever discovered in northern Peru. Thus, Pacatnamu offers "laboratory conditions" for a study of the art, architecture, and population of a major religious center, shaped by the dynamics of local development and foreign conquest.

Previous Research

Although Pacatnamu was mentioned by various explorers (e.g., Hutchinson 1873; Middendorf 1894), it was not studied in detail until 1925. At that time, Kroeber made a sketch map of several mounds in the central portion of the site and recorded some observations about the architecture (1930:88-89). Subsequently, the site was mentioned sporadically in the archaeological literature (Garcia Rosell 1942:123-124; Schaedel 1951:235; Ishida et al. 1960:435; Kosok 1965:123). Archaeological excavations at Pacatnamu were first conducted in 1937-1939 by the German archaeologist, Ubbelohde-Doering. He continued his excavations there in 1952-1953 and 1962-1963. Ubbelohde-Doering's work resulted in the partial excavation of two of the more than fifty pyramid complexes. In the process, he uncovered numerous tombs containing remarkable material, including textiles, basketry, cordage, leather, and plant remains. The human remains were exceedingly well preserved—some of the bodies were mummified and in some cases tattoos were still visible (Ubbelohde-Doering 1959, 1967; Keatinge 1978; Hecker and Hecker 1985).

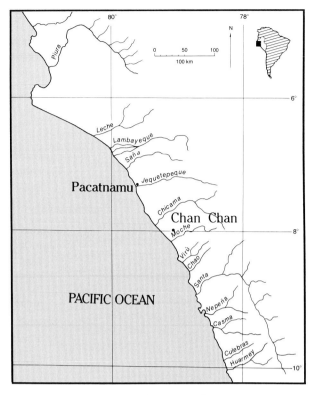

Figure 1.   Map of the North Coast of Peru.

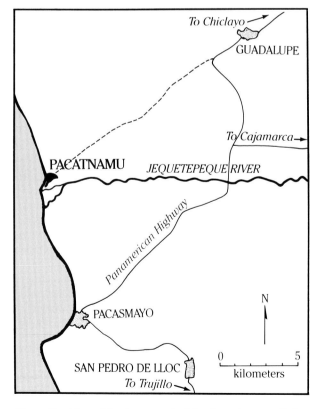

Figure 2.   Map of the lower part of the Jequetepeque Valley.

Wolfgang and Giesela Hecker accompanied Ubbelohde-Doering on his 1962-1963 expedition to Pacatnamu. They produced a general map of the site as well as maps of some of the major architectural features (Hecker and Hecker 1977, 1982, 1985).[1] Although these maps are useful, most were drawn without excavation of the architecture, and thus are not as accurate or detailed as maps made after partial clearing.

Richard Keatinge conducted an extensive surface survey of Pacatnamu in 1974, and subsequently published several brief reports on his findings (Keatinge et al. 1975; Keatinge 1977, 1982).

The Pacatnamu Project

In February 1983, the Instituto Nacional de Cultura in Lima formally approved a request by the Museum of Cultural History at the University of California, Los Angeles, for a five-year excavation permit at Pacatnamu. This was to be a multidisciplinary research effort, combining archaeological excavation with physical anthropology, botany, zoology, textile analysis, ethnography, and ethnohistory.

During the first three field seasons, which took place between June and September in 1983, 1984, and 1985, Pacatnamu was systematically surveyed, portions of it were surface collected, and excavations of various architectural features were completed. This work was very successful, producing abundant artifacts with excellent associations that provided valuable insights into the nature of the people who inhabited this spectacular site.

Considerable effort was focused on developing a chronology of the ancient occupation. This began with an analysis of the ceramics, which demonstrated that Pacatnamu had essentially two periods of occupation—an early period when Moche ceramics were in use, and a later period characterized by the use of Chimu ceramics.

A seriation of the mud bricks used to construct the architecture at Pacatnamu subsequently provided a four-phase chronological sequence that correlated with the Moche and Chimu occupations. This sequence has made it possible not only to identify Moche and Chimu architecture, but also to distinguish early from late construction within each of these periods.

The chronology based on ceramic and brick

---

1. The Heckers assigned numbers and letters to most of the architectural features at Pacatnamu. In almost all instances we have followed their designations.

Figure 3.   Air photo of Pacatnamu. Courtesy of Servicio Aerofotográfico Nacional, Lima.

seriation was augmented by chronologies based on controlled stratigraphic excavations, as well as a seriation of textiles and burial types. Radiocarbon determinations also support the chronology and permit the assignment of absolute dates to the periods of occupation.

Although the chronology is subject to change and refinement as more evidence is uncovered, our present information provides a consistent picture. It appears that Pacatnamu was unoccupied before the end of Moche IV or the beginning of Moche V (ca. A.D. 600). During the Moche occupation some ceremonial architecture was constructed, largely in the central portion of the site. Moche refuse was widely dispersed in this area and in some scattered areas to the north, but its distribution was considerably smaller than the spread of Chimu refuse during the later occupation. Although some relatively high-status Moche burials have been excavated at Pacatnamu (Ubbelohde-Doering 1967; Hecker and Hecker 1985), the vast majority of interments during this period appear to be of common people— they have neither the quantity nor quality of associated objects that characterize elite burials.

The motivation for the Moche occupation of Pacatnamu is difficult to determine. There is no evidence that the site was fortified at that time; thus, its natural defensive potential was probably not a factor. It is possible that the spiritual qualities of the site—its location on a high plateau with a dramatic view of both the ocean and the valley floor—may have motivated the local people to select it for religious purposes.

During the Moche occupation, ceramics clearly reflect some Huari influence, but this influence is not evident in the Moche textiles. Nor is it reflected in burial practices: Huari burials are seated and tightly flexed, while Moche burials at Pacatnamu are consistently extended and lying on their backs.

Near the end of the Moche occupation (ca. A.D. 900), new ceramic forms were added to the Moche assemblage. Most notable are jars with necks that depict an adult male with long tresses and a small moustache indicated at the corners of his upper lip. This is a form that Ubbelohde-Doering referred to as the "King of Assyria" (1967:24). They were also found by Disselhoff in Moro (1958:185) and by Hecker and Hecker at Pacatnamu (1977:30, Table 1, Photos 15A,B). These face-neck jars, often associated with cooking ollas with distinctive rim profiles, allow us to recognize refuse pertaining to the end of the Moche occupation at Pacatnamu.

Approximately A.D. 1050 there was a major break in the sequence between the Moche and the Chimu occupations. This hiatus, which coincides with major changes in nearly all artifact types, appears to correspond to a period of major flooding—presumably a niño whose severity would have created. a crisis for the population living in the area. As a result, Pacatnamu was probably abandoned, although it may have retained a small residual population.

In approximately A.D. 1100-1150 there was a second major floresence at Pacatnamu, with an altogether new inventory of ceramics, textiles, and bricks, and new architectural forms. The vast majority of the architecture visible today was constructed during the following two centuries.

This second floresence, which we refer to as the Chimu occupation, was at least partially motivated by the need for defense. Major walls were built across the northern and southern margins of the site to complement the high cliffs on the east and west. As a result, access to the central part of Pacatnamu could be easily controlled. The unfinished portions of major walls along the northern side suggest that the site was being expanded in this direction shortly before the Chimu occupation ended.

It is not yet known what caused the end of the Chimu occupation, which is tentatively dated at around A.D. 1370. However, it is tempting to speculate that it may, in part, have been related to the conquest of the lower Jequetepeque Valley by the Kingdom of Chimor, which had its capital at Chan Chan, approximately 150 kilometers to the south (Fig. 1).

After A.D. 1370 it is possible that a small population continued to live at Pacatnamu, but by the time the Inca conquered the North Coast (ca. A.D. 1470), the site was largely in ruins—most of the earlier architecture was heavily eroded, and windblown sand was banked against the leeward side of the walls and pyramid structures. A few Inca period offerings suggest that Pacatnamu still maintained some of its earlier ceremonial significance, but it clearly had been eclipsed as a major center.

Offerings continued to be made at Pacatnamu during the early part of the Colonial Period, and some small cemeteries from that time have been identified. It is unlikely, however, that the site was occupied at that time. No Colonial Period architecture or refuse have been found, and thus far no Colonial Period document has been discovered that mentions a settlement at that location.

Changing Perspective on the Function of Pacatnamu

Pacatnamu has traditionally been viewed as a ceremonial complex and pilgrimage center analogous to the site of Pachacamac on the Central Coast. Heinrich Ubbelohde-Doering (1959, 1960, 1967) first suggested this interpretation, and Richard Keatinge (1977, 1978, 1982) has been its most recent proponent.

Our first three field seasons have cast some doubt on the pilgrimage center hypothesis. To date, no ceramics or artifactual material have been found that clearly indicate that anyone other than members of the local valley population is buried at Pacatnamu. Furthermore, the vast majority of ceramic sherds found in test pits within the architectural complexes represent fragments of simple utilitarian vessels—not the elite ritual ware we would expect to find at a major ceremonial center.

Nevertheless, Pacatnamu clearly constitutes one of the largest concentrations of ceremonial architecture on the North Coast. During its second period of florescence, Pacatnamu undoubtedly served as a focus of ceremonial activity and political power for the population of the lower Jequetepeque Valley.

In this volume, only a small part of the research of the first three years of the Pacatnamu Project is presented. The reports are limited to aspects of the research that form relatively complete units at this time. Various studies that are still underway, such as ceramic chronology, evolution of architectural forms, and development of burial practices, are so predictably subject to change and refinement during the next few field seasons that their publication now is premature and would only lead to confusion when the final results are published.

The research during the past three years has been extremely rewarding. We have been able to achieve a good overall understanding of Pacatnamu along with some detailed reconstructions of how it functioned in ancient time. We anticipate that the next two field seasons will greatly expand and refine our current knowledge and ultimately help resolve major issues of Andean culture history.

RESUMEN:
Introducción

Pacatnamú es un importante sitio arqueológico, que posee características únicas. Está ubicado muy cerca a la desembocadura del río Jequetepeque, en la Costa Norte del Perú (Figs. 1,2). Bordeado por barrancos, en dos de sus lados, y resguardado por una alta muralla, en el tercero, es uno de los sitios arqueológicos más espectaculares del Perú y uno de los menos explorados y conocidos arqueólogicamente (Fig. 3).

La porción central del complejo arquitectónico tiene un área de, aproximadamente, 1 kilómetro cuadrado. Está dominado por la presencia de más de 50 pirámides truncas coronadas por cimas elaboradas. A los lados de las pirámides de adobes, se ubican complejos de habitaciones con corredores y plazoletas, posible alojamiento de la clase alta en el sitio; por último, los cementerios, se hallan dispersos tanto dentro como fuera de las murallas del sitio.

Debido a la aridez del clima y a que Pacatnamú se halla más alto que el nivel cultivable del valle, la conservación de los especímenes arqueológicos es bastante buena. Las paredes, frecuentemente, alcanzan casi su altura original, las fachadas pintadas sobreviven y las tumbas conservan todo su contenido—ataúdes de caña, vasijas de lagenaria y cerámica, adornos y vestidos exquisitamente tejidos, los que constituyen la más grande colección de textiles ornamentados jamás descubiertos en el norte de Perú. Por todo esto, Pacatnamú ofrece "condiciones de laboratorio" para el estudio del arte, arquitectura y estructura de la población en un gran centro ceremonial, sujeto a la dinámica de su propio desarrollo local y a las viscisitudes de la conquista foránea.

Investigaciones Previas en Pacatnamú

Aunque Pacatnamú fue mencionado por diversos exploradores del XIX (p. ej. Hutchinson 1873; Middendorf 1894), no fue comenzado a estudiar hasta 1925, cuando Alfred Kroeber delineó los mapas de algunas de las estructuras de la parte central del sitio, añadiendo algunos comentarios sobre la arquitectura (Kroeber 1930:88–89). Posteriormente, se hallan referencias esporádicas en la literatura arqueológica (p. ej. Garcia Rosell 1942:123–124; Schaedel 1951:235; Ishida et al. 1960:435; Kosok 1965:123).

Las primeras excavaciones arqueológicas

fueron realizadas por el arqueólogo alemán Heinrich Ubbelohde-Doering en 1937–1939, 1952–1953 y 1962–1963. Estas consistieron en la excavación parcial de dos de los más de 50 complejos de pirámides existentes en Pacatnamú. En el proceso, Ubbelohde-Doering descubrió numerosas tumbas conteniendo valioso material, el que incluía tejidos, canastas, cuerdas, cuero y restos de plantas. Los restos humanos estaban muy bien preservados, habiendo algunos momificados con tatuajes todavía visibles (Ubbelohde-Doering 1959, 1967, Keatinge 1978; Hecker y Hecker 1985).

Wolfgang y Giesela Hecker acompañaron a Heinrich Ubbelohde-Doering en su expedición a Pacatnamú en 1962–1963. Ellos elaboraron un mapa general del sitio, así como algunos planos de los principales complejos (Hecker y Hecker 1977, 1982, 1985).[1] Aunque ellos son muy útiles, la mayoría fueron confeccionados sin excavaciones, por lo que no son tan exactos como si se hubiesen hecho limpiando parcialmente las estructuras.

En 1974 Richard Keatinge realizó un extenso recorrido de superficie en Pacatnamú, publicando, posteriormente, varios reportes breves dando cuenta de sus observaciones (Keatinge et al. 1975; Keatinge 1977, 1982).

El Proyecto Pacatnamú

En Febrero de 1983, el Instituto Nacional de Cultura del Perú (INC), en Lima, aprobó una solicitud del Museo de Historia Cultural de la Universidad de California, Los Angeles (UCLA), de un permiso para excavaciones e investigaciones en Pacatnamú por un período de cinco años. El proyecto planteaba una investigación multidisciplinaria que combinase la excavación arqueológica con la antropología física, etnobotánica, etnozoología, análisis textil, etnografía y etnohistoria.

Durante las tres primeras temporadas de trabajo de campo, llevadas a cabo entre junio y setiembre de 1983, 1984 y 1985, se llevó a cabo una sistemática exploración del sitio, durante la cual se procedió a la recolección de elementos culturales en superficie, dentro de áreas seleccionadas previamente. Este procedimiento probó ser muy productivo, ya que se recuperaron abundantes artefactos que, asociados, han contribuido a una mejor comprensión del sitio.

Se dedicó especial atención al desarrollo de una cronología, la que se inició con el análisis de la cerámica, que demostró que Pacatnamú atravesó, esencialmente, por dos períodos de ocupación: un período temprano, durante el que se usó el estilo Moche, y un período tardío, caracterizado por la presencia de cerámica Chimú.

Posteriormente, la seriación de adobes usados en la construcción del sitio proveyó una secuencia cronológica de cuatro fases, que relacionan las ocupaciones Moche y Chimú. Esta secuencia hizo posible no sólo el identificar construcciones Moche o Chimú, pero, también, distinguir edificaciones Chimú temprano y tardío.

La cronología basada en la seriación cerámica y de adobes fue refinada por la información proveniente de las excavaciones estratigráficas, así como por la seriación de tejidos y tipos de entierros. Los fechados radiocarbónicos respaldan esta cronología y permiten asignar fechados absolutos a los diversos períodos de ocupación en Pacatnamú.

Aunque nueva evidencia y subsiguientes refinamientos puedan alterar la cronología, nuestra información actual provee una imagen consistente. Aparentemente, Pacatnamú no estuvo ocupado antes de fines de Moche IV o comienzos de Moche V (ca. 600 DC). Durante la ocupación Moche se erigieron algunas de las estructuras ceremoniales, principalmente en la porción central del sitio. Los basurales Moche están dispersos en esta área, así como en algunos sectores hacia el norte, pero su distribución es considerablemente más reducida que la de los basurales Chimú, correspondientes a la ocupación tardía. Aunque algunas tumbas de personajes de alto rango han sido excavadas en Pacatnamú (Ubbelohde-Doering 1967; Hecker y Hecker 1985), la mayoría de los entierros durante el período Moche parecen pertenecer a gente del común—no poseen ni la cantidad ni la calidad de ofrendas asociadas a los entierros de personajes de alto rango.

El motivo de la ocupación Moche en Pacatnamú es difícil de determinar. No hay evidencia que el sitio estuviese fortificado durante este período, por lo que su potencial defensivo parece no haber sido la razón. Es posible que su ubicación en una meseta—más alta que el valle y el océano—y sus posibilidades visuales, hayan apelado a las cualidades espirituales de la población local para emplazar allí un centro religioso.

Durante la ocupación Moche, la cerámica refleja alguna influencia Huari, pero esta no es evidente en los textiles. Tampoco se refleja en las prácticas funerarias—mientras que la posición

---

1. Los Hecker asignaron números y letras a la mayoría de las estructuras de Pacatnamú. En casi todas las instancias, hemos seguido sus designaciones numéricas.

cadavérica Huari es sentada y flexionada, los entierros Moche en Pacatnamú son consistentemente extendidos y descansando sobre las espaldas.

Cerca del fin de la ocupación Moche (ca. 900 DC), aparecen nuevas formas cerámicas en el inventario Moche. La más notable está representada por una vasija en forma de jarra con un cuello que representa en alto relieve a un adulto del sexo masculino con trenzas y pequeños bigotes en las esquinas del labio superior. Esta es una forma que Ubbelohde-Doering denominó "Rey de Asiria" (1967: 24). También fue encontrada por Disselhoff en Moro (1958: 185) y por los Hecker en Pacatnamú (1977: 30, tabla 1, fotos 15A y 15B). Estos cerámios, frecuentemente asociadas a ollas de cocina con bordes distintivos, permiten reconocer los estratos correspondientes al final de la ocupación Moche en Pacatnamú.

Alrededor del 1050 DC hubo una interrupción en la secuencia entre las ocupaciones Moche y Chimú. Este hiato, que coincide con importantes cambios en todos los tipos de artefactos, parece responder a un periodo de grandes inundaciones— presumiblemente un Niño cuya severidad habría creado una crisis cataclísmica para la población viviendo en el área. Como resultado, Pacatnamú fue probablemente abandonado, aunque es posible que haya retenido un número muy pequeño de residentes.

Hacia 1100 o 1150 DC se produce un segundo gran florecimiento del sitio, con un nuevo inventario cerámico, textil, adobes y formas arquitectónicas. La mayor parte de estructuras visibles en la actualidad fueron construidas durante los siguientes doscientos años.

Este segundo florecimiento, al que nos referiremos como ocupación Chimú, estuvo motivado, por lo menos parcialmente, por necesidades defensivas. Se construyeron grandes murallas en las porciones norte y sur del sitio, las que complementaron la inaccesibilidad por los barrancos ubicados al este y el oeste. Como resultado, el acceso a la parte central del sitio podía ser facilmente controlado. Las porciones de la muralla incompleta, al norte de Pacatnamú, sugieren que el sitio se estaba expandiendo en esa dirección muy poco antes del fin de la ocupación Chimú.

Todavía no se ha podido precisar qué causó el fin de la ocupación Chimú, fechada tentativamente hacia 1370 DC; sin embargo, es tentador especular que puede estar relacionado a la conquista del valle del Jequetepeque por el Chimor, cuya capital, Chan Chan, está ubicada a aproximadamente 150 kilómetros hacia el sur.

Después de 1370 DC es posible que haya permanecido un pequeño número de residentes en Pacatnamú, pero, al momento que los Inca conquistaron la Costa Norte (ca. 1470 DC), la mayor parte del sitio estaba en ruinas. Algunas ofrendas atribuibles al periodo Inca sugieren que Pacatnamú mantenía algo de su prestigio como centro ceremonial, pero es claro que sólo era pálido reflejo de su opulencia anterior.

Durante el período colonial temprano se continuaron depositando ofrendas en Pacatnamú y se han identificado algunos pequeños cementerios correspondientes a ese período. Sin embargo, no es probable que el sitio fue ocupado durante esa época. Hasta ahora no hemos podido identificar construcciones o estratos de ese período, así como no hay, hasta este momento, referencias documentales que mencionen población viviendo allí.

Cambio de Perspectivas Acerca de las Funciones de Pacatnamú

Pacatnamú ha sido tradicionalmente visto como un complejo ceremonial y centro de peregrinación análogo a Pachacamac, en la Costa Central. Heinrich Ubbelohde-Doering (1959, 1967) fue el primero en sugerir esta interpretación y Richard Keatinge (1977, 1978, 1982) ha sido su más reciente defensor.

Nuestras tres primeras temporadas de trabajo de campo han sembrado algunas dudas sobre la hipótesis del centro de peregrinación. A la fecha, ni la cerámica ni otros artefactos recuperados sugieren que nadie que no haya sido parte de la población del valle fue enterrado en Pacatnamú. Más aún, la gran mayoría de los fragmentos cerámicos hallados en pozos de prueba o en los complejos arquitectónicos es de tipo utilitario o doméstico— no los elaborados fragmentos comunmente asociados con alto rango o rituales que se esperan encontrar en un importante centro ceremonial.

De cualquier manera, Pacatnamú es claramente uno de los sitios con mayor concentración de arquitectura ceremonial en la Costa Norte del Perú. Durante su segundo florecimiento, Pacatnamú indudablemente sirvió como un importante centro ceremonial y de poder político para la población del bajo valle del Jequetepeque.

En este volumen se presenta sólo una pequeña parte de las investigaciones llevadas a cabo durante los primeros tres años del Proyecto. Los informes se limitan a aspectos que forman unidades en este momento. Diversos estudios continúan realizándose, como la cronología cerámica, evolu-

ción de las formas arquitectónicas y desarrollo de las prácticas funerarias; estos temas son tan susceptibles a ser modificados y refinados durante las próximas temporadas de trabajo de campo que su publicación ahora sería prematura y podría conducir sólo a confusiones cuando los resultados finales sean publicados.

Las investigaciones durante los primeros tres años han sido muy productivas y se ha obtenido una buena imagen general de Pacatnamú, al lado de algunas reconstrucciones detalladas de su funcionamiento. Se anticipa que durante las siguientes dos temporadas de trabajo de campo se incrementarán y refinarán nuestros conocimientos actuales y se podrán resolver algunas de las preguntas de la historia cultural de los Andes prehispánicos.

Brick Seriation at Pacatnamu

Donald H. McClelland

Sun dried mud bricks have been the fundamental building material of large architecture on the Peruvian coast for most of the last 3,500 years, and they are among the most plentiful and durable artifacts remaining at most coastal archaeological sites. Investigators at North Coast Chimu sites such as Chan Chan (Kolata 1978, 1982) and Chotuna (Bruce 1982) have found that brick characteristics such as size and shape evolved through time, and they suggest that this evolution can be used to trace the sequence in which a given structure was built, as well as the order in which different structures were built at a given site.

Since virtually all structures at Pacatnamu are made of mud bricks, a study was initiated to develop a brick typology and seriation that would lead to a better understanding of its construction sequence. More than 4,400 exposed bricks at approximately 90 locations at the site were analyzed.

Four main brick types have been identified at Pacatnamu. These correspond to the successive Moche, Intermediate,[1] and Chimu occupation phases, with the Chimu Phase being divided into two subphases, Initial and Terminal. These four brick types have been designated Moche, Intermediate, Standard Chimu,[2] and Terminal Chimu.[3] The brick typology developed to date has been useful in establishing the temporal relationships of several major construction units, as well as in identifying the contemporaneity of several seemingly unrelated structures.

Brick Typology at Pacatnamu

The bricks at Pacatnamu have been classified by form (shape and size) and composition. Factors that identify the various brick types are summarized in Figure 1 and below.

---

1. Ceramic associations suggest that both the "Moche" and "Intermediate" periods occurred during Moche V, the final phase of Moche culture. The Intermediate is probably late Moche V, but it will be referred to as "Intermediate" to distinguish it from the bulk of the Moche construction that preceded it.
2. These are called "Standard" Chimu rather than "Initial" Chimu because they constitute the main mass of most of the visible structures at Pacatnamu and because they were apparently used throughout the entire period of Chimu occupation from the Initial through the Terminal phases.
3. The Terminal Chimu bricks have been divided into several subtypes based on shape and composition.

BRICK TYPE		MOCHE	INTERMEDIATE	Std. Chimu	TERMINAL CHIMU							
SHAPE		Flat-Rectangular	Flat-Rectangular		Flat-Rectangular				Flat-Bottomed Ovoid			
COMPOSITION		River-Silt	Mottled		River-Silt	Hard-Silt	Color-ed	Congl-omerate	River-Silt	Hard-Silt	Color-ed	Congl-omerate
OCCURRENCE CHIMU	TERMINAL											
	INITIAL											
	INTERMEDIATE											
	MOCHE											
TYPICAL MEAN DIMENSIONS (cm)	L	28.6	27.0		33.7				29			
	W	19.4	17.9		18.2				22			
	H	10.7	11.3		10.4				15			
RANGE OF DIMENSIONS (cm)	L	23–36	23–38		25–43				26–35			
	W	15–23	13–22		13–25				18–24			
	H	8–14	8–15		7–15				13–18			
TYPICAL L/W		1.47	1.51		1.85				1.9			
STD. DEVIATION OF LENGTH (% of mean)		6.6%	7.7%		11.6%				—			
MANUFACTURING METHOD		Mold (Some cane marked)	Hand (Flat tool sometimes used to shape sides)						Hand			
MASONRY QUALITY		Accurate straight courses	Accurate straight courses		Frequent uneven courses and other irregularities							
IDEALIZED TYPICAL SHAPES									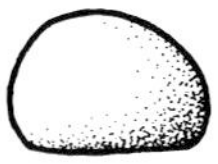 End View 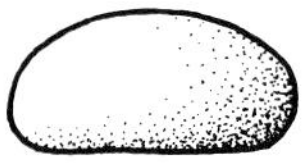 Side View			

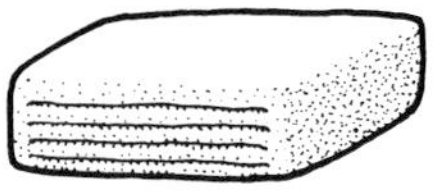

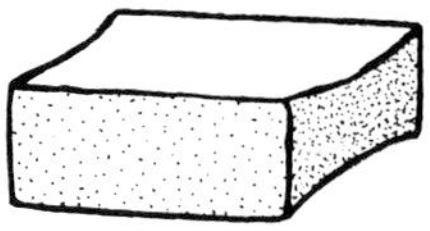

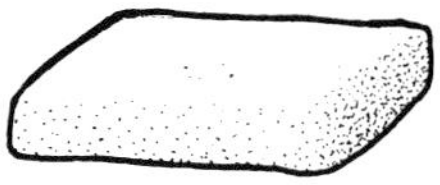

Figure 1.   Pacatnamu brick typology.

Figure 2.   Moche bricks from Huaca 31. Note circled cane mold marks on brick near lower right corner.

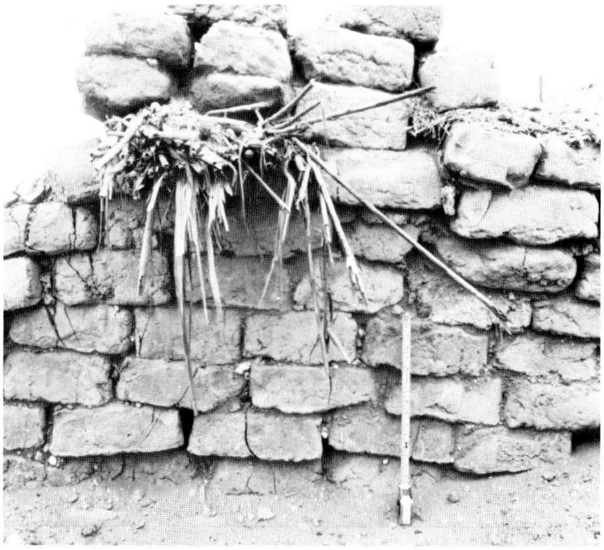

Figure 3.   Intermediate bricks from divider wall of Huaca 31 ramp.

Form

Two primary brick shapes are found at Pacatnamu: flat-rectangular and flat-bottomed egg-shaped ("ovoid"). Although many flat-rectangular Chimu bricks have slightly convex top surfaces, ovoid bricks are a distinct shape and apparently did not evolve from flat-rectangular bricks.[4]

Flat-rectangular Bricks

Throughout the Moche, Intermediate, and Initial Chimu occupations, only flat-rectangular bricks were used in exposed wall surfaces, and these continued to be used, along with ovoid bricks, through the Terminal Chimu Phase. Throughout the entire occupation of Pacatnamu, there was little change in average height and no clear-cut pattern in height-to-width ratio[5] of flat-rectangular bricks (see "Comparison With Other Sites," below). Bricks of the Moche, Intermediate, and Chimu phases, however, can be distinguished by a combination of other shape and size factors.[6]

Because of the errors associated with thickness measurements, the most satisfactory shape and dimensional criteria[7] for the flat-rectangular bricks seem to be:
1. Length,
2. Length-to-width ratio,
3. Standard deviation of length (expressed as a percentage of mean length), and
4. Shape (verticality of sides, flatness of surfaces, sharpness of edges, etc.).

Moche (Fig. 2) and Intermediate (Fig. 3) bricks have similar lengths and widths. Chimu bricks (Fig. 4) are longer and narrower than Moche and Intermediate bricks.[8] The range of sizes of Chimu bricks is almost twice that of Moche and Intermediate bricks (Fig. 5). This size range provides another useful criterion for distinguishing brick types, at least between groups of bricks large enough to allow significant statistical comparisons.

Both Moche and Chimu bricks tend to have rounded edges, while Intermediate bricks have a distinctive sharp-edged appearance and slightly concave sides (Figs. 1-4). Many of the best-preserved flat-rectangular Chimu bricks have trapezoidal cross sections with slightly sloping sides and ends, and they usually have slightly convex top surfaces (Figs. 1,4A). Moche and Intermediate bricks generally have vertical sides and flat surfaces.

There is unequivocal evidence only during the Moche Phase for the use of cane molds to make bricks, although cane mold marks are found on only a few Moche bricks (Fig. 2). The flatness of the sides of most other Moche bricks suggests that they may have been made in wood molds. A flat wood tool appears to have been used to partially smooth the sides of many Intermediate and Chimu bricks.

Ovoid Bricks

During the Terminal Chimu occupation at Pacatnamu, there was a proliferation of rounded, ellipsoidal, flat-bottomed bricks (Figs. 6-9). These "ovoid" bricks were used mostly in facing walls and in the uppermost layers of structures, but some of the latest structures at the site were built almost entirely of ovoid bricks. These bricks were apparently first used during the Initial Chimu Phase as filler material in case-and-fill walls.[9]

---

4. This is indicated by the lack of transitional shapes between flat-rectangular and ovoid and by the fact that both shapes were used during the Terminal Chimu Phase, often intermixed in the same structure.
5. The height of a thin flat-rectangular brick is a poor bench mark, because (1) the measurement errors are greater in absolute terms for the height than for the length or width since the top surface of the brick is often less flat and less accurately shaped than are the ends or sides, and (2) a given error is a greater percentage of the height than of the length or width.
6. The measurement process inevitably involves at least three categories of errors: (1) direct measurement errors arising from brick surface irregularities and from the mortar joint which obscures the brick's true dimensions; (2) statistical errors arising from a finite sample size; and (3) possible systematic errors arising from the impossibility of selecting a random sample for measurement. The first category is the largest and most serious, but probably averages less than

+/- 1.5 cm. The second category can be calculated from the standard deviation and sample size. It is well under +/- 1.0 cm except for very small samples.
7. It must be emphasized that these dimensional comparisons are based on the means of large samples, with the differences of means being much less than the dimensional ranges within the samples. The differences of means, however, appear to be statistically significant.
8. Intermediate bricks seem to be somewhat thicker than Moche and Chimu bricks, but the sample of Intermediate bricks is relatively small and the statistical significance is less certain.
9. Few ovoid bricks were measured because many structures containing them are heavily eroded, mortar obscures ovoid bricks more than flat-rectangular bricks, and size seems to be highly variable within any given structure. Since ovoid bricks were used mainly in the latest structures, dimensional distinctions would not provide additional chronological information.

Figure 4.   A. Typical Standard Chimu flat-rectangular bricks.   B. Standard Chimu bricks in east wall of Major Quadrangle.

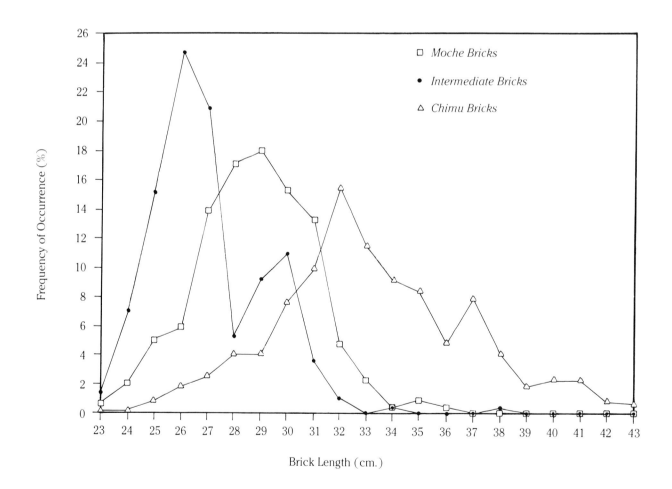

Figure 5.   Length frequency distribution of Moche, Intermediate, and Chimu flat-rectangular bricks.

Terminal Chimu
Construction

Moche Construction

*Figure 6. A. West half of Huaca 31 north face. B. Detail
of Terminal Chimu construction on Huaca 31 north
face showing ovoid bricks, including one gray
colored brick and the rest white conglomerate bricks.*

Composition

The builders of Pacatnamu had access to many sources of material suitable for making bricks. Five main types and several subtypes of material have been identified based on color and texture (Table 1):

1. From the Moche through the Chimu phases, the basic construction units are bricks made of a good quality brown to grayish silt, probably obtained from the nearby Jequetepeque River. This material will be referred to as "river-silt."
2. Bricks found in a few Moche and Intermediate locations have a distinctive mottled rust/gray color.[10] These will be referred to as "mottled."
3. During the initial Chimu occupation, chocolate brown, yellowish-green, and dark gray silts came into use and were prevalent during the Terminal Phase. These will be referred to as "colored."

4. A light gray, hard silt was used only in the Terminal Chimu Phase. These bricks will be referred to as "hard-silt."
5. Another material used only during the Terminal Chimu Phase is the red or white conglomerate strata that underlie the site and form the upper layers of the plateau. A small amount of clay, mud, or other binding material was probably added, because the pure conglomerate will not coalesce enough to form bricks or mortar. These bricks will be referred to as "conglomerate."

There is a wide color range within each category. Samples of each type were collected and the colors were identified with a Munsell soil color

---

10. This may be a heat oxidation effect and not a separate type of brick material because it seems to occur near areas where there is definite evidence of fire oxidation.

White Conglomerate   Red Conglomerate

Figure 7.   Unset white and red conglomerate bricks on summit of Huaca 29. Note mixture of ovoid and flat-rectangular bricks.

Brown Colored
Rectangular
Bricks

White
Conglomerate
Ovoid Bricks

Red
Conglomerate
Ovoid Bricks

Red Conglomerate Bricks in
Red Conglomerate Mortar

Figure 8.   Section of Outer Wall near Doorway 2 showing variety of brick types.

Figure 9. Outer Wall near Doorway 2 showing wall segmentation.

NAME	COLOR	MUNSELL CODE	TEMPER AMOUNT/TYPE
RIVER SILT	Brown to grayish brown	10YR 6/3 to 10YR 6/4	None to moderate/Sand & gravel
MOTTLED	Light gray with rust mottle	Variable	None to moderate/Sand
COLORED			
(Chocolate)	Dark brown	10YR 5/3 to 10YR 4/3	None to slight/Plant remains
(Yellow)	Pale yellow to greenish-yellow	2.5Y 7/4 to 2.5Y 6/4	None to heavy/Gravel
(Gray)	Dark gray	10YR 4/1 to 10YR 4/2	None to slight/Plant remains
HARD-SILT	Light gray	10YR 7/2	None to moderate/Plant remains
CONGLOMERATE			
(Red)	Pink to red	7.5YR 7/4 to 7.5YR 5/6	Heavy/Gravel & 2 cm. flat chips
(White)	White to light gray	10YR 8/2 to 10YR 7/2	Heavy/1–2 cm. limestone

Table 1. Brick material types based on color and temper.

chart.

A few river-silt bricks, a few colored bricks (particularly the dark gray), about one third of the hard-silt bricks, and the majority of the conglomerate bricks are ovoid shaped. The rest, which comprise the great majority of bricks at Pacatnamu, are flat-rectangular.

Summary of Brick Types

The four main brick types (Moche, Intermediate, Standard Chimu, and Terminal Chimu) are summarized in Figure 1 and below:

1. Moche. The earliest bricks at the site are late Moche, based on their association with Moche ceramics and burials. When found in structures containing other brick types, the Moche bricks always occupy the lowest levels. They are flat-rectangular, river-silt bricks, mostly mold-made, with fairly uniform dimensions. The greatest concentration found to date is at Huaca 31 and its associated structures.

2. Intermediate. The tentatively identified Intermediate bricks are similar to Moche bricks, but they are thicker and sharper-edged, often with slightly concave sides. They are usually either mottled or are made of a slightly yellowish river-silt with a gray patina. Their main location identified to date is in the ramp of Huaca 31.[11]

3. Standard Chimu. These are flat-rectangular, river-silt bricks. They are longer and narrower than Moche and Intermediate bricks and are less regular in shape and size. They often have trapezoidal cross sections with slightly convex top surfaces. They are called "Standard" Chimu rather than "Initial" Chimu, because they form the main mass of the visible structures at Pacatnamu, including the large huacas, the Major Quadrangle, and the Inner, Outer, and South Walls, and because they were used throughout the entire Chimu occupation. (See Map Insert

for the location of site features and structures.)

4. Terminal Chimu. The Terminal Phase of Chimu occupation is marked by the widespread use of colored and conglomerate bricks and ovoid bricks. They have been collectively called "Terminal" Chimu bricks.[12] They are common in the upper courses of walls, in facing layers, and in late structures such as the Outer Wall and Huacas 18, 23a, and 29.

Bricks have been assigned to the Chimu Phase on the basis of their association with Chimu ceramics and burials. When found in structures together with Moche and Intermediate bricks, they occupy the uppermost levels.

Wall Construction

Most bricks at Pacatnamu are set in alternating courses of runners and headers. Exceptions include walls set entirely with runners, which may be diagnostic of ceremonial structures, and bricks set on edge, which have been found only in Moche structures.

The straightness and regularity of courses are additional diagnostic factors. Moche and Intermediate bricks are laid accurately in straight, level courses.[13] Chimu walls, however, contain numerous irregularities.

There is a large variation in brick selection and arrangement of courses within the Terminal Chimu Phase. Some of the more common varieties are:

1. Random mixture of chocolate, yellow, and dark gray flat-rectangular bricks laid in regular courses. (Example: niches. See "The Huaca 1 Complex—Architectural Features," below.)

2. Walls consisting of mixtures of colored and conglomerate bricks laid in regular courses. (Example: Outer Wall near Doorway 2; Fig. 8, Map Insert).

3. Segments one to two meters wide, each

11. The assignment of the ramp to an Intermediate Phase was made because the ramp brick style is somewhat different from the Moche and Chimu brick styles, and because the ramp was apparently built after the Moche construction but before the later Chimu additions. This assignment is somewhat tenuous at this point. No Intermediate Phase pottery has been found in direct association with bricks in the ramp; however, several bricks similar to the ramp bricks were found in a test pit northeast of Huaca 31 in close

association with Intermediate Phase sherds.
12. They have been called Terminal Chimu bricks because they were used primarily during the Terminal Chimu Phase. The demarcation between phases was probably gradual, however, as indicated by the dashed line in Figure 1. Occasional examples of Terminal Chimu bricks are found in Initial Chimu construction.
13. This is in contrast to the construction at Huaca Galindo, another late Moche site (Conrad 1974:678).

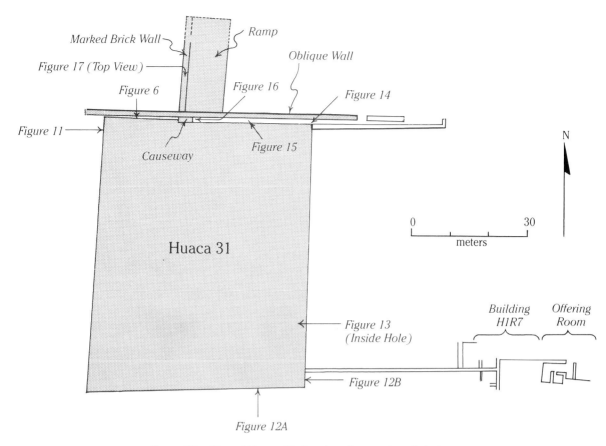

Figure 10.   Map of Huaca 31 showing view angles of photos.

of which contains primarily one brick type and one mortar type. (Example: Outer Wall near Doorway 2; Fig. 9).

4. Conglomerate ovoid bricks not laid in regular courses. (Example: wall blocking Doorway 3 in Outer Wall. See "City Walls—Outer Wall," below.)

5. Roughly-laid, irregular walls comprising most Terminal brick types. (Example: Inner Wall west of Huaca 1 courtyard. See "City Walls—Inner Wall," below.)

6. Structures consisting of hard-silt bricks in irregular courses with intermixed rectangular and ovoid bricks. (Example: H1M1 in the Major Quadrangle. See "The Huaca 1 Complex—Structures Within the Major Quadrangle, H1M1," below.)

7. Structures made almost entirely of red conglomerate bricks in regular courses. (Examples: most of the Huaca 23a quadrangle and some interior walls of the Huaca 49 Complex. See "Other Late Chimu Structures—Huacas 4, 49, and 50 and Huaca 23a," below.)

With further study it may be possible to seriate these variations in wall architecture. It would be appropriate to test the hypothesis that the fraction of conglomerate bricks increases with time.

Huaca 31 and Associated Structures

The construction of Huaca 31 (Map Insert) and its associated structures (Fig. 10) spans virtually the entire history of the occupation of Pacatnamu. The earliest portion is Moche and is the most extensive example of Moche brick construction yet found at Pacatnamu. It was repaired and expanded several times by later inhabitants through the final stage of occupation. The Chimu addition to the north face of the huaca is a classic example of Terminal Phase construction using white conglomerate ovoid bricks (Fig. 6).[14]

---

14. Ubbelohde-Doering (1967:22) noted the use of both flat-rectangular and "plano-convex" (ovoid) bricks in Huaca 31 and said that the latter are in higher and later layers.

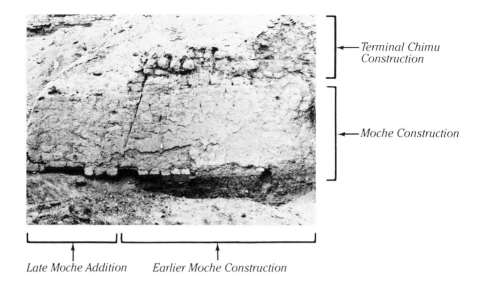

Terminal Chimu
Construction

Moche Construction

Late Moche Addition   Earlier Moche Construction

Figure 11.   West face of northwest corner of Huaca 31.

On-edge Bricks

Cane/Mortar Layer
Cane Marked Bricks

On-edge Bricks
Cane/Mortar Layer
Capping Layer

Original Platform

Foundation Layer

*Figure 12.   A. South face of Huaca 31 west of southeast
corner. Note cane mold-marked bricks in foreground.
B. East face of southeast corner of Huaca 31.*

Moche Construction Phase

The Offering Room and Building H1R7

The history of Huaca 31 begins with two closely related structures, called the Offering Room and Building H1R7 (Fig. 10; Map Insert), lying between Huaca 31 and Huaca 1. They are low enclosures or platforms. The brick shapes and construction style are Moche. The bricks in the Offering Room are mottled clay. Those in Building H1R7 are mostly grayish river-silt, although a few are mottled. The bricks in both areas appear to be mold-made; a few have cane mold marks.

Huaca 31

Construction of this pyramid was apparently preceded by the construction of two roughly parallel east-west walls. The south wall became part of the structure of the pyramid's south face and connected it to Building H1R7. The wall just north of the pyramid (called the Oblique Wall) remained freestanding. A causeway joined the Oblique Wall to the pyramid during the Moche Phase.

The Huaca 31 pyramid was apparently built in several stages. It was extended to the north at least twice by the addition of casing walls. The end of the most northerly addition is shown in Figure 11. Construction was probably completed in a short time because the bricks are similar in all parts of the structure and there is no weathering of the now-buried north faces of the casing walls. The Offering Room, Building H1R7, and the Huaca 31 pyramid appear to be roughly contemporary because their bricks are very similar.[15]

The southeast corner of the pyramid provides a good example of Moche construction techniques (Fig. 12). The earliest part was a platform of well-laid Moche bricks with sloping walls ten courses high. These were set on a foundation layer of headers, which protrudes about ten centimeters beyond the plane of the wall. The wall was capped with a single course of much larger bricks that may have been the topping layer of the original structure. This was overlaid by a thick layer of canes in mortar, above which are about eight more courses of normal-sized Moche bricks. One course consists of headers on edge—a common Moche brick arrangement. The cane layer is clearly shown in Fig-

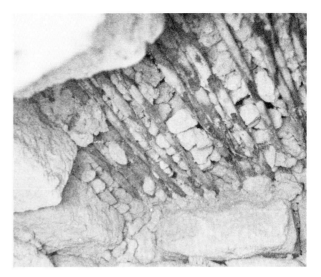

Figure 13. Hole in Huaca 31 east face showing structure of cane layer.

ure 13 through a hole that was dug in the east face of the pyramid sometime in the past.

Similar construction is evident at the northeast corner of the pyramid (Fig. 14). The northwestern corner (Fig. 11) is different; the courses of on-edge bricks are present, but the cane and mortar layer is not visible, possibly because of the excellent condition of the plaster surface on the exposed walls.

Structures North of the Pyramid

The Oblique Wall roughly parallels the north face of the pyramid. The center section of the wall forms the south terminus of the ramp (Fig. 10). Few bricks could be measured because of the intact plaster layer, but other characteristics of the wall, such as six courses of on-edge bricks, quality of construction, mortar and plaster techniques, and uniformity of dimensions, strongly resemble other Moche construction in Huaca 31. Immediately east of the center section, the brick alignment changes; apparently, a section of the Oblique Wall was removed and later restored (Fig. 15). The uppermost course is on-edge bricks, indicating that the section was restored during the Moche period.

The east wall of the causeway connecting the Oblique Wall with the north face of the pyramid is Moche construction (Fig. 16). It has an unusual brick arrangement consisting of headers laid flat and on edge, possibly because headers and on-edge bricks fill a narrow gap more easily than runners.

The north face of the pyramid, the south face of the Oblique Wall, and the east wall of the

---

15. Many of the bricks in Building H1R7 and in the west half of the south face of Huaca 31 are encrusted with a white crystalline material.

Terminal Chimu
Construction

On-edge Bricks

Cane/Mortar Layer

Moche Construction

Figure 14.   Northeast corner of Huaca 31.

A (on edge)
B (runners)
C (on edge)

A

B

C

Restored Section

Figure 15.   South face of Oblique Wall showing restored section (between cane and tape
measure). Note changes in alignment of brick courses at these locations. Original
courses of bricks (A, B, and C) can be seen on each side of the restored section.

Figure 16.   Causeway east wall between north face of Huaca 31 (on left) and south
face of Oblique Wall (on right). Note several courses of on-edge bricks (arrows).

causeway are all very similar with regard to brick shape, mortar thickness, and surface plaster. It seems unlikely that any great span of time elapsed between the construction of these features.

Intermediate Construction Phase

The ramp abutting the north face of the Oblique Wall seems to be a somewhat later addition. It comprises two parallel side walls and internal dividing walls, creating a series of cells filled with rubble to form the main body of the ramp.

The western side wall is the only structure yet found at Pacatnamu made of bricks with makers' marks (Fig. 17).[16] Only about five different marks are present. The marked Pacatnamu bricks and the neighboring unmarked bricks are otherwise identical.

The two side walls and the dividing walls of the ramp are made of mottled bricks or yellowish-brown bricks with a gray surface patina. These Intermediate bricks are more sharp-edged than Moche bricks and usually have slightly concave sides (Figs. 1,3). The ramp bricks are laid with thin mortar joints, while Moche walls often have thick mortar joints. Lengths and widths are similar to Moche bricks, but thicknesses are somewhat greater.

Chimu Construction Phase

The remains of the Chimu additions to Huaca 31 are extremely eroded. Several of these additions are constructed primarily of less durable conglomerate bricks, while others have been distorted by settling. The west half of the pyramid's north face, however, is a fine example of Terminal Chimu ovoid brick construction (Fig. 6). It is easy to see the abrupt transition between the earlier flat-rectangular and later ovoid bricks.

The east half of the north face is badly eroded, but the northeast corner is sufficiently intact to show the brick arrangement clearly (Fig. 14). Above the Moche construction are eight to ten courses of Terminal Chimu rectangular bricks, mostly colored, but intermixed with a few white conglomerate ovoids.

16. Mud bricks with makers' marks have been reported at other North Coast Chimu sites such as Chotuna (Bruce 1982:19), Huaca Galindo (Conrad 1974:683), and Pampa Grande (Shimada 1976:475). The makers' marks found in the Huaca 31 ramp are similar to some reported by Hastings and Moseley (1975:199) at the Moche sites of Huaca del Sol and Huaca de la Luna; however, the inventory of marks at Pacatnamu is far smaller than that reported by the investigators at Chotuna, Huaca Galindo, Pampa Grande, and Huacas Sol and Luna.

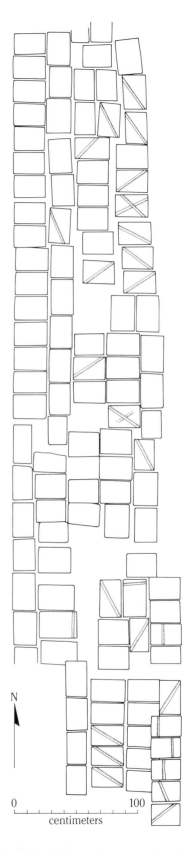

N

0   100
centimeters

Figure 17.   Bricks in Huaca 31 ramp with makers' marks.

Figure 18. Typical brick arrangement in east wall of Major Quadrangle.

The excavated portion of the northern part of the pyramid's upper surface appears to be a complex mixture of three construction phases: Moche, Initial Chimu, and Terminal Chimu. Much of the upper surface is paved with what appear to be Standard Chimu bricks or colored Terminal Chimu flat-rectangular bricks. A badly eroded mound on the north edge of the summit just south of the ramp is capped with a layer of conglomerate bricks. The upper surface of the ramp and part of its west face are covered with Terminal Chimu bricks, primarily red conglomerate. These upper-surface Terminal Chimu bricks are highly eroded—often only a powdery residue remains. Those that are well preserved are mostly ovoids.

Because of the erosion of the huaca's upper surface, it has not been possible to identify any substantial superstructures that are entirely Chimu. Instead, the Chimu additions seem to be repairs or facing layers applied to the original Moche structure.

The Huaca 1 Complex

Pacatnamu contains many units comprising pyramidal huacas with attached rectangular enclosures. The largest is the Huaca 1 Complex (Donnan, Huaca 1, this volume; Map Insert).

Huaca 1

Apparently, the bulk of the structure was built during the Initial Chimu Phase and was rather crudely expanded during the Terminal Phase. Excavation of the southeast corner of Huaca 1 exposed a Terminal Chimu Phase structural addition to the main body of the pyramid, which is a smoothly plastered Initial Chimu Phase construction, similar to the Major Quadrangle walls (see below). The Terminal Phase addition appears to consist only of internal stabilizing walls; the finished external casing walls were completely eroded. Near the top of the huaca are the eroded remains of Terminal Chimu red conglomerate bricks.

Major Quadrangle Walls

South of Huaca 1 is the Major Quadrangle. Its walls are among the least eroded structures at Pacatnamu, with the original plastered surface still intact in many places. The walls are laid with alternating courses of headers and runners. Generally speaking, the lower third of the walls consists mostly of Standard Chimu bricks, the middle third contains more colored bricks, and the upper third contains many conglomerate bricks. Standard Chimu bricks are in the majority at all levels except for the top few courses of the highest remaining portions of the walls, which are all conglomerate bricks (Fig. 18). These courses, which apparently were added during the Terminal Phase to increase the height of the walls, contain the only ovoid bricks in the wall surface. The change in brick usage and the slight surface contour changes between the lower, middle, and upper portions of the walls may indicate that they were built in at least three vertical increments. The interiors of the walls consist of field stones, mortar, and roughly-laid bricks, including ovoids.

Prominent vertical cracks mark locations where wall surface bricks were laid in segments, possibly by different groups.[17] The wall segment shown in Figure 18 contains a number of irregularities that are typical of Pacatnamu wall construction: a course that contains both runners and headers, a course that disappears, and adjacent courses of headers.

The Major Quadrangle wall bricks are somewhat crudely shaped and have highly variable dimensions (Figs. 1,5). These sizes are randomly distributed and are not correlated with height in the wall.[18]

Structures within the Major Quadrangle

Within the Major Quadrangle are several walled enclosures and other structures. Some still have prominent walls 1.5 meters to 2 meters high, while others are eroded almost down to ground level. The present height of a wall depends on its original height and thickness, as well as on the material from which it was made. The better-preserved areas are constructed mostly of Standard Chimu bricks, which are quite durable. The heavily eroded areas, such as Room Complex A in the southwest corner of the Major Quadrangle, abound in the less durable Terminal Chimu conglomerate and colored bricks.

Room Complex A and the Audiencia

The rectangular unit called Room Complex A is made up of numerous low, eroded walls consisting mostly of colored and conglomerate Terminal Chimu bricks, both flat-rectangular and ovoid. Near the center of the area is an open courtyard containing a U-shaped audiencia—a typical feature of North Coast Chimu ceremonial complexes (Kolata

Figure 19.   Side wall of audiencia in Area A of Major Quadrangle showing bricks set as runners.

1982:72-77; Bruce, this volume). The two side walls of the U (Fig. 19), together with the inside surface of the back wall, are laid entirely with runners, unlike almost all other construction at Pacatnamu. Similar construction was found on the summit of Huaca 18 (see below), a location of obvious ceremonial significance. Since the audiencia bricks are harder and the quality of masonry is better than in the surrounding structures, the audiencia is less eroded than other parts of this area. This might indicate that the audiencia's ceremonial importance warranted better construction than that of utilitarian structures.[19]

H1M1

In the southeast corner of the Major Quadrangle is a structure known as H1M1 (Verano and Cordy-Collins, this volume). The bricks are made of light gray hard-silt and are set with mortar of the same material. Most bricks are flat-rectangular; the rest are flat-bottomed ovoids. The hand-made bricks are crude, and the walls are rough and irregular. They were no doubt intended to be interior stabilizing walls. This is the only significant Chimu structure yet found at Pacatnamu that is constructed of a single brick material. It is the only place in the Major Quadrangle where ovoid bricks were used interchangeably with flat-rectangular bricks in the

---

17. Moseley (1975:193) suggested that this method of construction was used at Chan Chan as a means of exacting a labor tax from individual community groups.

18. This contrasts with the construction at Chan Chan, where the brick size decreases fairly uniformly in proportion to height in the wall (Kolata 1982:68).

19. It should be noted that the later U-shaped structures (audiencias) found in the Huaca 8 quadrangle had a conventional runner-header brick configuration. Those in the Huaca 23a quadrangle were too eroded to permit a definitive determination of brick arrangement.

lower courses of walls, which strongly suggests that the structure is Terminal Phase.

Architectural Features

Several of the compounds within the Quadrangle and west of Huaca 1 contain numerous niches, which have also been found at other North Coast Chimu sites (Kolata 1982:72-77). The niches are built mostly of flat-rectangular colored bricks and eroded niches have a distinctive greenish-brown color.

The West Corridor of the Major Quadrangle contains small rectangular structures that may have been intended to constrict traffic flow through the corridors (see Donnan, Huaca 1, this volume). The bricks of the constrictions seem to be of hard-silt material. These constrictions are the only structures in the Major Quadrangle other than H1M1 that have been found to contain bricks made from this material.

City Walls

Inner Wall

The Inner Wall (Map Insert) stretches across the site from the river valley cliff to the sea cliff. A deep trench north of the wall is crossed by causeways at the doorways through the wall.

Doorway 1, just north of Huaca 1, is wide and has a massive pilaster on its east side. A causeway across the trench provides access to the doorway. The original profile of the trench was an inverted trapezoid. The south wall of the trench was steepened by extending the north face of the Inner Wall down into the trench to a point about halfway between the ground level and the bottom of the trench.

The causeway is made of Standard Chimu bricks similar to, although somewhat grayer than, the Major Quadrangle wall. The north face of the Inner Wall is similar, but it also includes flat-rectangular gray and yellow colored bricks in the lower courses and conglomerate bricks, including ovoids, in the uppermost courses.

The pilaster is made mostly of flat-rectangular colored bricks similar to those used to build the niches in the Major Quadrangle, with some eroded conglomerate bricks on the upper surface.

The construction of the wall commenced with the digging of the trench. The causeway was built next, followed by the north face of the Inner Wall. It can be determined that this face is later than the causeway because the plaster surface of the cause-

way extends beneath the wall. Moreover, it contains more Terminal Phase bricks than the causeway. The pilaster, at least in its present form, was added later. This assumption is based on the almost exclusive use of colored and conglomerate bricks. It was apparently widened after its initial construction in order to make the doorway narrower (Donnan, City Walls, this volume).

The masonry style of the Inner Wall east of the pilaster and west of the Huaca 1 courtyard is an extreme example of Terminal Phase crudeness. The profile of the wall is convoluted, with numerous bends and curves. The brick inventory includes colored, hard-silt, and conglomerate rectangular and ovoid bricks.

Outer Wall

The Outer Wall is a massive structure that extends from the river valley about two-thirds of the way across the pampa toward the sea cliff (Map Insert). There are four doorways, as well as a gap where a ravine cuts through the wall.

The main structure of the wall appears to be case-and-fill construction. The exposed bricks are all Standard Chimu or Terminal Chimu and include both flat-rectangular and ovoid bricks. The fill material is cane, rubble, and Standard Chimu bricks laid without mortar.

The doorways through the Outer Wall are classic examples of Terminal Chimu masonry. They are adorned with a great variety of colored and conglomerate bricks, both rectangular and ovoid, and almost all colors of mortar. The bricks often are applied in segments one to two meters long. The effect now is quite decorative, but the walls were probably plastered when they were built, thus concealing this colorful appearance.

Doorway 2 is one of the most elegant Terminal Phase constructions yet found at Pacatnamu (Figs. 8,9). The lower courses of bricks that line the passageway seem to be Standard Chimu bricks, but all other bricks are Terminal Chimu. Some adjacent segments show interesting color reversals (e.g., a segment of red bricks with white mortar next to a segment of white bricks with red mortar; Fig. 9). Doorway 2 was built in at least two stages. Facing layers were added to the north and south faces of the wall east of the doorway, as evidenced by definite breaks on the east wall of the passageway. The original bricks have very rounded corners, as though they had been subjected to considerable wear before the facing layer was added.

Doorway 3 appears to be entirely late Terminal Phase, very hastily constructed with any available materials, including river stones. After it was built, it was completely blocked off by a wall made almost entirely of red conglomerate ovoid bricks, arranged randomly rather than being set in regular courses. Both the material and the masonry style of this blocking wall place it near the end of the Terminal Phase.

Doorway 4 has been largely obliterated by the road that passes through the wall at this point. Only the north end of the west passageway wall remains. This surface contains colored and conglomerate ovoid bricks. There are also a few red conglomerate and yellow colored flat-rectangular pavement bricks on the floor of the doorway.

South Wall

This low wall across the southern end of the plateau (Map Insert) consists of one or two courses of Standard Chimu bricks similar to those in the Major Quadrangle walls. The wall—originally of case-and-fill construction—has eroded almost to ground level. It is certainly Chimu, but the few remaining courses do not permit more accurate dating. Walls made almost entirely of Terminal bricks will often have one or two courses of Standard Chimu bricks as a foundation. Because Terminal Phase colored and conglomerate bricks seem to be much less durable than Standard Chimu bricks, a tentative assignment of the wall to the Terminal Phase can be supported indirectly by the almost complete erosion of the upper part of the wall.

Other Late Chimu Structures

Huacas 18 and 29

These two pyramids (Map Insert) are excellent examples of Terminal Chimu brick construction. Each pyramid has a ramp on its north side and extensive wall construction and other structural elements on its summit. A low wall on the summit of Huaca 18 is similar to and laid in the same manner as those of the Major Quadrangle audiencia side walls (Fig. 19). Many of the features of Huaca 18 are similar to but on a smaller scale than those of Huaca 29. The exposed surfaces of both contain many colored and conglomerate bricks, including ovoids.

Huaca 29 provides a "sampler" of most of the brick shapes and brick and mortar materials used at Pacatnamu, including white conglomerate bricks set in gravelly white conglomerate mortar; red conglomerate bricks in white conglomerate mortar; red conglomerate bricks in red mortar; and chocolate-colored flat-rectangular bricks, white conglomerate bricks, and red conglomerate bricks, all set in chocolate-colored mortar. The south face contains hard-silt bricks. The walls of Huaca 29 include both flat-rectangular and ovoid bricks.

On the summit of Huaca 29 there is a pile of unset ovoid and flat-rectangular red-and-white conglomerate bricks (Fig. 7). A similar pile of unset red conglomerate bricks lies near the northeast corner of Huaca 18. These unset bricks may have been piled waiting to be set in a wall, suggesting that they were placed there just before the pyramid was abandoned and confirming that the heavy use of conglomerate bricks was a late occurrence.

Huacas 4, 49, and 50

Huaca 4 is south of Huaca 8 and just north of the Inner Wall (Map Insert). Huacas 49 and 50 are aligned north to south, with the Huaca 23a quadrangle lying between them (Donnan, Huaca 23a, this volume). These three huacas each contain a low central structure and are surrounded by a complex of rooms and outer enclosing walls. The central structures of Huacas 4 (Keatinge, this volume) and 49 are C-shaped with the open part of the C oriented to the north. The central structure of Huaca 50 may have been similar, but it is now heavily eroded.

The oldest parts of these structures—generally the outer enclosure walls and the bases of the central structures—were apparently started in the Initial Phase, as they consist mostly of Standard Chimu bricks and colored bricks. Later, additions were made to the central structures and enclosure walls, and the complexes of rooms within the enclosure walls were built, using mostly conglomerate bricks.

Huacas 4 and 49 are similar architecturally and have similar brick inventories, indicating they were probably built at about the same time. Huaca 50 has a smaller fraction of Terminal Phase bricks and thus may be somewhat older, although one room in the complex appears to have been added near the end of the Terminal Phase.

Huaca 23a

This complex includes a pyramid with associated flanker mound and altar (Donnan, Huaca 23a, this volume). Its quadrangle extends to the south and east of the pyramid and encloses several rooms and two audiencias. This quadrangle lies between the Huaca 49 and 50 complexes. The bases of the pyramid, flanker mound, and altar are made mostly of Standard Chimu bricks, but they are overlaid with Terminal Phase bricks. The entire quadrangle is built almost exclusively with Terminal Phase bricks, mostly red conglomerate. It is possible that the original structures were built about the same time as the original structures of Huaca 49. The Huaca 23a quadrangle, however, seems to be later than either the Huaca 49 or 50 complexes, on the basis of brick content as well as wall abutment patterns (Donnan, Huaca 23a, this volume).

Huaca 8

Although Huaca 8 is the second largest pyramid at Pacatnamu, its associated quadrangle is much smaller and simpler than that associated with Huaca 1. The excavated portion of the quadrangle consists of two rooms in its southwest corner, neither of which has much internal structure. The room nearest the Huaca 8 pyramid is designated Room 2. It is constructed almost entirely of Standard Chimu bricks and appears to be contemporaneous with the pyramid. It contains a large west-facing audiencia, which is built with bricks in the normal runner-header pattern, unlike the audiencia in the Major Quadrangle.

Room 1 appears to be later, based on its higher percentage of Terminal Phase bricks. This room contains two audiencias. The northern one is built with Standard Chimu bricks; the other with Terminal Phase bricks. Thus, the northern audiencia is either the older of the two or it was made with reused bricks. Like the audiencia in the Major Quadrangle, it is better constructed than the surrounding structure.

Comparison With Other Sites

One goal of the brick study at Pacatnamu was to compare the bricks with those at other north coast Chimu sites. At Chan Chan (Kolata 1982:71) and Chotuna (Bruce 1982:16-19, 23) the height-to-width ratios of mud bricks varied through time from a lower value (thinner bricks) to a higher value (thicker bricks). The earliest bricks at those sites were flat-rectangular; later, the height-to-width ratio increased. Eventually, the bricks at Chotuna became round-topped (loaf-shaped; Bruce 1982:22). Round-topped bricks are noted by Kroeber (1930:58) at Chotuna, Purgatorio, and Huaca de los Estacos, and by Kolata (1978:62) at Chan Chan.[20] Round-topped bricks at other sites may not be identical to ovoid bricks at Pacatnamu, but they suggest a fairly widespread use of round-topped bricks by the Chimu. The shape changes at Pacatnamu do not align precisely with those at either Chan Chan or Chotuna, although the latest Chimu bricks are generally taller than the earliest.

Investigators at most other sites did not attempt to type bricks on the basis of composition. Kolata (1982:68) and Moseley (1975:192) recognized variations in soil types at their sites but did not find these variations significant for chronological purposes. Moseley (1975:193) comments that at Chan Chan mud bricks in adjacent wall segments differ in soil composition and size, indicating that they must have been made by different work parties. Bruce (1982:19) uses color as one of several secondary factors in arriving at a brick typology for Chotuna.

A cursory examination was made of mud brick architecture at Dos Cabezas, a major pyramid complex located on the valley floor south of Pacatnamu. It was felt that a comparison of the two sites would be enlightening because of their proximity, and because the alignment of Doorway 4 of the Outer Wall of Pacatnamu with the large flat mound at Dos Cabezas (Donnan, City Walls, this volume) suggests that Dos Cabezas may have had ceremonial significance for the builders of Pacatnamu. This alignment also suggests that Dos Cabezas preceded the Outer Wall and possibly the entire occupation of Pacatnamu. This supposition is supported by the prevalence of cane-marked bricks at Dos Cabezas compared with their relative scarcity at Pacatnamu. According to Hastings and Moseley (1975:198-202), cane-marked bricks are prominent in the Gallinazo period and decrease thereafter, virtually disappearing by the end of the Moche period.

Brick technology at the two sites is very different. Pacatnamu is characterized by many relatively low walls and pyramidal structures, case-and-fill construction, handmade bricks (except for Moche structures), ovoid bricks, and several colors of brick material. The brick structures at Dos Cabezas are fewer but taller and more massive. They involve solid brick construction made with accurately shaped, mold-made, flat-rectangular bricks having little variation in silt types. At Dos Cabezas brick size is correlated with elevation in the structure: lowest courses have very large bricks, with size diminishing at higher elevations. This characteristic is nonexistent at Pacatnamu.

20. Kolata refers to the round-topped bricks at Chan Chan as "tortuga" (tortoise) bricks but does not explain their relationship to the rectangular bricks.

Summary and Conclusions

Four construction phases (Moche, Intermediate, Initial Chimu, and Terminal Chimu) and four basic brick types that correspond to these phases have been identified at Pacatnamu.

1. Moche: flat-rectangular, river-silt bricks. They appear to be mostly mold-made, a few having cane mold marks.
2. Intermediate: flat-rectangular bricks. They often have sharp edges and slightly concave sides and are mottled or made of yellowish river-silt with a gray patina.
3. Standard Chimu: flat-rectangular, river-silt bricks used from the Initial through the Terminal Chimu occupation phase. They often have slightly sloping sides and ends, with a trapezoidal cross section.
4. Terminal Chimu: flat-rectangular and ovoid bricks of colored, hard-silt, or conglomerate material.

The assignment of brick types to these phases is based on ceramic and burial associations, wall abutment patterns, and relative positions of brick types within structures.

Moche occupation underlies much of the site of Pacatnamu. The largest Moche structure, and the best example of Moche architecture, is the original construction of Huaca 31 and its associated structures. There is firm evidence of the use of molds for making bricks only during the Moche Phase. In later phases, flat wood tools may have been used to help shape bricks.

The Intermediate Phase has been identified at only a few locations in the vicinity of Huaca 31. It is best represented by the Huaca 31 ramp.

The Initial Chimu Phase includes many of the larger structures at the site: Huaca 1, the Major Quadrangle walls, the Inner Wall trench and causeway (and possibly the Inner Wall facing), and probably many of the other large huacas.

Terminal Chimu is found throughout the site on the uppermost layers of most structures, such as Huaca 1, the Major Quadrangle walls, and Huaca 31. Huacas 4, 49, and 50 may have been started during the Initial Chimu Phase but they have substantial Terminal Phase structural additions. Other structures such as H1M1, the Outer Wall, the South Wall, the quadrangles of Huacas 8 and 23a, and Huacas 18 and 29 may be almost entirely Terminal Phase.

Terminal Chimu construction appears to be the latest at Pacatnamu for the following reasons:

1. It always seems to be applied after Initial Phase construction; e.g., as upper courses of walls, as outer facing layers, or to fill gaps in Initial Phase walls.
2. Wall abutment and alignment patterns indicate that complexes built primarily with Terminal Phase bricks are later than adjacent complexes built with fewer such bricks (cf. Huaca 23a and Huacas 49 and 50).
3. Stacks of unset conglomerate bricks beside Huaca 18 and on the summit of Huaca 29 suggest they were under construction at the time they were abandoned.

Several distinct wall construction styles are found within the Terminal Phase suggesting that it may be possible to seriate Terminal Phase structures based on the subtypes of bricks used and their arrangement in walls. It appears that the fraction of conglomerate bricks increased with time. Throughout the Chimu occupation, walls were often built in segments in a manner similar to other North Coast sites.

The quality of the brick material and masonry construction deteriorated during the Terminal Phase. This may point to a playing out of good silt sources in later times, or more likely to a reduction in the labor force available to bring good quality materials from the alluvial river valley, thereby forcing increased use of the poorer quality material found readily at hand on the plateau. It may also suggest a period in which haste was of the essence in completing the monumental architecture of Pacatnamu.

The bricks at Pacatnamu tell an interesting story about the site's history. The brick typology and seriation presented here, of course, apply only to Pacatnamu and not to North Coast Chimu sites in general. Although there is a generic similarity to the brick construction reported at some other North Coast Moche and Chimu sites, Pacatnamu has its unique characteristics. The evolution of brick shapes is different from that at Chan Chan and Chotuna, and more types of brick material are used at Pacatnamu than at the other sites. It is possible, of course, that Chimu occupation at Pacatnamu was too short to exhibit the full range of brick evolution found at the other sites. It is expected that the brick typology and seriation will continue to be useful as more structures are excavated. The data derived from continuing excavation will, in turn, make it possible to further refine the brick chronology.

RESUMEN:
Seriación de Adobes en Pacatnamú

Los adobes han sido, por más de 3500 años, el material de construcción fundamental en la costa del Perú. Dado que practicamente todas las estructuras de Pacatnamú han sido construidas con este material, se inició una investigación que estableciese una tipología que condujese a una mejor comprensión de la secuencia de construcción en el sitio.

Se han identificado cuatro fases de construcción: Moche, Intermedia, Chimú Inicial y Chimú Terminal o Final (Fig. 1):

1. *Las construcciones Moche están representadas por la plataforma original de la Huaca 31 (Fig. 2), las tres paredes paralelas asociadas a ella y el denominado Cuarto de las Ofrendas.*

2. *La fase Intermedia tiene un buen ejemplo en la rampa de la Huaca 31 (Fig. 3).*

3. *Durante la fase Chimú Inicial fueron construidas la mayor parte de las estructuras que se ven en la actualidad, incluyendo la Huaca 1 y su Cuadrángulo Mayor, el foso y las rampas de ingreso de la Muralla Interior y probablemente la mayoría de las huacas más grandes del sitio (Figs. 4A y 4B).*

4. *El Chimú Terminal se encuentra en las capas superiores de la mayoría de las estructuras, como en la Huaca 31 (Figs. 6A y 6B). Otras construcciones como la Muralla Exterior, la Muralla Sur y las Huacas 18 y 29, parecieran haber sido construidas completamente durante el Chimú Final. La evidencia sugiere que las Huacas 18 y 29 estaban bajo construcción cuando fueron abandonados (Fig. 7).*

Se han identificado cuatro tipos de adobes (Fig. 1):

1. Adobes Moche, *de forma plano-rectangular y hechos con barro de río, color marrón y marrón grisáceo (Fig. 2).*

2. Adobes Intermedios, *son también plano-rectangulares, pero irregulares, y moteados por la mezcla de materiales usada, gris claro con marcas color óxido y amarillos con superficie grisácea (Fig. 3).*

3. Standard Chimú *son hechos nuevamente con barro de río, marrón y marrón grisaceo, pero su forma tiene tendencia a ser parecida a un "pan de molde" (Figs. 4A, 4B).*

4. Chimú Terminal *son ovoides y con color marcado, marrón o gris obscuro y amarillo palido (Figs. 6A, 6B). Se pueden dividir hasta en 7 sub-tipos, de acuerdo a la forma y el material usado.*

Por la mezcla en el uso de tamaños y disposición en las estructuras, el análisis de grupos de adobes provee mejor y más confiable información, que el análisis de adobes individuales (Figs. 5, 8).

Los adobes hechos con molde pertenecen solo al Período Moche.

Durante el Período Chimú, las paredes fueron construidas por segmentos, como en otros sitios de la Costa Norte (Fig. 9).

La Fase Chimú Terminal se caracteriza por modificaciones encima de la superficie de las estructuras existentes, mas que por reconstrucciones extensivas. Esto podría sugerir que el Chimú Terminal es bastante corto en Pacatnamú (Figs. 6A, 11, 14).

La calidad de los adobes y de las técnicas de construcción muestran un significativo deterioro durante el Chimú Terminal.

Aunque hay una similaridad genérica con los adobes reportados en otros sitios de la Costa Norte, Pacatnamú posee sus propias características a este respecto. La evolución de la forma de los adobes es diferente que en Chan Chan o Chotuna, y el uso de más tipos de material resalta en contraste con éstos y otros sitios. Tampoco se halla todo el rango de adobes Chimú conocidos a la fecha, lo que podría tener implicancias para el entendimiento de este período en el sitio.

The City Walls at Pacatnamu

Christopher B. Donnan

The site of Pacatnamu is roughly triangular in plan, with two sides defined by cliffs that rise from the beach on the west and from the valley floor on the southeast (Fig. 1). These high cliffs effectively restrict access to the site on two sides of the triangle, but the third side, to the north, is easily approachable. The southern tip of the site, where there is a gentle slope instead of a sheer cliff face, is also vulnerable. To protect these two exposures, ancient inhabitants expended considerable effort to construct formidable barriers to span the site from east to west.

Although some of the barriers were abandoned before they were completed, they were meant to restrict access by means of high walls. In most instances, these walls were to have had a trench along the outer side, the depth of which would have enhanced their height and thus increased their effectiveness.

The walls along the north side of the site may have been built at different times, possibly in response to the expanding size of the settlement. The earliest of these would have been the Inner Wall. It runs from east to west across the site, through the central area of monumental architecture (Figs. 2,3). The Outer Wall was built to the north of the Inner Wall. It begins at the eastern cliff face and extends approximately half the distance across the site, connecting there with a deep ravine that cuts down to the beach. The Outer Wall has two extensions that continue west of the ravine, but both of these appear to have been abandoned before they were completed.

North of the Outer Wall is an unfinished attempt at building a third major barrier (Figs. 2,3). It consists solely of sections of a trench; the construction of the adjacent wall apparently had not begun when the project was abandoned. Like the Outer Wall, this third barrier was designed to connect with the deep ravine that cuts across the western half of the site. This barrier will be referred to as the Unfinished Wall.

In addition to these three walls, there is another wall near the southern tip of the site that extends from the eastern to the western cliff face. Although less massive than the walls on the north side of the site, it would have served as a formidable barrier along the southern margin. It will be referred to as the South Wall.

The three walls on the north side of the site and the one at the southern tip would have been very effective in restricting access to the central portion of Pacatnamu. We will now turn to a more detailed discussion of each.

Figure 1. Air photo of Pacatnamu.

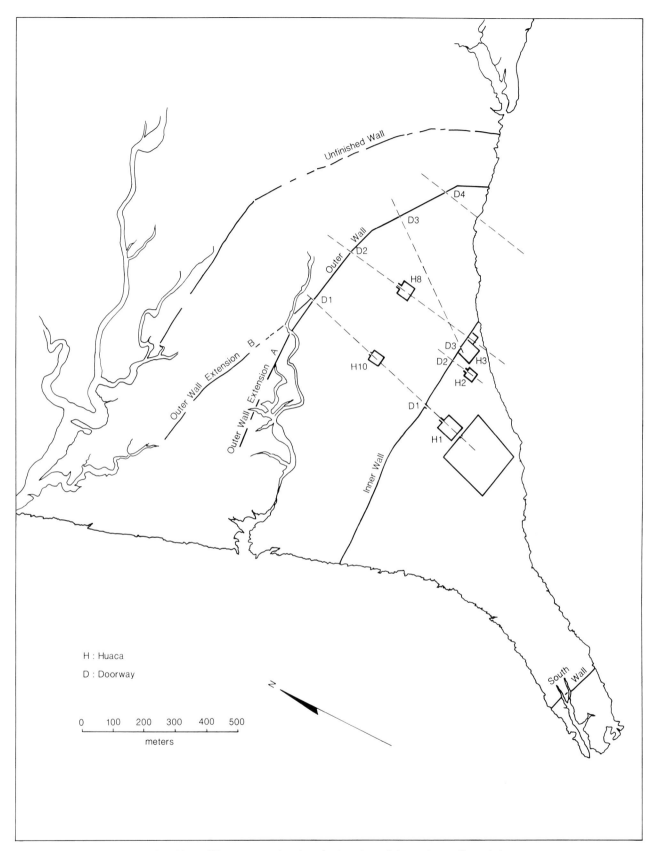

Figure 2.   *Map of Pacatnamu showing the location of the major walls and doorways
as well as some of the structures aligned with the doorways.*

Figure 3. Air photo of Pacatnamu looking west, indicating the location of the Inner Wall, Outer Wall, and Unfinished Wall.

The Inner Wall

The Inner Wall appears on air photographs of Pacatnamu as a light-colored line (Figs. 1,3). Viewed on the ground, it is a nearly continuous band of white, windblown sand. Because it appears to be both linear and relatively level, it has been mistakenly referred to as a road by previous researchers (Hecker and Hecker 1977, 1982). Actually, the line is a deep trench filled with windblown sand, which extends from the east side to the west side of the site. Our excavations along this trench provided seven profiles across its width that are remarkably similar to one another in size and form. The trench has a trapezoidal cross section, with an average depth of approximately 2.4 meters. The width at the top is approximately 3.3 meters, and at the bottom, which is nearly flat, it averages approximately 1.1 meters.

A massive wall made of case and fill was constructed along the southern edge of the trench. This appears to have been built in segments—each architectural complex located along the southern

edge of the trench having an independently constructed portion of the wall. Thus, there is considerable variation in the size and quality of the wall at different places along its length.

The best preserved and most massive section is immediately north of Huaca 1, forming the northern side of the courtyard in front of the huaca. This wall is approximately 6.5 meters thick at the base and still stands to a height of 3 meters. Given the massive thickness of its base, the original height may have been as much as 5 meters. It is straight and well constructed. In contrast, the section of wall immediately west of the courtyard has numerous curves, and the masonry is irregular.

East of Huaca 1, the wall appears to have been part of the courtyard in front of Huaca 2. It is considerably narrower and less impressive than the section in front of Huaca 1 and today is more extensively eroded. The section in front of Huaca 3 is actually the north side of the huaca itself.

On the west side of the site it is difficult to identify sections of the Inner Wall, even though the trench is clearly visible. In most areas, there is only

Figure 4. Air photo of Huaca 1, looking south. The location of the Inner Wall, with Doorway 1, is indicated.

a low mound of earth where the wall would have been. In part, this is because the erosion of standing architecture on the west side is greater than on the central or east sides, due to the greater moisture and salt content of the ocean air, which accelerates decomposition of adobe. In addition, the materials used to construct the wall on the west side may have been less substantial—perhaps thinner casing walls and more fill. It is also possible, however, that sections of the wall had not been completed. Both the Outer Wall and the Unfinished Wall appear to be noticeably less effective on the west side of the site than on the east. Perhaps this was also the case with the Inner Wall, which today is clearly more imposing on the east.

There are three doorways that provide access through the Inner Wall. The largest of these is Doorway 1, located north of Huaca 1, the largest and most imposing structure at Pacatnamu (Fig. 4). Here a causeway spans the trench, its upper surface forming a ramp that rises from the north to the threshold of the doorway (Fig. 5). The location of Doorway 1 is clearly related to the position of

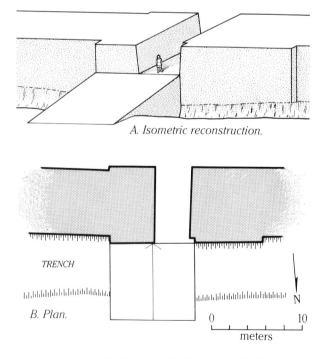

A. Isometric reconstruction.

B. Plan.

TRENCH

N

0   10
meters

Figure 5. Doorway 1 of the Inner Wall.

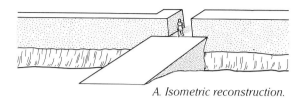

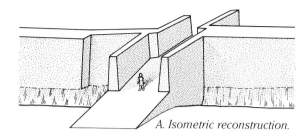

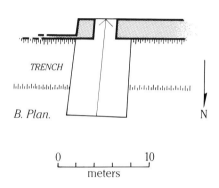

A. Isometric reconstruction.

TRENCH

B. Plan.

N

0   10
meters

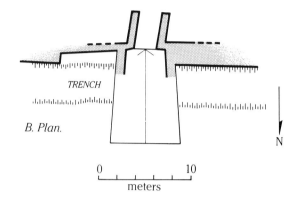

A. Isometric reconstruction.

TRENCH

B. Plan.

N

0   10
meters

Figure 6.   Doorway 2 of the Inner Wall.

Figure 7.   Doorway 3 of the Inner Wall.

Huaca 1. It provides access to the courtyard in front of the huaca, and because it was built in alignment with the ramp on the huaca's north side, it creates a very elegant entry to this ceremonial complex. Doorway 1 was originally 5.75 meters wide and aligned with the ramp. It was subsequently constricted by adobe construction along the east side, thus reducing its width to 3.8 meters and leaving it somewhat out of alignment with the ramp. The reduction of the doorway also involved the construction of a pilaster on the east side, but no matching pilaster was built on the west (Fig. 5).

Doorway 2 provides access to the courtyard in front of Huaca 2 and is in alignment with the ramp leading to its summit. The doorway is 2.5 meters wide and has a square pilaster on its east side (Fig. 6). A causeway across the trench forms a ramp that rises from the north to the threshold of the doorway.

Doorway 3 is in front of Huaca 3. In contrast to the other two doorways, it does not provide access to a courtyard. Instead, the causeway spanning the trench forms the main ramp of Huaca 3 and thus leads directly to an upper level of the huaca (Fig. 7). The doorway is 4.5 meters wide and is flanked by narrow walls that form a 90° angle with a wall

along the front side of the huaca.

Although the design and construction of the three doorways along the Inner Wall exhibit considerable variation, the causeways that span the trench in front of these doorways are quite similar. Each is built of case and fill with side walls made of adobe. All of the lowest courses of the walls are set on the floor of the trench, suggesting that the three causeways were built soon after the trench was excavated.

The Outer Wall

Although there are numerous similarities between the Inner Wall and the Outer Wall at Pacatnamu, there are also several basic differences. The Outer Wall is more massive than the Inner Wall. The adjacent trench is wide but very shallow, and it does not appear to have added substantially to the creation of a barrier (Fig. 8). Instead, it may have served as a convenient source for fill used in constructing the wall, or possibly as a source of material from which some of the bricks were made. The trench varies from 3 to 11 meters in width and from 0.2 to 2.3 meters in depth. In general, it has a shallow, flat bottom, but in one part it is stepped on the

Figure 8. View looking west along the Outer Wall (left) and its adjacent trench.

south side, adjacent to the wall.

It is difficult to assess how much of the trench was entirely manmade and how much may have been a modified natural erosion channel. Clearly, a major erosion channel extends from the center of the site to the western cliff face, and part of the trench on the eastern half of the site may have been a natural channel as well.

Although the trench that extends along the north side of the Outer Wall is shallow, the wall itself is massive. It averages approximately 9 meters in width at its base and in some portions still stands to a height of 4.5 meters. Its original height was probably more than 7 meters. The wall was constructed of case and fill. The casing walls were built in segments, with distinct bricks and mortar utilized in adjacent sections (McClelland, this volume).

One section of the Outer Wall, labeled Outer Wall Extension A (Fig. 2), continues west of the ravine, but it appears to have been abandoned before it was completed. Today, it can be recognized as segmented portions of a trench that do not continue to the western cliff face. Only the eastern portion of this trench has an adobe wall along its southern edge.

Segmented portions of another trench, labeled Outer Wall Extension B (Fig. 2), can be seen appended to the Outer Wall near the central part of the site. It extends toward the west to intersect with one branch of another deep ravine that cuts through the western cliff face. Its segmented state and the lack of any adjacent walls suggest that it was abandoned soon after it was begun.

Outer Wall Extension B would have enclosed a triangular portion of the site which has manmade surface features clearly visible in the air photographs (Fig. 1). Surface survey of this area reveals well-planned rectangular architectural units and indicates a very short, late occupation on the periphery of the site near the close of the site's occupation. Perhaps Outer Wall Extension B was an attempt to enclose this new community within the major walls. If so, the cessation of construction may be associated with a general abandonment of this section of the site.

There are four doorways through the Outer Wall (Fig. 2). The portion of the trench on the north side of these doorways was left unexcavated, thus eliminating the need to build causeways.

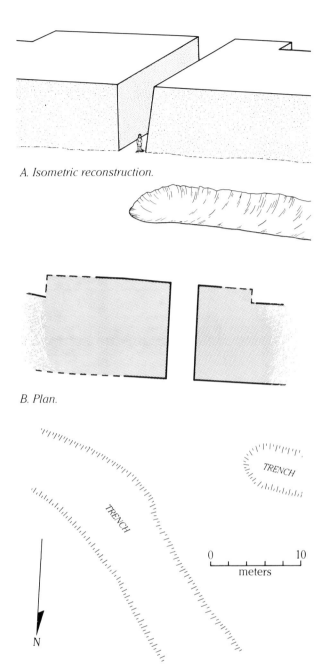

A. *Isometric reconstruction.*

B. *Plan.*

TRENCH

TRENCH

0   10
meters

N

Figure 9.   Doorway 1 of Outer Wall.

The Unfinished Wall

North of the Outer Wall, and roughly parallel to it, is the Unfinished Wall. It consists of a man-made trench extending from the eastern cliff face to a major ravine that cuts through the western cliff face and leads down toward the beach. The trench is quite large at the eastern cliff face, but as it extends westward it soon becomes segmented, and near the center of the site it appears to have barely been started. There is no evidence of a wall along the south side of the trench. Instead, it appears that the project was abandoned shortly after it got underway.

The South Wall

The South Wall does not have an adjacent trench and appears to have been less substantial than the other city walls. Only a low remnant is visible on the surface of the site. It was originally built of adobe casing walls filled with rubble and rounded cobbles, which have spilled out as the walls eroded. It is fairly consistent in width, averaging 2.1 meters at the base. It was built directly on the hard conglomerate that forms the geological base of the site.

There are three distinct sections of the South Wall. The longest extends from the eastern cliff face to the ravine where the present road is located. A second section extends west to the next ravine, and a third section extends from that point to the western cliff face.

There are only two places along the South Wall where doorways could have been located. One is where the first and second sections meet in the eastern ravine, and the other is where the second and third sections meet in the western ravine. Unfortunately, heavy erosion at these points has destroyed all traces of the wall, along with any evidence of doorways. Nevertheless, the fact that the present road passes through the South Wall at the eastern ravine suggests there was an ancient doorway at this location.

Chronology of Wall Construction

It is clear that all of the major walls were built during the Chimu occupation of Pacatnamu, which begins after A.D. 1100 (Donnan, Introduction, this volume; McClelland, this volume). No evidence has yet been found that would indicate that the site had similar walls or trenches during the Moche occupation.[1]

---

1. The Heckers (1985:39) have pointed out that there appears to be an east-west wall connecting Huacas 5, 6, 7, 8, and 9, located in the northeast portion of Pacatnamu. Moreover, they have postulated that this wall may have been built prior to the construction of the huacas. Careful examination of the bricks used in constructing this wall, however, indicates that it is Chimu, and portions of it may even be Terminal Chimu, as defined by McClelland (this volume). It does not appear to be a defensive wall since it has no adjacent trench, nor does it span the width of the site from east to west. Thus it is not considered in this report as a city wall.

Figure 10. *View looking south through Doorway 2 of Outer Wall, showing the perfect alignment with Huaca 8.*

Figure 11. *View looking north from the center of the ramp at the summit of Huaca 8. Note the perfect alignment of Doorway 2 of the Outer Wall with the conical peak of the Cerros de Catalina (Charcape) in the background.*

Doorway 1 of the Outer Wall is located about midway between the eastern and western cliff faces. Its exact position appears to have been carefully selected since it is aligned with the altar and ramp of Huaca 10, Doorway 1 of the Inner Wall, the ramp of Huaca 1, and the doorway of the Major Quadrangle (Fig. 2; Donnan, Huaca 1, this volume). The doorway is 3 meters wide and has two large interior pilasters of differing size and form (Fig. 9).

Doorway 2 is approximately 175 meters east of Doorway 1. It aligns with the ramp of Huaca 8, the second largest huaca at Pacatnamu (Figs. 2,10). Moreover, from the center of the ramp of Huaca 8 looking north through this doorway, there is an exact alignment with the summit of a conical peak located in the Cerros de Catalina (Charcape), 10.5 kilometers north of Pacatnamu (Fig. 11). This doorway is 1.8 meters wide and has several post holes flanking it about 20 centimeters in front of the interior side of the wall (Fig. 12A). These suggest the possible existence of a gate or removable barrier used to close the doorway. Large vertical posts would have been ideal for supporting horizontal beams set one on top of the other between the posts and the wall to span the doorway. No evidence of post holes similar to those at Doorway 2 have been found at other doorways at Pacatnamu.

Doorway 3 of the Outer Wall is approximately 175 meters east of Doorway 2. It is in alignment with the ramp of Huaca 3 (Fig. 2). The doorway is 3.8 meters wide, with a large, interior pilaster on its west side (Fig. 13). Sometime after its construction, Doorway 3 was deliberately closed off with an adobe wall built across its interior. This wall was flush with the north face of the Outer Wall, but because it was only 5 meters thick, it left a niche on the southern face (Fig. 13). It is not clear why Doorway 3 was closed. It should be noted, however, that a natural erosion channel flows against the north side of the Outer Wall near Doorway 3. Perhaps heavy rainfall on the plain north of Pacatnamu during a niño caused water to flow into the city through this doorway. If so, the doorway may have been closed off to prevent subsequent flooding.

Doorway 4 of the Outer Wall is approximately 165 meters east of Doorway 3. Today the road from Guadalupe to La Barranca passes through the Outer Wall at this location, and the original doorway has been bulldozed to widen it for modern use. Nonetheless, careful excavation revealed its original size and form. It was 2.7 meters wide and appears to have had no interior pilasters (Fig. 14). It was deliberately built to be diagonal rather than per-

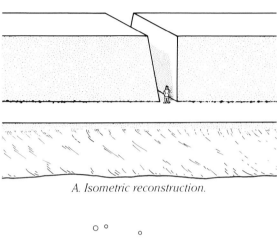

A. Isometric reconstruction.

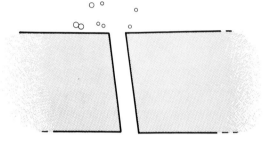

TRENCH

B. Plan.

N

0   10
meters

Figure 12. Doorway 2 of the Outer Wall.

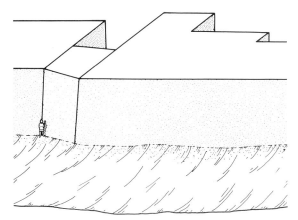

A. Isometric reconstruction.

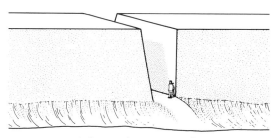

A. Isometric reconstruction.

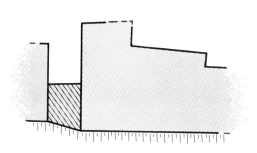

TRENCH

B. Plan; crosshatching indicates the
section added to close off the door.

N

0   10
meters

Figure 13.   Doorway 3 of the Outer Wall.

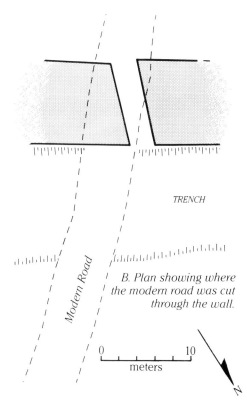

TRENCH

B. Plan showing where
the modern road was cut
through the wall.

Modern Road

0   10
meters

N

Figure 14.   Doorway 4 of the Outer Wall.

pendicular to the Outer Wall. Its alignment is not toward any major construction at Pacatnamu but rather to the archaeological site of Dos Cabezas, located on the floor of the Jequetepeque Valley, approximately 2.2 kilometers to the south.

Since the Inner Wall would not have been necessary for defensive purposes once the Outer Wall was completed, it was probably built before the Outer Wall. The Outer Wall appears to have been finished before the Unfinished Wall was begun, at least as far west as the ravine at the central part of the site. Outer Wall Extension A and Outer Wall Extension B may have been constructed as sequential projects, with each being abandoned as another wall, incorporating more site area, was begun further to the north. The Unfinished Wall appears to have been the last in this sequence of ever more northward wall constructions, but it clearly was abandoned long before it was completed.

If the sequence of Inner Wall, Outer Wall, and Unfinished Wall is correct, it suggests that the motivation for wall construction was to create a major barrier along the northern margin of the site, and that this margin was being pushed further north by a rapidly growing settlement. It also suggests that this growth ended rather suddenly during the construction of the Unfinished Wall and probably shrank back rapidly to the area inside the Outer Wall.

It is difficult to place the construction of the South Wall within the hypothetical sequence of construction along the northern margin of the site.[2] On one hand, it seems reasonable that the South Wall would have been built at about the same time as the Inner Wall to secure this margin of the site that otherwise would have been left open to entry from the valley floor. The relatively small size of the South Wall, however, and the absence of an adjacent trench, suggest that attack from the southern side of the site was considerably less threatening than attack from the north. This being the case, it could be argued that the South Wall could have been built any time during the construction of the northern walls, depending on when the people at Pacatnamu felt sufficiently threatened to commit the labor and materials for its construction.

Function of the City Walls

Although it is assumed that the city walls at Pacatnamu were built for defense, there are some aspects of their design and construction that suggest this may be an oversimplification.

While the deep trench along the Inner Wall would have formed a formidable barrier across the entire width of Pacatnamu, the wall itself appears to have been rather minimal along the western half of the site, leaving it more vulnerable to attack. If defense alone motivated the construction of the Inner Wall, one would expect the entire wall to have had the same defensive potential.

The Outer Wall is similar to the Inner Wall in being considerably less effective along the western side. It is massive from the eastern cliff face to the central part of the site where it connects with the large ravine. From that point to the western cliff face, the wall is incomplete and only the ravine itself provides a boundary. Today, most parts of the ravine are relatively shallow and can be crossed without difficulty, so the ravine itself would provide little or no defense against an invading army. The only way it could have been effective in the past was if its southern edge had been deliberately cut to form a deep vertical face. There is no evidence that this was done, but erosion since the site was abandoned could have removed all traces of such alteration.

The Unfinished Wall also appears to have been planned to connect with a ravine on the western side of the site. Therefore, it too would have provided a rather weak defense unless the sides of the ravine had been altered.

Another factor that seems curious if the walls were to function defensively is the multiple doorways. Certainly a single doorway in each wall would have been easier to defend while not greatly lengthening the distance traveled to enter or leave the site. Since each of the three doorways along the Inner Wall is aligned with a specific huaca, perhaps access to the huaca was the critical factor in the creation of multiple entrances in this wall. On the Outer Wall, however, the distance from the doorways to the huacas with which they are aligned is considerable, and in the case of Doorways 3 and 4, alignment is not with any structure readily accessible to a person entering Pacatnamu.

One possible explanation for the four doorways in the Outer Wall is found in the writing of Filipe de Medina who, in 1650, described a Pre-Columbian ceremonial site near Huacho that had

---

2. McClelland (this volume) has suggested that it may have been built during the Terminal Chimu phase, but the evidence is not conclusive.

four entrances—one for males from the coast, one for females from the coast, one for males from the sierra, and one for females from the sierra (Medina 1904[1650]:215; Rostworowski 1981:117). Perhaps the doorways in the Outer Wall at Pacatnamu were also designed for use according to sex and origin.

It should be noted that no two of the seven doorways discussed above are alike. Most similar are Doorway 2 and Doorway 4 in the Outer Wall, since neither has interior pilasters. But even these two are different: Doorway 2 is perpendicular to the wall, and the trench is several meters away from its north side; Doorway 4 is diagonal to the wall, and the trench is adjacent to the north side. Each of the other five doorways has one or more interior pilasters, but size and form are unique to each doorway. Also, the pilasters are all asymmetrical, as though there was a deliberate attempt to make the two sides of the doorway dissimilar. The reason for this is not clear, but it may well be that it is related to their use by distinct groups of individuals.

While the multiple doorways and relatively weak western portions may suggest that the city walls were not constructed solely for defense, they have various features that indicate defense was at least an important factor. Primary among these is their immense scale. The Outer Wall averages 9 meters in width at its base and may have been 7 meters high. Portions of this wall, where the sides are preserved, indicate it was trapezoidal in cross section, with the sides tapering inward toward the top.[3] If our 7-meter estimate for the height is correct, the top would have been approximately 6 meters wide. This would have been ample width to serve as a terreplein from which to defend the site from attack. A small wall might have been built along the north side of this terreplein to serve as a parapet to shield the defenders from objects thrown by attackers. Walls with terrepleins and parapets have been reported from other sites on the North Coast (Bawden 1977, 1982; Topic and Topic 1978).

The Inner Wall also has portions thick enough to have served as a terreplein. This is particularly evident in the section that borders the courtyard north of Huaca 1 where the wall is 6.5 meters thick and may have been 5 meters high. The top would

have been approximately 5 meters wide, sufficient for a terreplein.

The Outer Wall, and the thickest portions of the Inner Wall, are unique at Pacatnamu. All other walls are less than 2.2 meters wide at the base, and their width at the top would have been too narrow to serve as a terreplein.[4]

The deep trench along the entire length of the Inner Wall provides additional evidence that this wall had a defensive function. Excavation of this trench would have required the removal of more than 4,500 cubic meters of the hard conglomerate that forms the base of the site, which would have been an enormous undertaking. For defense, however, the trench would have been extremely effective. Even with a relatively minimal wall along its south side, defenders could have easily prevented attackers from crossing this barrier. Only at the three causeways would crossing have been possible, but here defenders had the advantage of thick, pilastered doorways, defensive walls, and an elevated position relative to the attacking force.

Therefore, although the city walls of Pacatnamu have some features that seem inappropriate to a defensive function, other features indicate that defense was a primary motivation for their construction.

Labor Requirements

Calculations of the amount of manpower required to build Pacatnamu's walls are difficult since the architecture is heavily eroded and estimates of original size must be approximated. Nevertheless, there was unquestionably a great deal of effort put forth in the construction of these walls, and it is worthwhile to attempt to assess what that effort may have been. In doing so, focus will rest primarily on the Outer Wall, since it is reasonably complete and clearly represents the largest and most labor-intensive project.

Excavations suggest that the average thickness of the Outer Wall at its base was approximately 9 meters. The wall now stands to a height of 4.5 meters in several sections and almost certainly had an average height of more than 7 meters. Its length,

---

3. The Heckers (1985:40,41; fig. 4) have suggested that the Outer Wall was stepped along its south side to form these distinct levels. We were not able to find any evidence of this.
4. The large walls enclosing the Major Quadrangle of the Huaca 1 Complex vary between 1.8 and 2.2 meters in width at the base, and their original height was probably about 5 meters. Given their trapezoidal cross section, their width at

the top would have been between 0.50 and 1.20 meters—clearly insufficient to serve as a parapet. These walls, therefore, must have functioned simply to demarcate the boundaries of a sacred precinct, to provide privacy, and to assure restricted access. They do not appear to have been built for defensive purposes.

from the eastern cliff face to the ravine near the center of the site, is approximately 830 meters. Therefore, the volume of masonry construction in this section alone would have been about 43,000 cubic meters.

I am reluctant to make a hypothetical estimate of how many man-days of labor were required to complete the monumental task of constructing the walls at Pacatnamu. Such calculations have been attempted by various scholars dealing with other sites and other projects and have generally resulted in widely varying conclusions. I do, however, feel it is valid to compare the construction of the city walls with other monumental constructions at the same site.

Huaca 1, the largest truncated pyramid at Pacatnamu, consists of approximately 40,000 cubic meters of case-and-fill masonry, while Huaca 8, the second largest, has approximately 25,000 cubic meters. One must bear in mind, however, that these truncated pyramids were often built on top of earlier pyramids, some of which date to the Moche occupation of Pacatnamu. They appear to have grown to their present size through a series of enlargements over a long period of time. The construction of the city walls, however, was presumably a single project that took place during a period of a few years. In this respect, they clearly represent a quantum leap in the scale of construction at Pacatnamu. No other corporate labor project or group of projects ever approached the magnitude of this one, or demanded such intense concentration of large numbers of workers at a single time.

Conclusion

Clarifying the function of the city walls of Pacatnamu makes possible a clearer and more detailed analysis of the nature of the site during its Chimu occupation. The numerous pyramid mounds provide clear evidence that one of the primary functions of the site was ceremonial, and most published reports focus on this aspect. Some have even suggested that Pacatnamu served as a pilgrimage center similar to Pachacamac on the central coast, and had religious devotees coming to it from great distances, bringing tribute and seeking spiritual fulfillment (Keatinge 1978).

Although this may have been the case, the city walls indicate that a major concern at Pacatnamu during its late occupation was defense. The residents of Pacatnamu were able to create a formidable fortification by incorporating natural ravines and the cliff faces on the east and west, and by constructing major walls and trenches to provide protection along the exposed northern and southern sides of the site. The amount of effort and material invested in the construction of the walls and trenches, when compared with that required to build even the largest pyramid mound, provide ample evidence of the need for security from attack. This need, impressively demonstrated by the city walls, clearly had a profound effect on the location, size, and form of Pacatnamu during its Chimu occupation.

RESUMEN:
Las Murallas de Pacatnamú

Por la ubicación y la forma triangular de Pacatnamú (Fig. 1), los barrancos que lo rodean protegen el sitio por dos de sus 3 lados. Con la finalidad de cerrar el tercer acceso, al norte, y asegurar el sur, los habitantes pre-hispánicos de Pacatnamú invirtieron considerable esfuerzo en la construcción de 4 murallas que uniesen los barrancos ubicados al este y oeste del sitio (Figs. 1 y 2).

La Muralla Interior

Aparentemente se trata de la más temprana. Se compone de:
1. Un foso trapezoidal con medidas promedio: 2.4 mts. de profundidad, 1.10 mts. de ancho en el fondo, y 3.30 mts. de ancho en la superficie.
2. Una muralla este-oeste, que en la parte mejor preservada—en frente de la Huaca 1—mide 6.50 mts. de ancho en la base y 3 mts. de alto. Se piensa que podría haber medido 5 mts. de alto.

Hay tres entradas que permiten atravesarla:
1. Puerta 1 (D1; Figs. 2 y 5), frente a la Huaca 1.
2. Puerta 2 (D2; Figs. 2 y 6), frente a la Huaca 2.
3. Puerta 3 (D3; Figs. 2 y 7), frente a la Huaca 3.

La Muralla Externa

Es más tardía que la Interior y debió ser construida obedeciendo a la expansión del sitio. Posee los mismos componentes básicos:
1. Un foso, cuyo ancho varía de 3 a 11 mts. y su profundidad de 0.20 a 2.30 mts., por lo que podría ser parcialmente un canal de erosión natural y no construido como el de la Muralla Interior (Fig. 8).
2. Una muralla este-oeste, con dos extensiones (A y B, Fig. 2) inconclusas. Mide 9 mts. de promedio en la base y todavía alcanza una altura de 4.50 mts. Quizá la altura original fue de 7 mts.

Tiene 4 entradas cuidadosamente planeadas:
1. Puerta 1 (D1; Figs. 2, 9), está alineada con la rampa de la Huaca 10, Puerta 1 de la Muralla Interior y la rampa de la Huaca 1.
2. Puerta 2 (D2; Figs. 2, 12), está alineada con la rampa de la Huaca 8, la de segundo tamaño en Pacatnamú, desde donde, mirando hacia Puerta 2, se ve que está alineada con un pico cónico de los Cerros de Charcape (Fig. 11).
3. Puerta 3 (D3; Figs. 2, 13), está alineada con la rampa de la Huaca 3. Fue clausurada con una pared de adobes, poco tiempo después de su construcción.
4. Puerta 4 (D4; Figs. 2, 14), hoy pasa por allí la trocha que viene de Guadalupe; mediante excavaciones se determinó que está alineada con la Huaca Dos Cabezas, a 2.2 kms. al sur, al otro lado del río.

La Muralla Inconclusa

Está al norte de la pared exterior (Fig. 2) y parece que el proyecto fue abandonado a poco de comenzar.

La Muralla Sur

No posee foso y parece haber sido de menores dimensiones que las otras. Mide un promedio de 2.10 mts. de ancho en la base. No se pudieron ubicar las entradas, debido a la erosión y al paso de la trocha que viene de Guadalupe.

Cronología

Todas las murallas se construyeron durante la ocupación Chimú, después de 1100 DC. La seriación de adobes y el análisis del mortero usado, sugieren que se construyeron dentro de un período de tiempo relativamente corto. Primero lo fue la Interior, seguida de la Exterior y de la Inconclusa; sin embargo, no es posible asignar un lugar en esta secuencia a la Muralla Sur, pero se supone que fue construida al mismo tiempo que la Interior.

Funciones de las Murallas

Aunque se asume que tuvieron funciones defensivas, los alineamientos que presentan, así como el excesivo número de entradas, sugeriría que también estuvieron relacionadas a las funciones rituales del sitio.

Inversión de Trabajo en la Construcción

No se pretende establecer cuantos días hombre fueron necesarios para su construcción, pero una comparación de una sección de 830 mts. de la Muralla Exterior—aprox. 43,000 mts. cúbicos, con el volumen de la pirámide más grande en Pacatnamú, la Huaca 1—aprox. 40,000 mts. cúbicos, o con la Huaca 8—aprox. 25,000 mts. cúbicos; que fueron construidas sobre pirámides más tempranas, deja en claro que la construcción de las murallas fue el trabajo de mayor envergadura emprendido por los habitantes de Pacatnamú.

The Huaca 1 Complex

Christopher B. Donnan

Huaca 1 is the largest and most impressive pyramid structure at Pacatnamu and is the center of an architectural complex that dominates the central portion of the site (Map Insert, Fig. 1). Because of the obvious importance of this complex and its relatively good state of preservation, it was decided that it would be a major focus of the first two seasons of excavation. During the 1983 season, the large rectangular enclosure on the south side of Huaca 1 was extensively excavated and a nearly complete map of its internal architecture was created. This structure, which will henceforth be referred to as the Major Quadrangle, was further excavated in 1984 in order to understand the function of some of the rooms. The primary effort in 1984, however, was to clear the architecture on the west and east sides of Huaca 1, the two altars on its north side, and the large flanking pyramid to the northeast, which will henceforth be referred to as the East Pyramid. An effort was also made to clear the ramp and summit of Huaca 1 so that it could be accurately mapped and an assessment could be made of how it may have functioned.

Our efforts to excavate and record the Huaca 1 Complex were greatly facilitated by the previous work of Giesela and Wolfgang Hecker, who were members of the German archaeological expedition that worked at Pacatnamu in 1962-1963 under the direction of Heinrich Ubbelohde-Doering. The Heckers produced an excellent plan of the Huaca 1 Complex, based almost entirely on surface observations. They subsequently published this plan, along with a detailed description of the architecture and excellent observations as to how it may have functioned (Hecker and Hecker 1977, 1982, 1985).

Our efforts at the Huaca 1 Complex were intended to provide "ground truth" testing of the Heckers' work by means of careful excavation. In many instances we merely trenched along the upper portions of walls to locate corners of rooms, to test for presence of doorways, benches, and ramps, and in general to add the architectural details necessary to transform the Heckers' plans and hypotheses into drawings complete enough to reconstruct the form and function of the architecture.[1]

---

1. The importance of the Heckers' work cannot be overstated. The accuracy of their plans, the clarity of their observations, and the logic of their assumptions about this architectural complex were of tremendous help, and many of our achievements would have been difficult, if not impossible, without their pioneering efforts.

Figure 1.   Oblique air photo of the Huaca 1 Complex.

Definition of the Complex

The Huaca 1 Complex includes the numerous courtyards and clusters of rooms that surround Huaca 1, as well as the East Pyramid on the northeast, the two altars in the North Courtyard, and the Major Quadrangle on the south (Fig. 2).

The west and south sides of the complex are clearly defined by massive walls without doorways. The north margin of the complex is also quite clear—it consists of a massive wall with a deep trench on its northern side, which extends east-west across the central portion of Pacatnamu (Donnan, City Walls, this volume).

The east side of the Huaca 1 Complex is more difficult to define because the agglutinated architecture in this area appears to merge subtly into other major ceremonial compounds to the east. This situation is compounded by the relatively poor preservation of some of the walls in this area, thus making it difficult to determine the presence or absence of doorways that might connect portions of the architecture on the east side with the Huaca

1 Complex. We have chosen to define the east side of the complex as the east wall of the Major Quadrangle and to include some of the rooms and courtyards on the east and south side of the East Pyramid. It should be noted, however, that this definition is somewhat arbitrary and may not precisely correspond to the way in which the ancient inhabitants would have defined this complex.

Primary Entrance and North Courtyard

The primary entrance to the Huaca 1 Complex is from the north, by crossing the trench on a causeway and passing through a massive wall by means of a narrow door (Figs. 2,3). The door was originally 5.75 meters wide, but its width was deliberately reduced to 3.8 meters by subsequent construction on the interior of the east side. The location of this primary entrance is directly in front of, but is not precisely aligned with, the ramps leading to the summit of Huaca 1.

Just inside the primary entrance is a large courtyard containing two low altars. These altars are rectangular, with a primary east-west axis. They are made of case-and-fill construction, with carefully plastered exteriors. Each has a low flat summit, sloping sides on the east and west, and nearly vertical sides on the north and south (Figs. 4,5). The west altar is somewhat larger than the east altar and has small ramps on its north and south sides. Although neither of these altars is in alignment with the ramp of Huaca 1, they are both in alignment with the ramps of the East Pyramid. A large stream of unidentified liquid had flowed down the ramp that formed the east side of the west altar, leaving a reddish-brown residue (Fig. 6).[2]

East Pyramid

This two-level structure has a roughly rectangular footprint (Figs. 2,3). A central ramp on the west side leads up to the first level. From there, another ramp leads to the second level, which forms the summit of the pyramid. A low platform extends along the entire east side of the summit. Along the back of this platform is a low wall which is of particular interest because it was deliberately built with curves in its length. It is the only wall so constructed that has been recorded at Pacatnamu.

The East Pyramid was built with case-and-fill construction. Erosion along the upper surfaces has exposed some of the interior walls that were built to stabilize the fill that forms the structure's interior. There is no evidence of rooms or buildings on either level of the East Pyramid, with the exception of a small room on the north side of the mound. This room could have been entered from the first level of the huaca by passing through a narrow doorway.

East and Northeast Courtyards

Near the northeast corner of Huaca 1 is a narrow doorway that leads from the North Courtyard to a corridor extending along the east side of Huaca 1. Walking south along this corridor to the north side of the Major Quadrangle, one can then turn east and enter a series of large courtyards. The largest of these, East Courtyard I, is unusual in having a dense accumulation of ceramic fragments that cover nearly its entire surface in some areas.

Excavation in the area revealed a very shallow deposit of refuse on top of sterile soil.

Most of the east wall is completely eroded, but it is likely that originally it created a division between East Courtyards I and II. From a corridor that starts at the southwest corner of East Courtyard III, it was possible to gain access through a narrow door in Northeast Courtyard III to numerous other rooms and courtyards located along the south and east sides of the East Pyramid. The Heckers suggested that there may have been an entrance to Northeast Courtyard III through a doorway in the east wall (1982:51). We were unable to either confirm or deny the presence of a doorway here because the architecture was badly eroded.

West Complex

On the west side of Huaca 1 is a complex of rooms and open courtyards that forms a distinct architectural unit (Figs. 2,3,7). The only access to it is through a narrow doorway near its northwest corner. Its large central courtyard is most impressive, consisting of three walls, with twelve niches in each side.[3] The total of thirty-six niches is the greatest number found in any single location at Pacatnamu. These niches occur in various locations within the Huaca 1 Complex; they vary considerably in size as well as in architectural detail (see "Niches," below).

South of the large central courtyard is a series of rooms, three of which have niches along their walls. Two of these have baffled doorways connecting them with rooms on their north sides.

Huaca 1

Huaca 1 is the largest solid structure at Pacatnamu (Figs. 1-3). It measures approximately 70 x 70 meters at the base and is more than 10 meters high at the summit. It has a ramp leading up from the North Courtyard to a large platform that constitutes the north side of the huaca. The east side of this platform is divided into several rooms, whereas the west side is open. In the center of the platform is a second ramp that leads up to a large courtyard in the central portion of the huaca. This second ramp is somewhat narrower than the first and ap-

---

2. Samples of this residue were obtained and are currently being analyzed at the University of California, Los Angeles.
3. The Heckers (1985:159) have stated that the east side of this

room had eight columns. Our excavation in that area indicates that the "columns" are actually the eroded remains of niches. To date, no columns have been found at Pacatnamu.

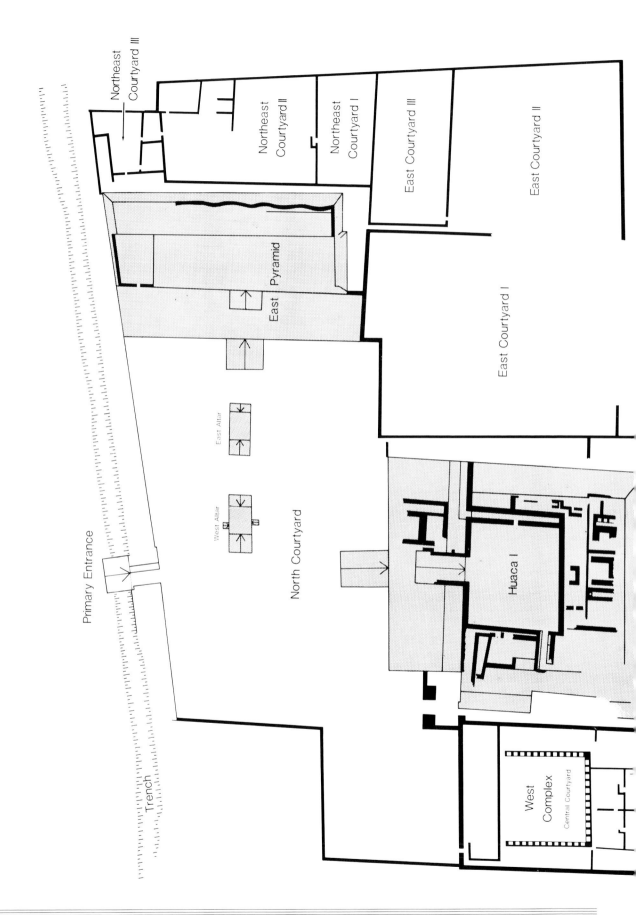

Northeast Courtyard III

Northeast Courtyard II

Northeast Courtyard I

East Courtyard III

East Courtyard II

East Courtyard I

East Pyramid

East Altar

West Altar

North Courtyard

Primary Entrance

Trench

Huaca I

West Complex

Central Courtyard

Figure 2. Plan of the Huaca 1 Complex.

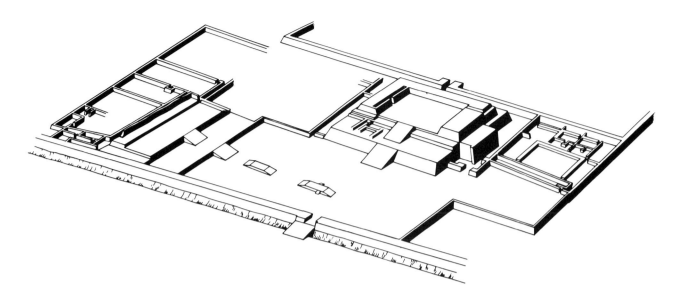

Figure 3. Isometric reconstruction of the northern part of the Huaca 1 Complex, looking southeast.

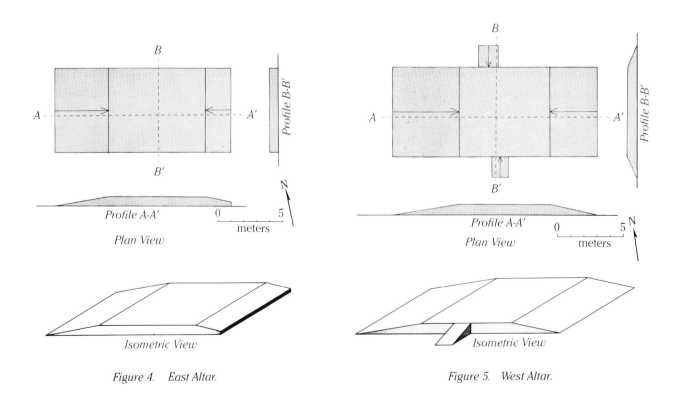

Figure 4. East Altar.

Figure 5. West Altar.

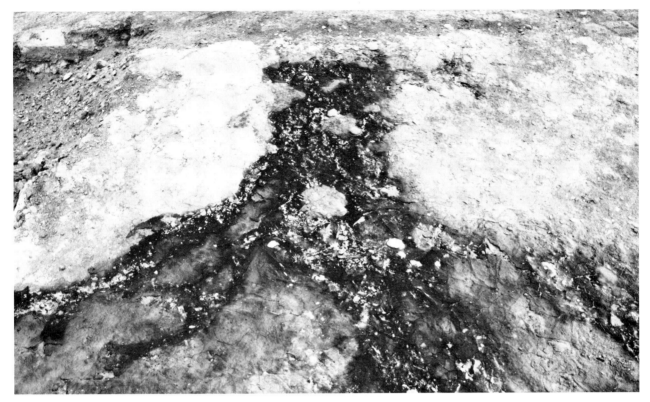

Figure 6. Residue on the east ramp of the West Altar.

pears to have had walls that served as balustrades.

There are two doorways leading off the large central courtyard. One, located near the center of the east wall, leads only into a narrow north-south corridor that has no other exit. The other, near the southwest corner of the courtyard, provides access to a corridor that leads toward the western edge of the huaca, turns toward the south, and subsequently disappears because of extensive erosion in this area. It is likely, however, that this corridor originally continued toward the southern face of the huaca and then turned east, ultimately providing access to a series of rooms located high up along the south side of the huaca. At least one of these rooms contained a series of niches along one wall.

The highest part of Huaca 1 is an east-west section that divides the large central courtyard from the series of rooms along the south side. This high area still has some architectural remains, including a three-sided structure in the center. Additional remains were found along the high elevated area on the east side of the mound and on the northwest portion. However, they were so badly eroded that their original form could not be reconstructed.

Routes to the Major Quadrangle

On the south side of Huaca 1 is an enormous rectangular enclosure, with a single entrance near the center of its north wall (Fig. 2). To gain access to this doorway from the primary entrance to the Huaca 1 Complex, one walks south through the North Courtyard and continues along either the east or the west side of the huaca. Of these two possible routes, the west side is by far the most impressive architecturally. Here massive pilasters create a monumental doorway near the northwest corner of the huaca. The doorway leads into a room with a second doorway on its south side. This second doorway gives access to a corridor leading south to the north wall of the Major Quadrangle, and from there, east to the Quadrangle's main entrance. It seems likely that any important individuals entering or leaving the Major Quadrangle would have proceeded along this route.

The route along the east side of Huaca 1 presents a much more humble approach, suggesting it may have been used by people of lower rank— perhaps servants and/or others who were support personnel for staging ceremonies and maintaining the architectural complex.

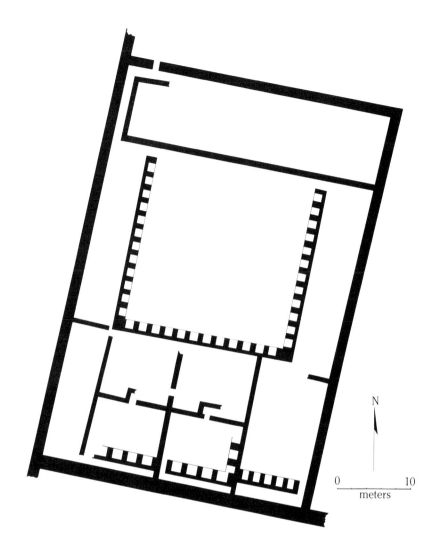

Figure 7.   Plan of the West Complex.

Major Quadrangle

This enormous rectangular enclosure, situated immediately south of Huaca 1, measures approximately 170 meters east-west and 175 meters north-south (Fig. 2). It is defined by large perimeter walls—2.2 meters wide at the base and still standing in some areas to a height of more than 3.5 meters. The original height was probably about 5.0 meters.

There is only one entrance to the Major Quadrangle—a narrow doorway near the center of the north wall. The size of this entrance was altered on several occasions: at one time the threshold was raised 1.3 meters, and subsequently the width was constricted from 2.3 to 1.9 meters. Two large pilas-ters of dissimilar size and form were located on the inside of the wall flanking the doorway. A wall extending south and then west from the eastern pilaster directed incoming traffic into corridors leading toward the west (Fig. 2). From this point, various parts of the Major Quadrangle could have been reached by following convoluted routes through long hallways and doorways. The overall plan of the Major Quadrangle is characterized by a wide variety of architectural units, none of which are equal in size or identical in form. There is no bilateral or radial symmetry, and the major segments are not organized along either the north-south or the east-west axis.

Blind Corridor

One of the most curious features of the Major Quadrangle is the extremely long corridor that dead-ends at the northwest corner (Fig. 2). Its single entry is near the midpoint of the south wall. From there it runs for more than 220 meters—nearly half the length of the south wall and the entire length of the west wall. Its function remains an enigma.

West Corridor

Another long corridor begins at the north side of the Major Quadrangle near the main entrance. It extends along the north wall to the northwest corner, then turns south and continues parallel to the first corridor and the west wall. Midway along the west side of the Quadrangle it makes a series of right-angle turns around two large patios, eventually ending in a room complex at the southwest corner of the Major Quadrangle.

This corridor is unique in having pilasters constricting its width in five places (Fig. 2). The pilasters are U-shaped casing walls filled with refuse, built adjacent to the corridor walls. Except for Constriction 1, they occur in pairs, located on opposite sides of the corridor.

The two pilasters that form Constriction 2 are unique in being of unequal size. They are also the only ones that were built while the corridor was under construction, as evidenced by some of the bricks actually bonded into the corridor walls. This is particularly evident in the pilaster on the east side of the corridor.

The casing walls of Constriction 4 were built after the corridor walls were completed but before they were plastered. The other three constrictions were built after the corridor walls had been completed and plastered, suggesting that they were added after Constrictions 2 and 4 were in place and functioning.

H1M1

The southeast corner of the Major Quadrangle is a large open area dominated by an extensively looted and weathered mound. This mound, designated H1M1, is made of case-and-fill construction, apparently to create an elevated platform. Although the architectural design is distinct from the burial platforms at Chan Chan, there are also similarities that make them analogous (Conrad 1982; Verano and Cordy-Collins, this volume).

Domestic Areas

With exception of the area around H1M1, the east side of the Major Quadrangle appears to have been used primarily for domestic activities rather than ritual or administrative functions. There is abundant evidence of architecture, but the walls are much less substantial than those in the other parts of the Quadrangle and are more extensively eroded. Moreover, the area has deep deposits of habitation refuse that have served to bury many of the walls.

Room Complexes

Five distinct room complexes dominate the central portion of the Major Quadrangle as well as its southwest corner. Each is defined by surrounding walls and contains multiple rooms, at least two open courtyards, and interior walls with multiple niches (Fig. 2). These five room complexes appear to be the most important architectural units in the Major Quadrangle and will be described individually.

Room Complex A

This complex, shown in detail in Figure 8, is located in the southwest corner of the Major Quadrangle. Its primary entrance is at the southern end of the West Corridor. Once inside Room Complex A, narrow hallways and baffled doorways provide access to numerous rooms and courtyards. The largest courtyard is near the center of the complex and is oriented on the east-west axis. Its main doorway, located near the center of the west wall, is on this axis, directly opposite a U-shaped structure known as an audiencia. Audiencias have been reported from Chan Chan and Farfan and are thought to have served administrative functions. They often have dedicatory burials beneath their floors. Excavation beneath and in front of this audiencia revealed not only dedicatory burials but a series of deep pits that apparently had been filled with offerings. Unfortunately, these had been looted prior to our excavation, but the looted material scattered around them indicates the importance of the associated architecture (Bruce this volume; Donnan, Elaborate Textile, this volume).

By walking along the south side of the audiencia and passing through a series of corridors and small rooms, it is possible to reach a set of rooms with platforms, niches, and a small ramp (Fig. 8). This is the most elaborate architecture in Room Complex A and is the only section with niches along the walls.

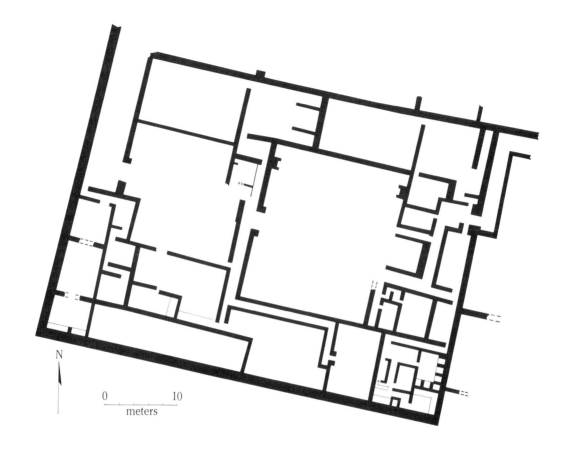

Figure 8. Plan of Room Complex A.

A secondary entrance to Room Complex A is provided by a pilastered doorway near the northeast corner. This doorway can be reached from either the long corridor along the west side of Room Complex B or from the area that includes the southeast corner of the Major Quadrangle where H1M1 is located (Fig. 2).

Room Complex B

This complex is located northeast of Room Complex A. Room Complex C notches the northeast corner of its otherwise rectangular shape (Fig. 9). Although a great deal of effort was expended in searching for the entrance to Room Complex B, it was not found. The reason for this may be that the original entry had a high threshold, which today would be indistinguishable from the lowest remaining portion of the heavily eroded walls; or perhaps the doorway was closed off sometime after

construction. The most likely location for the doorway would have been the center of the north wall, which today is eroded to only one brick high.

Two areas inside Room Complex B have multiple niches (Fig. 9). The most impressive are in the pair of rooms near the southwest corner. One of these rooms has niches on all four sides and a single entry near the center of the north wall. Immediately opposite the doorway to this room is another room, with niches along its south and west walls.

Niches are also found in a corridor near the northeast corner of Room Complex B, and in a room adjoining this corridor on the west.

Room Complex C

This complex intersects the northeast corner of Room Complex B (Fig. 9). It is rectangular in form with a single entrance leading through a

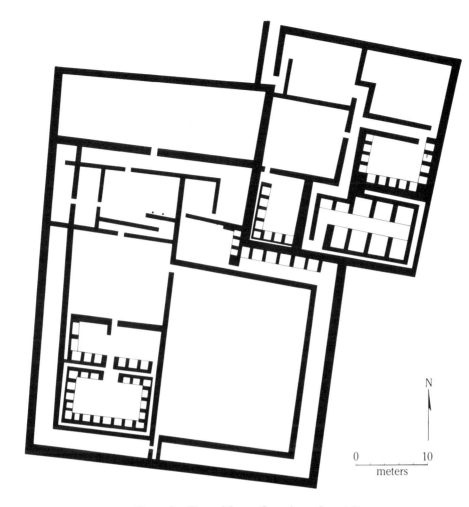

Figure 9.   Plan of Room Complexes B and C.

baffled doorway near the northwest corner. Curiously, the only access to the entrance is from the area of domestic activity that occupies the eastern part of the Major Quadrangle (Fig. 2).

Inside Room Complex C are three rooms with niches (Fig. 9). The first, located near the center of the east wall, has a series of niches along its west, south, and east walls. The second, in the southwest corner of the complex, has niches along its south and west walls. The third, at the southeast corner of the complex, is very unusual because of the layout as well as the size of most of the niches. The niches, located near the center of the room, are separated by a corridor. Between the niches and the walls is a narrower corridor which surrounds the niche formation. Seven of the nine niches in the room are considerably larger than any others found thus far at Pacatnamu (see "Niches," below).

Room Complex D

This complex, north of Room Complex C, has high perimeter walls defining its four sides (Fig. 10). It has a single entrance near the center of the north wall that can be approached only through a long, narrow corridor with two right-angle turns (Fig. 2).

The interior of Room Complex D is divided into quadrants of nearly equal size by two walls (oriented north-south and east-west), intersecting near the center. The northeast quadrant is a large, open courtyard, accessed through a narrow doorway at the northwest corner. At the southeast corner of this space there is a baffled doorway leading into the southeast quadrant.

The southeast quadrant is divided into several rooms of varying size, accessible only by making multiple turns through other rooms, baffled door-

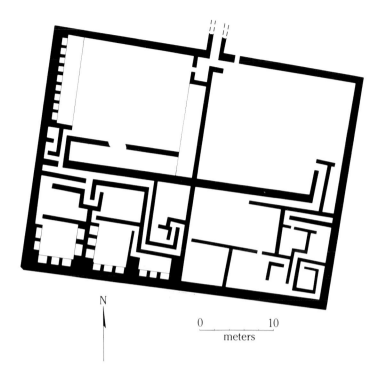

Figure 10. Plan of Room Complex D.

ways, and short corridors. One of the most curious architectural features is located in the southeast corner of the quadrant. Here, walls create an inwardly spiraling corridor that ultimately reaches a small rectangular room.

Like the northeast quadrant, the northwest quadrant of Room Complex D lacks major internal divisions. However, it does have a low platform and a row of niches along its west side, a low platform along its east side, and a narrow room along its south side. A passageway at the southwest corner provides access to a small room with a baffled entrance and to a doorway leading into the southwest segment of the complex.

The southwest segment is divided into six small rooms, with twisting corridors leading to each. The room in the northeast corner of the quadrant has the most circuitous access, which requires making multiple right-angle turns along a narrow corridor and completing a full spiral before nearing the innermost room. Excavation of the interior of this room revealed a clean clay floor, with no evidence of how the room may have functioned.

The three rooms along the south wall of this quadrant are also difficult to reach. Baffled doorways and short, twisting corridors combine to create

seclusion for each. All three have multiple niches along one or more walls.

Room Complex E

This complex is northwest of Room Complex D, near the entrance to the Major Quadrangle (Fig. 2). It is not as easily demarcated as the other complexes because it has an irregular form, and part of the perimeter is defined by a change in elevation rather than a freestanding wall. Nevertheless, it has many features in common with the other room complexes, and probably served many of the same functions.

Portions of Room Complex E are constructed on a solid masonry structure. The summit is approximately 3 meters above the floor level of the Major Quadrangle. It is a large rectangular area, with a narrow extension to the north at the northeast corner.

Three ramps provide access to the summit (Fig. 11). Each has two or more right-angle turns. One ramp is located on the east side, and another is at the north end of the narrow northern extension. Both lead to a set of adjoining rooms that occupy the major portion of the summit. The third ramp terminates near the southeast corner of the

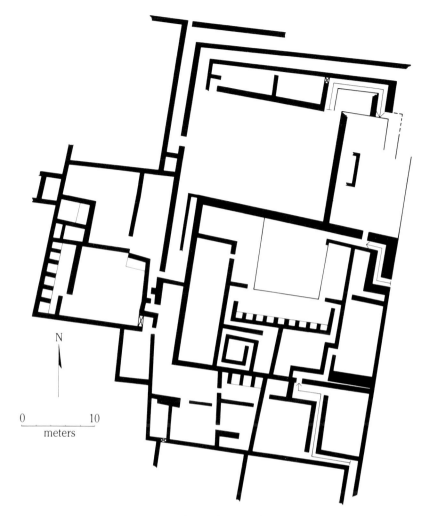

Figure 11. Plan of Room Complex E.

summit and provides access to only two of the rooms on the east side of the complex. It is odd that these two rooms, although immediately adjacent to the other summit architecture, are not immediately accessible from the other rooms. Reaching any adjacent room would require descent from the summit, and a long walk along corridors to the ramp on the west side of the summit. The purpose of this distinct two-part division of the summit architecture is not clear.

The largest room at the summit is centrally located and is entered at its northeast corner. A low bench extends along the west, south, and east walls. The south wall has a series of niches along its entire length. Rooms behind these niches are accessed around either end of the wall. The westernmost room is of particular interest because it is

divided into narrow corridors that spiral inward to a small secluded space, similar to that in the southwest quadrant of Room Complex D (Fig. 10). Excavation of the interior of this room revealed a clean clay floor, and no evidence of how the room may have functioned.

On the south and west sides of the summit architecture are clusters of contiguous rooms that are below the height of the summit but still about 1.5 meters above the floor level of the Major Quadrangle. Although the elevation and the position of these rooms may suggest a functional relationship to the summit architecture, this is contradicted by the long and convoluted access. One room, on the west side of the western cluster, is narrow and has niches along its west wall.

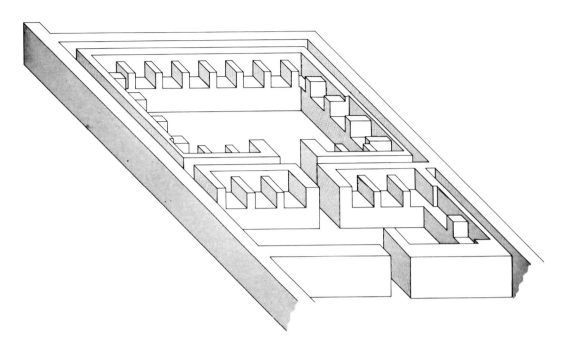

Figure 12.   Isometric reconstruction of the niches in the Southwest corner of Room Complex B, looking southwest.

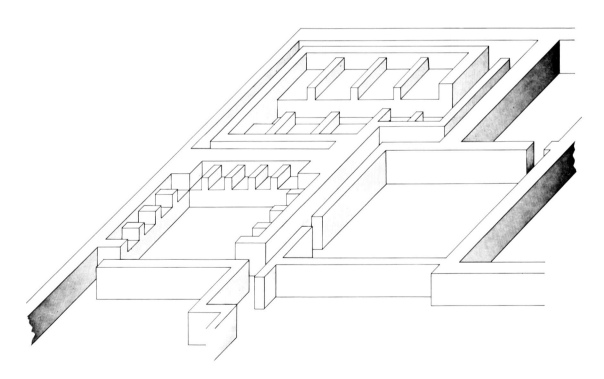

Figure 14.   Isometric reconstruction of the niches in the Southeast corner of Room Complex C, looking southeast.

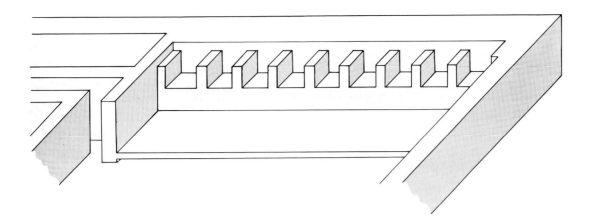

Figure 13. Isometric reconstruction of the niches in the Northwest corner of Room Complex D, looking southwest.

Altar

Near the north side of the Major Quadrangle, about midway between the entrance and the west wall, is a low structure situated in the center of a room (Fig. 2). It appears to have been approximately 1 meter high, with a flat top and nearly vertical sides. It has a small ramp at the center of its south side, which gives access to the summit. Its similarity in both size and form to the two altars in the North Courtyard inspires its designation as an altar.

Niches

The Huaca 1 Complex is distinguished by the sets of niches found in the room complexes in the Major Quadrangle, in the West Complex, and at the south side of the summit of Huaca 1. Most of these niches elaborate walls of small rooms (Fig. 12). Some are located along the walls of courtyards (Fig. 13). In one instance (the southeast corner of Room Complex C), the niches are along two sides of a blind hallway (Fig. 14, upper); in another case (the northeast portion of Room Complex B), they are along one side of a corridor (Fig. 9).

In nearly all instances, niches were added after the walls they abut were completed and plastered. The lower parts of the niches were built like bins: front walls were 65-110 centimeters high; side walls were higher, but extensive erosion prohibits exact determination of their original height. They may have been built to the ceiling (Fig. 15A), or had lintels that formed their upper portions (Figure 15B), or simply had walls that terminated well

below ceiling height (Fig. 15C). We have chosen to depict them with the latter form in Figures 12, 13, 14, and 16, but it should be noted that the other two possibilities are equally plausible.

Once the front and side walls were constructed, the lower, binlike portion of the niche was filled to the height of the front wall with rubble consisting of dirt, sand, and broken mud bricks. The horizontal surface of the niche was achieved by capping this fill with a thin (ca. 2 cm) layer of clay plaster. All other exposed interior and exterior surfaces were then finished with plaster.

In Room Complex D, each row of niches had a horizontal cornice along the front wall, just below the shelf portions of the niches (Fig. 16). This feature was unique to this location. The enigmatic placement of niches in the West Complex and in Room Complexes B and C created a very narrow passageway between the backs of the niches and the walls of the rooms (Figs. 7, 9). The purpose of this corridor is not known.

In view of their similar size, form, and construction, it is assumed that all niches served a similar function. What that function was is difficult to determine. The plaster surface that formed the shelf of the niche was thin and fragile and could not have supported much weight; nor could it have sustained the wear of objects repeatedly scraping against it. There was, in fact, no evidence of abrasion on the shelf surfaces of the niches, nor did they show signs of having been burned or soiled by materials spilling onto them. Their most likely function would have been to hold relatively lightweight objects. Perhaps niches in the open courtyard and patio areas held wood idols. Niches along the

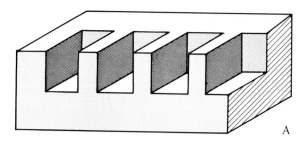

A

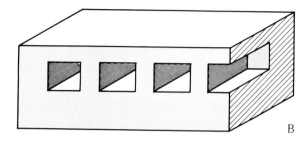

B

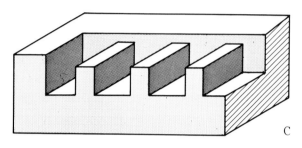

C

Figure 15. *Three possible forms of niches.*

inner walls of small rooms may have held ceremonial paraphernalia.

Chronology

The Huaca 1 Complex clearly dates to the Chimu occupation of Pacatnamu, A.D. 1100-1400. None of the bricks used in its construction can be attributed to the Moche occupation, nor to what we are currently calling the Intermediate Phase. Most of the Huaca 1 Complex was built with Standard Chimu bricks, although the upper portions of the perimeter walls, H1M1, and most of Room Complex A were built with Terminal Chimu bricks. This implies that these areas were added near the end of the Chimu occupation (McClelland, this volume).

The brick evidence is supported by four radiocarbon determinations from the Huaca 1 Complex, each of which is within the A.D. 1100-1400 time frame:

1. Beta-12282 = A.D. 1320 (630 ± 70 BP)
   Textile from a burial in H1M1 (Verano and Cordy-Collins, this volume).
2. Beta-12283 = A.D. 1260 (690 ± 60 BP)
   Wood from a branch used as fill inside H1M1 (Verano and Cordy-Collins, this volume.
3. Beta-12284 = A.D. 1270 (680 ± 60 BP)
   Wood from a branch used as fill inside H1M1 (Verano and Cordy-Collins, this volume).

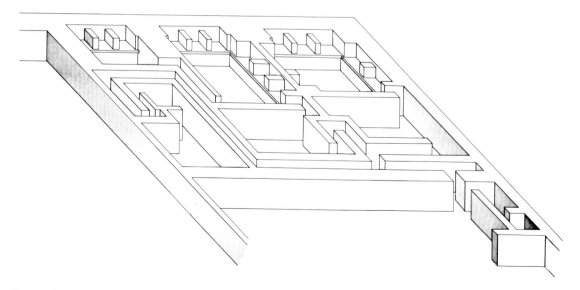

Figure 16. *Isometric reconstruction of the niches in the Southwest corner of Room Complex D, looking southwest.*

4. Beta-10740=A.D. 1270 (680 ± 110 BP)
Bone from one of the mutilated individuals in the trench outside the Primary Entrance (Verano, this volume).

General Observations

The Huaca 1 Complex is a relatively isolated architectural entity with very restricted access. Its perimeter walls clearly separate it from the agglutinated rooms, corridors, huacas, and courtyards that surround it.

Restricted Access

The Primary Entrance, on the north side, is small and formidable. It requires those entering to cross a deep trench by means of a narrow causeway and to pass through a massive wall. The only alternative entrance is on the northeast side. Unfortunately, the architecture in this area is not sufficiently well preserved to distinguish the form, or even the precise location, of this doorway. It is clear, however, that entry from this side was secondary, and would have lacked the architectural impact that characterizes the Primary Entrance.

Once inside the Huaca 1 Complex, restricted access continues to be manifested in the design of the distinct components. Both Huaca 1 and the East Pyramid have single means of access to the summits. At the summit of Huaca 1 there is only a single corridor providing access to rooms along the south side. Similarly, there is a single entrance to the West Complex.

The Major Quadrangle is perhaps the most pronounced example of restricted access at Pacatnamu. High, formidable perimeter walls define a quadrangle with an interior area of nearly 30,000 square meters. Access to this enormous space is possible only through a single narrow doorway, barely wide enough to allow two people to enter at the same time. Within the Major Quadrangle, long narrow corridors (some with constrictions) and pilastered and/or baffled doorways would have served to restrict access to various internal areas.

Architectural Grandeur

The massive scale of many walls, courtyards, and doorways, as well as the impressive volume of Huaca 1 and the East Pyramid, were deliberate attempts to achieve architectural grandeur. Expectations were also enhanced by the long and often convoluted corridors and baffled doorways that preceded access to interior rooms and courtyards. Multiple niches in some areas would also have provided a sense of grandeur, most notably in the Central Courtyard of the West Complex.

Differential Routing

In several instances, as one proceeds from the Primary Entrance through various parts of the Huaca 1 Complex, there is a choice of following a route to the right (west) or to the left (east). When this option occurs, the route to the right proceeds through large, often pilastered doorways and elegant corridors to well-planned, carefully constructed, and frequently massive structures. In contrast, the route to the left proceeds through relatively small, unpilastered doorways and sometimes narrow, irregular corridors to areas often irregular in plan and poorly built. Spaces reached by the right-hand route imply ceremonial or administrative functions, while those accessed by the left-hand route normally have refuse and thus imply a domestic function or an area where ceremonial food and drink was prepared and/or stored.[4]

An example of right-hand and left-hand alternatives is evident in the two ways of progressing from the Primary Entrance of the Complex to the entrance of the Major Quadrangle (see above). Another occurs when one enters the Major Quadrangle: proceeding to the right gives access to courtyards and room complexes that reflect high-status ceremonial and administrative functions; proceeding to the left provides entrance to the large area of domestic refuse and irregular architecture in the eastern portion of the Major Quadrangle (Fig. 2). The summit of Huaca 1 may be seen as another example of the right-hand versus left-hand dichotomy. A door to the left leads to a narrow room that may have been used for storage, while the door to the right ultimately leads to rooms high along the south side of the huaca, at least one of which contained niches.

This right-left dichotomy has been observed in other architectural complexes at Pacatnamu such as Huaca 23a (Donnan, this volume)—the right-hand route is consistently more elegant and leads to higher status architecture than the route to the left. This suggests that it may have been an important tenet of Chimu architecture at Pacatnamu.

---

4. The right-hand versus left-hand routing through the architecture at Pacatnamu was first brought to my attention by Cristobal Campana when he visited the site during our 1983 field season. He stated that it seemed to be used frequently in the monumental architecture at Chan Chan. It has also been discussed by Rostworowski (1977a) in relation to the concept of hanan and hurin on the Peruvian coast.

It should be noted that the Huaca 1 Complex is not unique at Pacatnamu. The basic components, as well as their size and location relative to one another, are repeated in several other complexes at the site. Among the clearest examples are Huaca 8 (the second largest complex at Pacatnamu) and Huaca 23a (Donnan, this volume). Additional examples include Huacas 9, 10, 12, 13, 16, and 17, and it may be that still others will be recognized as more architecture is cleared and mapped.

It is interesting that the Huaca 1, 8, and 23a complexes not only share the same inventory of architectural components but also contain the only six audiencias yet identified at Pacatnamu. In each case the audiencias are located in large rectangular enclosures on the south side of the main huacas.

The function of the Huaca 1 Complex has yet to be determined. In part, this is because only enough of the architecture was cleared to define its form, since the purpose of most of the excavation was to obtain a complete plan of the overall complex. Very few areas were cleared to original floor level, and most of those that were revealed clean clay floors with no evidence of activity. Therefore, most of what can be said about how the complex functioned must be inferred from the architecture itself. Only in certain instances can our understanding be enhanced by associated cultural material (Donnan, Elaborate Textile, this volume).

It seems clear, however, that the Huaca 1 Complex functioned primarily as an area for the staging of ceremonies. Restricted access, monumental scale, and general lack of evidence of domestic activity all imply a religious rather than a secular function.

The North Courtyard, with Huaca 1 and the East Pyramid flanking two sides and the two low altars near the center, seems ideally suited for ceremonies to be witnessed, or participated in, by large groups of people. The summits of Huaca 1 and the East Pyramid would have offered impressive locations as well. The Central Courtyard of the West Complex would have provided a smaller but still very impressive staging area.

As noted previously, East Courtyard I is unusual in having its entire surface nearly covered with ceramic fragments. These sherds, plus a shallow deposit of refuse, imply food preparation in this area. Since this activity was occurring in a large, open courtyard, it does not suggest a domestic, single family activity, but rather food preparation on a massive scale. Perhaps these activities were meant to provide food to be consumed on

ceremonial occasions.

The Major Quadrangle, although clearly a part of the Huaca 1 Complex, is a distinct area that may have functioned in a different way than the rest of the Complex. It has more small rooms, some of which may have been for domestic purposes. Those in the five room complexes may well have been, at least in part, the living quarters of elite individuals. The numerous courtyards suggest that some ceremonial activities took place in this area. The large area of domestic refuse along the east side of the Quadrangle indicates preparation of food, and the relatively simple architecture in this area may have been the living quarters of individuals who served the elite.

Numerous courtyards in the central and western portion of the Major Quadrangle may have been for ceremonial activities. There is also evidence that aspects of ceremonial life included weaving, llama sacrifice, and dancing (Donnan, Elaborate Textile, this volume).

Comparison with Chan Chan

The site of Chan Chan, located in the Moche Valley approximately 150 kilometers south of Pacatnamu, served as the capital of the Kingdom of Chimor during the Late Intermediate Period. Its sprawling architectural complexes, extending over an area of more than six square kilometers, include ten large rectangular enclosures called ciudadelas that appear to be similar to the Major Quadrangle at Pacatnamu. Given our present understanding of the Major Quadrangle and of the Huaca 1 Complex of which it is a part, it is worthwhile to assess the degree of similarity between it and the cuidadelas at Chan Chan.

The most obvious similarity between the ciudadelas at Chan Chan and the Major Quadrangle at Pactanamu is their overall form—both are rectangular walled enclosures oriented on a north-south axis, with a single small entrance near the center of the north wall. In both instances, the walled enclosures are divided into numerous rooms and open courtyards, connected by long corridors, generally entered through pilastered and/or baffled doorways. Both also have blind hallways.

At this point, however, similarities cease. Ciudadelas at Chan Chan are divided into northern, central, and southern sectors, each with characteristic interior architectural features and a distinct primary function (Day 1982:57). The Major Quadrangle at Pacatnamu has no tripartite division, and the only clear functional distinction is between the eastern area, which appears to have been primarily domestic, and the remaining area which appears to have been largely ceremonial.

Each ciudadela at Chan Chan has several audiencias, most often clustered in the central sector, which control access to numerous rooms with bins lining the walls that were presumably used as storage facilities (Day 1982:59-60). In the Major Quadrangle there is only one audiencia (in Room Complex A), and it is not associated with rooms containing storage bins. In fact, there are no storage bins anywhere in the Major Quadrangle, nor is there any indication that storage was an important function of this area.

Each ciudadela at Chan Chan has a burial platform, generally located in its central sector, which is thought to have been for royal burial (Conrad 1982:87-118). H1M1, located in the southeast corner of the Major Quadrangle, at first seemed to be a similar structure. Excavation of this mound, however, indicated that it lacks certain diagnostic features of the burial platforms at Chan Chan (Verano and Cordy-Collins, this volume).

Finally, the niches characteristic of many rooms and courtyards in the Major Quadrangle at Pacatnamu are similar to niches found at Chan Chan. At Chan Chan, however, niches are frequently used to elaborate the interiors of audiencias—a use not seen in any audiencias at Pacatnamu.

In summary, while there are many similarities between the ciudadelas at Chan Chan and the Major Quadrangle at Pacatnamu, a systematic comparison of the two reveals many important differences. These differences become even more pronounced when one considers that ciudadelas at Chan Chan are essentially complete architectural units, while the Major Quadrangle at Pacatnamu is but one component of the overall Huaca 1 Complex and clearly meant to function as part of the larger whole. The other components of the Huaca 1 Complex include numerous courtyards, rooms, and corridors, as well as altars, a massive huaca, and the East Pyramid. Altars like those in the Huaca 1 Complex have not been observed at Chan Chan, and although some large huacas are present, they are never directly associated with ciudadelas (Day 1982:62).

The significant differences between the Major Quadrangle and the Chan Chan ciudadelas reflect distinct architectural concepts, implying that they served distinct functions. Moreover, their differences suggest that they had distinct evolutionary antecedents.

RESUMEN:
El Complejo de la Huaca 1

La Huaca 1 es la pirámide más grande e impresionante en Pacatnamú. Ocupa la parte central del sitio y domina el espacio que la circunda (Fig. 1, Map Insert). Por su aparente importancia y buen estado de preservación, se dedicaron las temporadas de 1983 y 1984 a su estudio.

Los trabajos efectuados se vieron grandemente facilitados por las investigaciones de Giesela y Wolfgang Hecker (1982, 1985)—miembros de la expedición arqueológica alemana de 1962–1963, dirigida por Heinrich Ubbelohde-Doering—quienes levantaron un excelente mapa de la Huaca 1, basado en observaciones y mediciones en superficie. Como resultado de nuestro trabajo, se introdujeron correcciones menores y se ganó en comprehensión de las funciones del Complejo.

Definición del Complejo

Huaca 1 incluye un conjunto de patios y agrupaciones de cuartos que rodean a la pirámide principal, así como una pirámide secundaria al nor-este, dos altares al norte y el Cuadrángulo Mayor al sur.

Los lados oeste y sur del Complejo de la Huaca 1 están claramente definidos por paredes macizas que carecen de entradas; así mismo, la parte norte está definida por la Muralla Interna y el foso que atraviesa la parte central del sitio en dirección este-oeste (Donnan, este volumen).

La parte este del Complejo es más difícil de definir, por la presencia de arquitectura aglutinada que se mezcla con las construcciones de otros complejos al este. Además, la erosión hace difícil determinar la presencia de paredes o puertas que hayan servido de división y conección entre las estructuras ubicadas en este sector.

Entrada Principal y Patio Norte

La entrada principal está ubicada en la porción norte. Se cruza el foso por una rampa de acceso y se atraviesa la muralla usándose una entrada relativamente estrecha (Figs. 2, 3). Esta entrada—directamente en frente de la rampa de la Huaca 1, aunque no alineada con ella—tuvo originalmente 5.75 mts. de ancho, pero fue reducida a 3.80 mts., mediante una construcción en la parte interna de la porción este de la muralla. Al entrar se encuentra un gran patio con dos altares bajos, orientados este-oeste (*Figs. 4,5*); no están alineados con la Huaca 1, pero lo están con la rampa de acceso a la Pirámide Este.

Pirámide Este

Es una estructura de dos niveles y plano rectangular; posee dos rampas que conducen del nivel del piso a los dos niveles de la estructura. La cima está formada por el segundo nivel y está limitada hacia el este, por una pared baja. Deliberadamente construida de manera curvada, es única en su genero hasta este momento en Pacatnamú.

Patios Este y Nor-Este

Hacia el lado este de la Huaca 1 y de la Pirámide Este hay una serie de patios que denominaremos: Patio Este I, II y III, y Patio Nor-Este I, II y III. Para entrar a ellos hay que seguir un corredor paralelo al lado este de la Huaca 1, hasta la pared norte del Recinto Amurallado, donde se dirige hacia el este, hasta llegar a una entrada que sirve de acceso común para los 6 patios (*Fig. 2*).

El más grande, el Patio Este I presenta una densa acumulación de fragmentos de cerámica que cubre casi completamente su superficie. Los pozos de cateo muestran un depósito de pocos centímetros de basura encima del suelo estéril. La razón de la acumulación de fragmentos de cerámica no ha podido ser determinada.

Complejo Oeste

Hacia el oeste de la Huaca 1 hay un complejo de habitaciones y patios que parecen formar una unidad arquitectónica. El único acceso pareciera estar ubicado en la esquina nor-oeste de este complejo. El patio principal, formado por tres paredes, posee 36 nichos, 12 en cada una de las paredes, el mayor número registrado en un solo recinto en Pacatnamú. En la parte sur del Complejo Oeste hay una serie de cuartos, de los cuales tres tienen nichos a lo largo de sus paredes.

Huaca 1

Es la estructura sólida más grande en Pacatnamú; mide aproximadamente 70 x 70 mts. y un poco mas de 10 mts. de alto. Una rampa lleva desde el Patio Norte a la primera plataforma, la que está dividida en varias habitaciones, mientras el lado oeste está abierto. En el centro de la plataforma hay una segunda rampa que conduce a un patio abierto en la parte central del segundo nivel. Esta segunda rampa es un poco más angosta que la primera y parece haber tenido paredes laterales.

El patio abierto tiene dos puertas. Una, ubicada cerca del centro de la pared este conduce sólo a un angosto corredor norte-sur que carece de salida. La otra, cerca de la esquina sur-oeste, provee acceso a un corredor que conduce al borde occidental de la Huaca, torciendo en ángulo recto hacia el sur, donde desaparece debido a la erosión. Posiblemente, este último corredor haya conducido a las habitaciones que se encuentran ubicadas en la parte sur de la estructura, a una altura mayor que el nivel del patio abierto, donde por lo menos uno de estos últimos recintos muestra evidencias de haber tenido nichos en una de sus paredes.

La parte más alta de la Huaca 1 es una sección este-oeste, que separa los recintos mencionados del patio abierto. Esta área elevada conserva algunas paredes, incluyendo una estructura en forma de U en el centro.

Rutas al Cuadrángulo Mayor

Adosado a la parte sur de la Huaca 1 se halla un imponente Complejo Amurallado con una sola entrada, en su lado norte. Se accede a él dirigiéndose hacia el sur por el lado este o el oeste de la Huaca 1, siendo esta última ruta la más elaborada arquitectónicamente.

Cuadrángulo Mayor

Mide 170 metros en su parte este-oeste y 175 metros en la norte-sur (*Fig. 2*). Está definido por grandes paredes o murallas perimétricas, con un ancho máximo de 2.20 mts. en la base y una altura actual de 3.50 mts., por lo que podrían haber alcanzado mas de 5 mts.

Hay un solo acceso al Cuadrángulo Mayor: una angosta entrada ubicada cerca del centro de la pared norte del recinto, a espaldas de la Huaca 1. El ancho de esta entrada pareciera que ha sido modificado varias veces, habiéndose constreñido el ancho de 2.30 a 1.90 mts.

Desde la entrada, se pueden alcanzar distintas áreas del recinto siguiendo los diversos corredores que desde allí comienzan, ninguna de las cuales es igual en tamaño o forma; tampoco hay simetría radial o bilateral, ni organización del espacio en función de los puntos cardinales.

Corredor Ciego

Una de las más curiosas características en el Cuadrángulo Mayor es la existencia de un largo corredor que no conduce a sitio alguno (Fig. 2).

Corredor Oeste

Conduce desde la entrada al Cuadrángulo, al sector sur-oeste. Corre paralelo a la pared norte del recinto, para luego doblar al sur y seguir paralelo al Corredor Ciego y la pared oeste. Su recorrido termina en un complejo de habitaciones de la esquina sur-oeste del Cuadrángulo. Posee 5 constricciones adosadas a las paredes del corredor, las que fueron erigidas después que las paredes, pero antes que éstas fuesen enlucidas.

H1M1

Ubicado en la esquina sur-este del Cuadrángulo, se halla erosionado y extensivamente huaqueado. Es un montículo artificial que contuvo entierros humanos, pero no es una plataforma funeraria análoga a las de Chan Chan (Conrad 1982) y Farfán (Keatinge y Conrad 1983; ver Verano y Cordy-Collins, este volumen).

Area Doméstica

Con la excepción del área alrededor del H1M1 el lado este del Cuadrángulo parece haber sido un área doméstica, no de funciones administrativas o rituales. Hay abundancia de paredes, pero éstas son menos sólidas y están más erosionadas; así mismo, hay gran cantidad de basura cubriendo muchas paredes.

Complejos de Habitaciones

En el Cuadrángulo hay 5 complejos de habitaciones definidos por paredes que los circundan; contienen diversos recintos, por lo menos dos patios y paredes interiores con nichos o asientos (Fig. 2). Estos, parecieran ser las unidades arquitectónicas más importantes en el Cuadrángulo.

Complejo A

Ubicado en la esquina sur-oeste del Cuadrángulo (Fig. 8) presenta, entre otras características, una audiencia o estructura en forma de U. Ha sido huaqueado extensivamente, pero pareciera que contuvo un entierro dedicatorio y pozos para ofrendas (Bruce, este volumen).

Complejo B

Ubicado al nor-este del Complejo A, no se localizó su ingreso, el que podría haber estado en un dintel elevado. Posee dos sectores con múltiples nichos; uno de ellos los tiene en las cuatro paredes (Fig. 9).

Complejo C

Intersecta la esquina nor-este del Complejo B (Fig. 9). De forma rectangular, posee un solo acceso, por el área doméstica al este del Cuadrángulo. Posee tres habitaciones con nichos, donde hay un grupo con siete nichos, que son los más grandes ubicados hasta hoy en Pacatnamú.

Complejo D

Ubicado al norte del Complejo C, tiene paredes altas definiendo su perímetro (Fig. 10), con una sola entrada que conduce a través de un largo y angosto corredor. El interior está dividido en cuadrantes de casi igual tamaño.

Complejo E

Localizado al nor-oeste del Complejo D, cerca de la entrada al Cuadrángulo (Fig. 11), no es tan fácilmente demarcable por su forma irregular. Parte de su perímetro se define por cambios de elevación del piso, más que por la existencia de paredes.

Altar

En la parte norte del Cuadrángulo, a mitad de camino entre la entrada y la pared oeste, hay una estructura baja en el centro de un recinto. Parece haber tenido 1 mt. de alto, con la superficie plana y los lados casi verticales. Tiene una rampa en el lado sur y sus características son similares a las de los altares ubicados frente a la Huaca 1 y la Pirámide Este.

Nichos

Hay 6 habitaciones con nichos en el Cuadrángulo Mayor, Complejo Oeste y el lado sur de la cima de la Huaca 1. Generalmente están dentro de habitaciones chicas (Fig. 12). Otros están en una o más paredes de patios (Fig. 13). En un caso—Complejo C—los nichos se hallan a lo largo de dos lados de un recinto ciego (Fig. 14), mientras, en otro caso—en la porción nor-este del Complejo B—están a lo largo de un corredor.

En la mayoría de los casos, fueron construidos después que las paredes. Podrían haber tenido la misma altura que la pared (Fig. 15a), haber tenido dinteles (Fig. 15b), o haber sido muy similares a como fueron encontrados (Fig. 15c). Esta ha sido la forma escogida aquí para ilustrarlos (Figs. 12, 13, 14, y 16). Pero hay que tener en cuenta que las otras formas son también posibles.

En el Complejo C, cada hilera de nichos tenía una corniza horizontal, ubicada en la pared frontal, justo debajo del "asiento" (Fig. 16), una característica que no se ha registrado en otras parte del sitio.

Cronología

El Complejo de la Huaca 1 corresponde a la ocupación Chimú del sitio, entre 1100 DC y 1400 DC. La mayor parte ha sido construida con adobes Chimú Standard y algunas con adobes Chimú Terminal (ver McClelland, este volumen). Esta evidencia corresponde con cuatro pruebas de carbono 14:

1. Beta-12282 = 1320 DC (630±70 BP)
   Tejido proveniente de un entierro en el H1M1.
2. Beta-12283 = 1260 DC (690±60 BP)
   Madera usada como relleno en el H1M1.
3. Beta-12284 = 1270 DC (680±60 BP)
   Madera usada como relleno en el H1M1.
4. Beta-10740 = 1270 DC (680±110 BP)
   Hueso de un cuerpo mutilado en el foso frente de la Huaca 1.

Observaciones Generales

Una característica que llama la atención en el Complejo de la Huaca 1, es la posibilidad, en muchas ocasiones, de escoger una ruta por la derecha (oeste) o por la izquierda (este). Cuando esto sucede, la ruta de la derecha es más elegante, bien planificada, construida cuidadosamente y atraviesa arquitectura voluminosa. En contraste, la ruta de la izquierda pasa a través de pequeños e irregulares corredores, sin elegancia, hacia áreas de construcción y planeamiento irregular. Mientras los espacios alcanzados por la ruta de la derecha implican funciones administrativas y ceremoniales, los que se acceden por la izquierda implicarían funciones domésticas o un área donde era preparada o depositada comida y bebida ceremonial. Esta dicotomía puede observarse también en la Huaca 23a (Donnan, este volumen).

Los componentes básicos del Complejo de la Huaca 1 pueden ser observados también en otros complejos del sitio. Entre los ejemplos más claros están la Huaca 8 (la de segundo tamaño en Pacatnamú), Huaca 23a (Donnan, este volumen), 9, 10, 12, 13, 16 y 17, y quizá, otras donde estas características esperan ser reconocidas.

Comparación con Chan Chan

La similitud más obvia entre Chan Chan y el Cuadrángulo Mayor es la forma general—recinto amurallado rectangular, orientado norte-sur, con una sola entrada en el lado norte. En ambos casos, el interior está dividido en numerosos recintos y patios, conectados por largos corredores. Sin embargo, éstas son todas las similitudes, ya que en Chan Chan el espacio está dividido claramente en tres porciones: sur, centro y norte; el Cuadrángulo Mayor de Pacatnamú carece de esta división tripartita, y su división pareciese más bien ser entre este y oeste.

De la misma manera, hay diferencias con la audiencia, nichos, plataforma funeraria (Verano y Cordy-Collins, este volumen) y la asociación pirámide-recinto amurallado, que no existe directamente en Chan Chan.

Estas diferencias entre el Cuadrángulo Mayor y las ciudadelas de Chan Chan, reflejan conceptos arquitectónicos diferentes, lo que implicaría distintas funciones; además, sugerirían que tuvieron antecedentes evolutivos diferentes.

H1M1: A Late Intermediate Period Mortuary Structure at Pacatnamu

John W. Verano and Alana Cordy-Collins

Pacatnamu is characterized by a large number of looted cemeteries found both throughout the architectural complex and outside the Outer Wall. There are also several heavily looted mounds, the surfaces of which are littered with human skeletal material and fragments of textiles and ceramics. The material remaining on the surface indicates that these mounds once contained numerous burials and suggests that they may have served principally as mortuary structures. One of these mounds, H1M1, is located in the southeast corner of the Major Quadrangle of the Huaca 1 Complex (Fig. 1). During the 1983 field season, it was surface collected and partially excavated.

The appearance of H1M1 prior to excavation was that of a roughly circular mound, approximately 30 meters in diameter, with a maximum height at the center of 2.5 meters above the present ground surface. There were numerous looters' pits and a scatter of human bone together with fragments of textiles and ceramics littering the surface of the mound (Fig. 2). A comparison of air photos of Pacatnamu taken in the 1940s with those taken in the 1970s, as well as discussions with local informants, indicated that H1M1 had experienced a long history of sporadic looting.

After initial surface collection, a one-meter-wide exploratory cut was made in the east side of the mound to locate the external wall of the structure (Fig. 3). The cut was extended into the center of the mound, but no evidence of an eastern external wall was encountered. Numerous whole and fragmentary mud bricks and rubble found throughout the cut suggest the wall was destroyed either by looting or by the deliberate removal of bricks. Several intact segments of brick wall were found in the center of the mound. These were cleared and followed outward in an attempt to locate a relatively intact portion of the structure. Although this strategy was successful in revealing some architectural features of H1M1, the majority of the structure appears to have been destroyed.

Architecture

Despite extensive excavation, the external limits of H1M1 remained elusive; only a portion of what appeared to have been the western external wall of the structure was preserved (Fig. 3). However, the basic internal structure of H1M1, consisting of sand and rubble fill held in place by a series of interior walls, could still be identified. The interior walls were heavily damaged by looting, and most appeared to be only fragmentary segments of

Figure 1.   Location of H1M1, in the southeast corner of the Major Quadrangle.

Figure 2.   View of H1M1 as excavation began, looking northwest toward Huaca 1 (in background).

an original series of intersecting walls. The lower courses of these walls contained both flat-rectangular and ovoid bricks used interchangeably, suggesting that the structure is Terminal Phase. Both types of bricks were made of light-gray hard-silt (McClelland, this volume). Only one wall segment was plastered and there were no signs of weathering or exposure. The walls gave the impression of having been erected rapidly and carelessly, without much attention to symmetry or appearance. Their orientation was predominantly north-south and east-west, but the alignment of some wall segments differed significantly (Fig. 3). Judging from the layout of the preserved interior walls, H1M1 did not have a coherent internal plan.

Although much of H1M1's structure was destroyed by looting, intact fill was found in several areas. In most cases fill consisted of sand and rubble, alternating with thin layers of cornstalks, branches, and leaves (Figs. 4,5). The plant material presumably functioned to stabilize the fill.[1] In other areas, fill consisted of solid mud bricks or brick fragments. The variety of material used to fill different areas of the structure may reflect either the preference of distinct labor teams or the limited availability of fill materials. The absence of weathering on interior walls and the crude and rough finish suggest that H1M1 was built and filled in a single construction sequence.

Burials and Other Features

Textile, copper, wood, and gourd fragments were found scattered throughout the disturbed areas of H1M1, indicating that several burials may have been looted. Human skeletal material on the surface of the mound and distributed throughout the looted areas comprised the partial remains of at least ten individuals (see Appendix).

Four identifiable burials were recovered in the mound (Fig. 3); all but Burial 4 had been disturbed by looters. Burial 1 was essentially complete, with only minor damage to the textiles around the head. It was located in looters' backdirt at a depth of 30 centimeters, close to the center of the structure. The burial consisted of a textile bundle measuring 46 x 107 centimeters, containing the flexed body of a female approximately 20-25 years of age (see Appendix). The body lay on its back with the legs

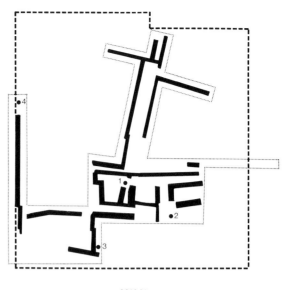

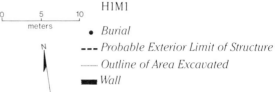

H1M1

• Burial
--- Probable Exterior Limit of Structure
.... Outline of Area Excavated
▬ Wall

Figure 3. Plan of H1M1.

Figure 4. An intact section of fill showing the alternating layers of sand and rubble, and plant material.

---

1. This type of case-and-fill construction is common at Pacatnamu and is also seen in other Late Intermediate Period architecture of the North Coast.

Figure 5. Detail of a layer of plant material from the fill of H1M1, in this case consisting primarily of cut branches. Samples of these branches were collected and radiocarbon dated.

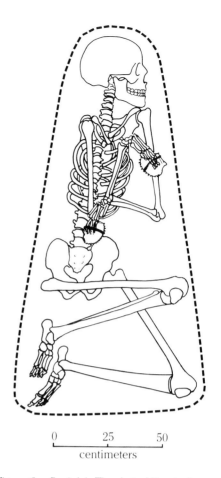

0   25   50

centimeters

Figure 6. Burial 1. The dotted line indicates the outline of the textile bundle.

Figure 7. Detail of the inner shroud of Burial 1. The double band design is composed of two motifs: a crested bird in profile carrying a baton and a truncated bird in profile with identical head and tail crests. Scale is 5 cm.

Figure 8. Miniature loincloths found with Burial 2. Longest 9.6 cm.

flexed and the knees drawn up to the left side (Fig. 6). The arms were crossed over the chest, and a valve of *Spondylus princeps* shell was tied to the palm of each hand with a sheer cloth band.[2] The body was wrapped in an inner layer of plain weave cloth with a resist design (Fig. 7) and an outer layer of warp ikat.

Burial 2 was located just below the surface in the south-central area of the structure (Fig. 3). It was heavily disturbed and scattered over a two square meter area. Less than 50% of the skeleton was found, but it was possible to identify the individual as an adolescent female, approximately 15-18 years of age (see Appendix). Associated with the partial skeleton were numerous elaborate textiles, including colorful slit tapestry miniature garments (Fig. 8).[3] Also associated with the burial were two round tweezers, three square bangles,

and two tubular sheaths, all made of copper (Fig. 9), as well as several turquoise and yellow iridescent feathers.

Burial 3 was located in looters' backdirt on the south side of H1M1 at a depth of 50 centimeters (Fig. 3). What was originally a single bundle containing the remains of a 6 to 12-month-old infant was found in two parts, with the contents disturbed (Fig. 10). Body position could not be determined with certainty, but the infant appears to have been laid on its back with the arms extended along the sides and the legs flexed. The body was wrapped in an outer layer of natural beige cotton plain weave and an inner layer of white cotton plain weave. Yellow wool yarn was wrapped around the wrists, green wool yarn around the ankles. One of the partial bundles contained a small, undecorated gourd bowl. It had been broken and repaired with twine. An additional object found with Burial 3 is of particular interest: a circular ring, 7 centimeters in diameter, constructed of tightly wrapped plant fibers, lay against the occipital bone of the skull (Fig. 11). A shallow depression and areas of pitting on the

---

2. The two valves of the *Spondylus* shell articulated, indicating that they represent a single animal.
3. The miniature textiles are described by Bruce (in press).

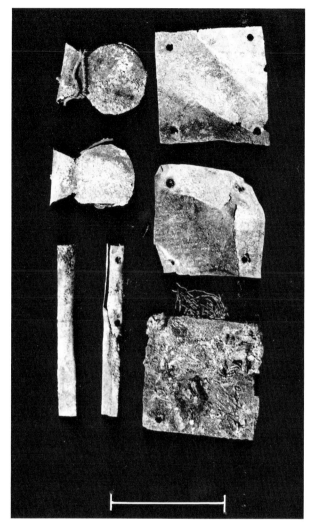

Figure 9. *Copper objects associated with Burial 2. Scale is 3 cm.*

Figure 10. *Burial 3 with shrouds intact. Scale is 10 cm.*

surface of the occipital bone indicate that the ring was exerting pressure on the skull during life. The ring appears to be part of an apparatus used to affix the infant's head to a cradleboard or to artificially deform the head, or perhaps both. Weiss describes and illustrates a similar ring made of cotton found tied in place on the head of a mummified child from Cerro Colorado in the Ica Valley on the South Coast (1961:93-94).

Burial 4 was located at a depth of 25 centimeters near the western limit of H1M1 (Fig. 3). The shallow burial appeared to be undisturbed and in primary context. It consisted of a textile bundle containing the remains of a newborn to six-month-old infant (Fig. 12). The textile wrappings consisted of an outer plain weave cotton shroud and an inner blue-striped cotton plain weave. In addi-

tion, the body was surrounded by an inner layer of cotton padding. Burial position was on the back with the arms extended along the sides and the legs loosely flexed. Tied to each hand was a piece of animal hide with fur.

Burials 3 and 4 are distinct from Burials 1 and 2 in the quality of their grave goods. The associations found with Burials 3 and 4—plain weave textiles and a repaired gourd—imply low-status burials. While the original context of Burial 3 is unknown, Burial 4 was located at a very shallow depth on the periphery of H1M1. Since isolated intrusive infant burials have been found in architectural features and occupational refuse elsewhere at Pacatnamu, it is likely that Burials 3 and 4 do not pertain to the original construction and use of H1M1.

In addition to the four human burials, a textile

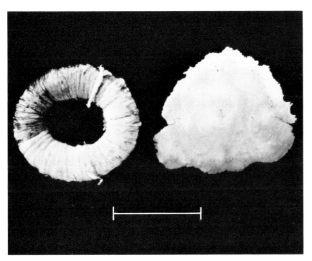

Figure 11. Above: Occipital bone of Burial 3 with fiber ring in the position it was found. Below: Fiber ring removed. Scale is 5 cm.

Figure 12. Burial 4 with shrouds intact. Scale is 10 cm.

bundle containing the remains of a green parrot (preliminary identification) was found just below the surface in a disturbed area near the center of the structure. The original context of this bundle is unknown.

Chronology

The brick type used in the construction of H1M1 (McClelland, this volume) and numerous diagnostic ceramic sherds found in the fill of the structure indicate a Chimu occupation (ca. A.D. 1100-1400) for H1M1. A single complete Chimu ceramic vessel was encountered during excavation, lying upright alongside one of the internal casing walls of the structure (Fig. 13).

The three radiocarbon determinations on H1M1

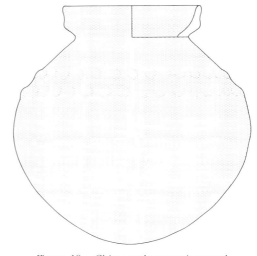

Figure 13. Chimu style ceramic vessel from H1M1. Height: 24 cm.

material cluster tightly and indicate a relatively late date for the structure. Two of the radiocarbon determinations were done on separate samples of a tree branch recovered from an undisturbed section of fill. The branch was collected from a layer of plant material interposed between repeated strata of refuse fill. It had the appearance of being freshly cut and still had leaves attached. The two samples produced radiocarbon dates of A.D. 1260 and 1270.[4] The consistency of the results suggests that the date is reliable.

The third radiocarbon determination was made on a sample of cotton textile from Burial 2. It produced a date of A.D. 1320, which is within one standard deviation of the other two radiocarbon dates.[5] This date provides evidence that Burial 2 was in fact contemporary with H1M1 and that the body may have been interred during or shortly after the building of the structure.

Analogous Structures

A number of North Coast mud brick structures have been identified as Chimu burial platforms on the North Coast of Peru (Conrad 1974, 1982; Keatinge and Conrad 1983; Pozorski 1971). With one exception, all the examples are found at Chan Chan in the Moche Valley. Conrad (1974), who has published the most extensive studies of these structures, divides the platforms at Chan Chan into two types: royal burial platforms associated with the ten large, walled compounds, and burials-in-platform structures, which are less elaborate constructions located in the zone of intermediate architecture.[6] All burial platforms at Chan Chan have been heavily damaged by looting, but survey and excavations by Conrad and Pozorski have revealed many details about their construction and contents. Characteristic of all platforms studied was an internal structure consisting of a series of prepared burial cells with access from above. Within each platform these cells were a consistent size and shape. They were laid out in an orderly arrangement around a single, centrally located T-shaped chamber, which presum-

ably housed the principal burial of the platform.

Keatinge and Conrad (1983) also identified a mud brick platform at the site of Farfan in the Jequetepeque Valley as an Imperial Chimu burial platform. This identification is based primarily on location and context, the fact that it was heavily looted, and the presence of fragments of elaborate grave goods and human bone in the looters' backdirt. Unfortunately, the platform at Farfan has not been fully excavated and its internal structure is not known.

Conclusions

The architectural design of H1M1 is clearly distinct from that of burial platforms at Chan Chan. At Chan Chan, an orderly arrangement of burial cells occupied the interior of the platform; the interior of H1M1 contained nothing but internal walls and fill. Beyond the architectural differences, however, the location and context of H1M1 are similar to the burial platforms at Chan Chan. H1M1 is located within the Major Quadrangle at Pacatnamu, which shares many architectural characteristics with the large walled compounds at Chan Chan. It is the only platformlike structure found within the Quadrangle, and it is known to have contained burials with elite grave goods, including *Spondylus* shell and elaborate textiles. Hence, it is probable that H1M1 served as a burial structure for the occupants of the Quadrangle analogous to that of the burial platforms in the walled compounds at Chan Chan.

APPENDIX:
Human Skeletal Material from H1M1

Below is a summary of the human skeletal material recovered from H1M1. The material described includes not only the four identifiable burials (B1-B4) but also material collected from the surface of the structure and isolated bones encountered during excavation.

I. Burials
    Burial Number: H1M1 B1
        Age: 20-25 years
        Sex: Female
    Comments: Preservation of the skeleton is excellent; there is some soft tissue preservation as

---

4. Sample 1: Beta-12283: 690 ± 60 B.P.
   Sample 2: Beta-12284: 680 ± 60 B.P.
5. Sample 3: Beta-12282: 630 ± 70 B.P.
6. Conrad argues that the royal burial platforms at Chan Chan are the burial places of the Kings of Chimor. The burials-in-platform structures contain Chimu-Inca ceramics and therefore postdate the royal burial platforms. Conrad suggests that these structures are the burial places of local lords during the period of Inca domination.

well, including hair, skin, and fingernails. All long bone epiphyses and the basilar suture of the skull are closed, but the medial epiphyses of the clavicles are incompletely united. The most notable pathology is a well-healed fracture of the left nasal bone and nasal process of the left maxilla. Apparently this individual suffered a blow to the face at some point in her life.

Burial Number: H1M1 B2
        Age: 15-18 years
        Sex: Female

Comments: The early epiphyseal group is closed, but the late group is still open (McKern and Stewart 1957). Crowns of the lower third molars are complete, but the teeth have not erupted. The burial was badly disturbed by looters and only approximately half the skeleton is present. Among the missing bones is the pelvis. Sex attribution is based on the maximum transverse diameter of the head of the femur (38 mm), which lies at the lower limit of the female range at Pacatnamu. The left femur and right tibia of this individual show patches of periosteal bone on the surface of the shafts (left tibia, right femur; fibulae not present). Bilateral involvement of the periostitis suggests a systematic disorder rather than a traumatic origin.

Burial Number: H1M1 B3
        Age: 6-12 Months
        Sex: Indeterminate

Comments: Although disturbed by looters, the skeleton is complete and well preserved. Age is estimated by the lack of any dental eruption and a maximum femoral length (without epiphyses) of 106 mm. The occipital bone shows some bony reaction (porosities) in a circular pattern corresponding to the location of a donut-shaped ring recovered with the burial. This porosity appears to be a pressure atrophy reaction to the ring.

Burial Number: H1M1 B4
        Age: 0-6 Months
        Sex: Indeterminate

Comments: Age at death is estimated on the basis of dental calcification and long bone length. No evidence of bony pathology was noted.

II. Isolated Human Skeletal Material.

Comments: Over 100 isolated human bones were recovered from the surface and looters' backdirt of H1M1. A minimum of ten individuals are represented by the material. Ages range from infant to old adult, and both males and females are present.

RESUMEN:
H1M1: Una Estructura Funeraria del Período Intermedio Tardío en Pacatnamú

H1M1 está ubicado en la esquina sur-este del Cuadrángulo Mayor (Fig. 1). Antes de las excavaciones, se veía como un montículo circular de 30 mts. de diámetro y 2.5 mts. de altura, con evidencia de una larga historia de huaqueo esporádico (Fig. 2). Sin embargo, en la parte central había varios segmentos íntegros de paredes de adobe, que sugería que la arquitectura básica no había sido completamente destruida.

Arquitectura

Los límites externos no pudieron determinarse; sólo fue localizada una porción de lo que pareciese ser la pared externa occidental (Fig. 3). La estructura interna, formada por tabiques de división y relleno diverso, pudo ser identificada, aunque muy dañada por el huaqueo. Esta estuvo construida con adobes pertenecientes a la ocupación Chimú (McClelland, este volumen). El alineamiento de los tabiques internos es norte-sur/este-oeste, aunque hay variaciones en algunos segmentos (Fig. 3).

Mucho del relleno, formado por desmonte de construcción alternado con capas de plantas de maíz (ramas y hojas), se encontró intacto (Figs. 4, 5); este tipo de relleno es común en Pacatnamú, así como en otros sitios tardíos de la Costa Norte.

Entierros y otros Hallazgos

En las áreas disturbadas de H1M1 se hallaron fragmentos de tejidos, cobre, madera y mates, indicando que muchos entierros habían sido destruidos por los huaqueros.

Se recuperaron 4 entierros identificables, aunque éstos estaban disturbados por los huaqueros:

Entierro 1

Esencialmente completo, con poco daño en los textiles alrededor de la cabeza. Estuvo en el desmonte dejado por los huaqueros, a 30 cms. de la superficie. El cuerpo correspondió a un individuo del sexo femenino, de 20 a 25 años de edad; estuvo flexionado y las rodillas ligeramente a la izquierda (Fig. 6). Estuvo envuelto en un manto de 46 x 107 cms.; tenía las manos cruzadas sobre el pecho, y en cada una de ellas, una valva de un mismo ejemplar de Spondylus princeps. *Adentro del manto el cuerpo estuvo envuelto en 2 otros tejidos, uno de ellos un ikat, y el otro con diseño de figuras antropomorfas (Fig. 7).*

Entierro 2

Ubicado a pocos cms. de la superficie de la parte sur-central de la estructura (Fig. 3). Estuvo muy disturbado y sólo se recuperó el 50% del esqueleto de un individuo del sexo femenino, de 15 a 18 años de edad; asociado a él se hallaron fragmentos de tejidos elaborados y ropa en miniatura (Fig. 8), objetos de cobre (Fig. 9), algunas plumas amarillas y turquesas.

Entierro 3

Estuvo en el desmonte de los huaqueros, en la parte sur de la estructura, a 50 cms. de profundidad (Fig. 3). Aparentemente fue un fardo conteniendo los restos de un infante de 6 a 12 meses de edad, el que estuvo fragmentado en dos partes (Fig. 10). El cuerpo estuvo envuelto en 2 capas de tejido de algodón. De especial interés fue el hallazgo de un anillo de 7 cms. de diámetro hecho de fibra vegetal que estuvo apoyado en el occipital (Fig. 11); una depresión en el mismo hueso sugiere que el anillo estuvo ejerciendo presión en el cráneo, en vida del individuo.

Entierro 4

Fue ubicado a 25 cms. de la superficie, cerca al límite occidental de la estructura (Fig. 3). Aparentemente no estuvo disturbado y consistía de un fardo conteniendo los restos de un infante cuya edad era entre recién nacido y 6 meses (Fig. 12).

Además de los entierros humanos, se recuperó un pequeño fardo conteniendo los restos de un loro verde (identificación preliminar), en un contexto disturbado.

Cronología

Los tipos de adobes usados en la construcción (McClelland, este volumen) y los fragmentos de cerámica, permiten ubicar esta estructura en la ocupación Chimú (1100–1400 DC). El único cerámio completo fue una olla Chimú (Fig. 13).

En los fechados radiocarbónicos se usaron dos ramas de árbol provenientes del relleno no disturbado, que arrojaron 1260 DC y 1270 DC, cifras bastante consistentes. La tercera muestra provino de un pedazo de tejido de algodón llano del entierro 2, que dió 1320 DC, lo que está dentro de la desviación standard de las otras dos cifras.

Conclusión

El diseño arquitectónico de H1M1 es claramente distinto al de las plataformas funerarias de Chan Chan, aunque la ubicación y el contexto sugiere algunas similitudes. Por ello, es posible que H1M1 haya cumplido una función similar para los habitantes del Cuadrángulo Mayor.

The Audiencia Room of the Huaca 1 Complex

Susan Lee Bruce

During the excavation and mapping of the Huaca 1 Complex, the Audiencia Room in the southwest corner of the Major Quadrangle proved of special interest. When shallow trenches were dug along the walls in this area, various objects were uncovered, including a spectacular collection of miniature textiles. Although this material was looted from its original context, it had been protected by a covering of melted adobe that resulted from the erosion of the architecture. Subsequent excavation in the Audiencia Room revealed three looted burial chambers that almost certainly were the source of the looted materials. The following report describes the Audiencia Room excavations and presents the results of these efforts.[1]

The Audiencia Room

The Audiencia Room is located in Room Complex A, near the southwest corner of the Major Quadrangle (Figs. 1,2).[2] It is composed of a large open courtyard with an alcove near the center of its east side. The courtyard measures approximately 21 meters north-south by 19 meters east-west. The alcove, which contains the U-shaped audencia, measures approximately 6 meters north-south by 7 meters east-west. Access to the Audiencia Room is either through a pilastered doorway in the center of its west wall, or through a small door and hallway at the northeast corner of the alcove (Fig. 2). Although the adobe walls forming the perimeter of the room are presently eroded to near floor level, at the time of construction they were most likely of sufficient height to insure privacy. The walls were originally plastered, but there is no evidence of friezes or other surface decoration. Remains of cane, reed, rope, and cane-impressed clay suggest the Audiencia Room was at least partially roofed.

On the north side of the courtyard are two

1. As a member of the Pacatnamu Project, my research was made possible primarily by project funds. Supplementary support was provided by the Fulbright-Hays Foundation, the Organization of American States (OAS), The American Museum of Natural History (New York) Lounsbury Pre-Doctoral Fellowship, the UCLA Museum of Cultural History Altman Award, the UCLA Department of Anthropology, and UCLA Friends of Archaeology. Donna McClelland conducted the initial excavation of the audiencia, and John Verano analyzed the human skeletal material discussed in this report. Sharon Gordon Donnan conserved the miniature crown and many other textiles excavated in the Audiencia Room.
2. Richard Keatinge's report of surface surveys conducted at Pacatnamu discusses this Audiencia Room (1982:215-219; fig. 9.2). The map of the room drawn by Keatinge is superseded by Figures 1 and 2 in this volume.

Figure 1. Map of the Major Quadrangle. The Audiencia Room (A) is located near the southwest corner.

adobe projections that extend about one meter out from the west and east walls (Fig. 2); their function is unknown. A wall near the southeast corner of the courtyard serves to baffle the entrance to a series of small rooms.

The U-shaped audiencia in the alcove is opposite the main doorway to the courtyard (Fig. 2). It is formed by a thick rear wall and two thinner projecting side walls, creating an approximately four-square-meter interior. Unfortunately, so much of the interior has been destroyed by looting that its architectural components are difficult to identify. It appears, however, to have had a bench along the rear wall and a low step across the front. It may have also had low benches along the side walls. These features are similar to other audiencias that have been excavated at Pacatnamu.

Our excavations included digging shallow trenches to floor level along the walls forming the room and the audiencia (Fig. 2). In the interior of the courtyard, ten 1 x 1 meter test units, two long trenches, a looted burial chamber, and a 1 x 1 meter section of a second burial chamber were excavated to sterile. A looted burial chamber in the U-shaped audiencia was excavated to sterile, and the remainder of the audiencia was cleared to floor level. In the hallway outside the west wall of the Audiencia Room we also excavated a 1 x 2 meter test unit to sterile and cleared the remainder of the hallway to floor level (Fig. 2).

The excavations showed clear evidence of two stratigraphic levels. The lower level, consisting of loosely packed refuse, occurred immediately above sterile soil. It was approximately 30 centimeters thick and contained Moche IV-V sherds, plant remains, one spindle with cotton yarn, and other cotton yarn fragments. There was no evidence of adobe architecture associated with this level.

The upper level corresponded to the Chimu occupation. It was separated from the lower level by a clay floor. In the courtyard the floor was completely eroded except for a narrow (50-200 cm) strip along the perimeter walls. Miniature textiles, textile fragments, ceramics, gourds, plant remains, and skeletal material were recovered from the upper level. Preservation of this material was considerably better than that in the lower level.

Analysis of the bricks used in the construction of the Audiencia Room confirms the fact that it was built during the Chimu occupation at approximately the same time as the exterior walls of the Major Quadrangle (McClelland, this volume).

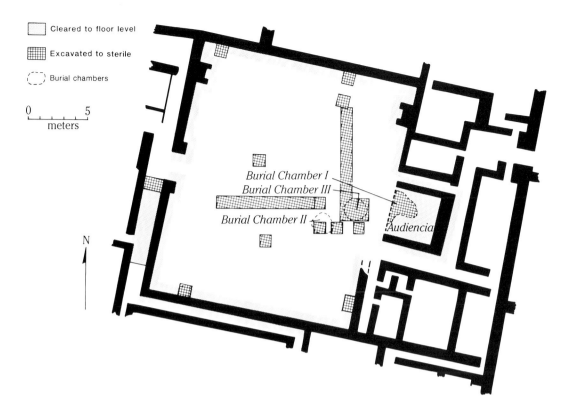

Cleared to floor level

Excavated to sterile

Burial chambers

0   5
    meters

N

Burial Chamber I
Burial Chamber III
Burial Chamber II
Audiencia

*Figure 2. Map of the Audiencia Room showing excavation units and burial chambers.
The U-shaped audiencia is located on the east side of the large courtyard.*

The shallow trenches along the perimeter walls of the courtyard yielded the bulk of the looted artifacts—the remainder were found in the upper (Chimu) level of the other excavation units. Since many of the artifacts are similar to those found in the looted burial chambers, it is likely that the chambers originally held much of the looted material.

It is difficult to determine when the burial chambers were looted, but it clearly was sometime after the Quadrangle was abandoned. The evidence suggests that there were at least two episodes of looting. The first is represented by the artifacts found under the fallen adobe walls and just above the floor level along the perimeter of the courtyard. The position of these objects indicates that the chambers were looted shortly after the abandonment of the room. Furthermore, since the textiles were so well preserved, only a short period of time could have elapsed before the walls began to erode and collapse, forming a protective covering.

The second looting must have taken place much later, after most of the courtyard floor had been eroded by both rain and wind. Textiles and other perishable artifacts were found in the middle of the courtyard near the present surface, protected by a deposit of adobe melt and windblown sand. Since it is unlikely that these textiles could have survived the climatic conditions that eroded the floor, they must represent a later looting of the burial chambers.

At the time of excavation, the surface of the courtyard appeared flat and undisturbed. In contrast, areas of Pacatnamu that have been looted during the last fifty years are characterized by mounds of backdirt and open pits. This difference suggests that the second looting occurred more than a half century ago.

Burial Chambers

Burial Chamber 1

This chamber, located in the center of the U-shaped audiencia, appears to have been approximately 1.5 meters in diameter and 50 centimeters in depth (Fig. 2). Looting has destroyed evidence of the chronological relationship of the chamber to the architecture. However, audiencias in ciudadelas at Chan Chan have subfloor burials believed to be contemporary with their construction (Keatinge 1982:216), and thus it is likely that burials beneath this audiencia also date to the time of its

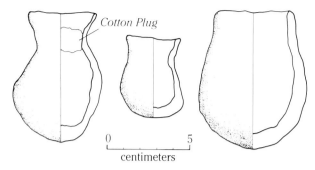

Figure 3. Drawing of miniature ceramic ollas (ofrendas) recovered from various locations in the Audiencia Room.

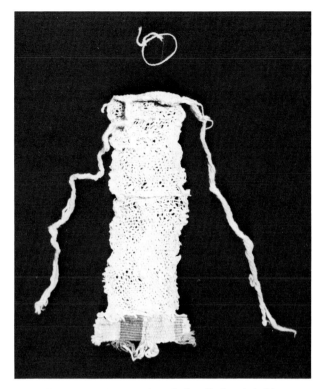

Figure 4. Miniature loincloth rolled and tied into a bundle with a length of cotton yarn, found in the U-shaped audiencia. White cotton plain weave with fringed band. 16 cm.

construction.

Human bones found in Burial Chamber 1 represent one female, 11-13 years old, and at least four other individuals, 15-20 years old, whose sex could not be determined. The size and shape of the chamber implies that the individuals were in a flexed burial position. The bodies appear to have been wrapped in textiles at the time of interment—some of the bones had adhered to large fragments of simple plain weave cloth, a type often used as a burial shroud. A large shell (*Conus fergusoni*) with a textile band around it was associated with the skeletal material.

Mixed with the human bones were whole and broken bricks, broken and some charred *Spondylus* shells, ceramic sherds, llama and small animal bones, plant remains, textile fragments, string, gourd fragments, wood spindle fragments, a copper spindle whorl, a small piece of copper sheet, perforated espingo seeds (*Quararibea* sp.), and shells (*Thais, Donax,* and *Tegula atra*).

Several oxidation-fired ofrendas were excavated from Burial Chamber 1 and from the area immediately surrounding it (Fig. 3). They are crudely made and range in height from 4-8 centimeters. These vessels resemble jars and are thought to be miniature offerings. Two of them had cotton plugs. Similar ofrendas or ofrenda fragments were found in almost every excavated area of the audiencia complex, the heaviest concentrations being associated with the looted burials (see descriptions of Burial Chambers 2 and 3).

The remainder of the U-shaped audiencia was cleared to floor level. Among the artifacts recovered were miniature textiles, which appeared to be associated with Burial Chamber 1. These textiles included two bags, two loincloths, three tunics, two rectangles, and one square. One of the loincloths was folded and tied with a length of yarn (Fig. 4); a rectangle and a square, in a fine open plain weave,

were folded and tied together to form a bundle (Fig. 5). Many of these textiles are similar to those found elsewhere in the Audiencia Room.

Burial Chamber 2

During the excavation of the test units and trenches in the interior of the courtyard, two other burial chambers were located. Burial Chamber 2 was discovered approximately 4.5 meters in front of the south wall of the audiencia (Fig. 2). The circular chamber was approximately 2.0 meters in diameter and 1.3 meters in depth. It contained the partial remains of at least one individual, 12-14 years in age, whose sex could not be determined. The skeletal material included a femur, a mandible, a clavicle, a radius, several ribs, and finger phalanges. Human hair was also noted. Although it was not possible to determine the burial position from the skeletal remains, the size of the chamber could have accommodated either extended or flexed burials.

The fill in the chamber contained at least fifteen broken gourd bowls, 16-20 centimeters in diameter and 6-8 centimeters deep. It is likely that

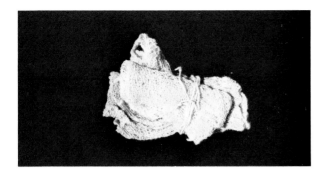

Figure 5. A. Miniature bundle tied with a length of cotton yarn from the audiencia. B. When opened, the bundle was found to contain a miniature square and rectangle of open plain weave cotton cloth. Square: 16 cm; rectangle: 15 cm.

Figure 6. Miniature gourd drum with skin covering and cord handle from another area of Pacatnamu. 7 cm.

Figure 7. Moche stirrup spout vessel showing figure holding drum. Courtesy of Field Museum of Natural History, Chicago.

originally there were many more. Other gourd remains include small rings about 6 centimeters in diameter with two perforations and traces of white pigment on the exterior surface. Some of the perforations still have cotton yarn threaded through them. A more complete specimen found in another area of the site has a skin covering stretched across the opening of the ring (Fig. 6). This specimen resembles the drums suspended by cords, which are depicted on Moche ceramic vessels (e.g., Fig. 7) and suggests that the small gourd rings from Burial Chamber 2 are miniature drums.[3]

Whole and fragmentary ofrendas, similar to those found in Burial Chamber 1 (Fig. 3), were scattered throughout the fill. Other oxidation-fired sherds were identified as Moche, Lambayeque, and Chimu.

Reduction-fired ceramics were also excavated from Burial Chamber 2. Two whole double spout and bridge vessels (Fig. 8A,B) and fragments from four others were found, along with several reduction-fired sherds with press-molded designs.

Fragments of copper ornaments made from hammered sheets, four *Spondylus* beads, and a carved wooden finial (Fig. 9) were also recovered from the burial chamber.

Textile fragments were encountered throughout the fill of Burial Chamber 2, but it could not be determined if any were miniatures. Only one band and several tassels were identifiable. The remainder of the textiles consisted of unraveled alpaca yarn dyed in bright colors.[4] It is clear from the amount and type of yarn that many elaborate and brightly colored textiles must have originally been present. Much of this material is similar to that used in miniatures found elsewhere in the courtyard and thus it is possible that Burial Chamber 2 originally contained miniature textiles.

Precise dating of Burial Chamber 2 is impossible, given that Moche, Lambayeque, and Chimu sherds were recovered. It seems likely, however, that Moche ceramic fragments found in the looted chamber were from the earlier Moche midden in this area and that the chambers were dug and utilized only during the Chimu occupation. In this regard, it should be noted that no Moche style textile fragments were found.

Burial Chamber 3

This was located in the courtyard approximately 1.5 meters in front of the audiencia (Fig. 2). The burial chamber was nearly circular, measuring approximately 1.85 meters in diameter; its depth was 1.1 meters below the present surface. The burial chamber fill included hardened melted adobe,

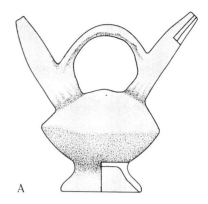

A

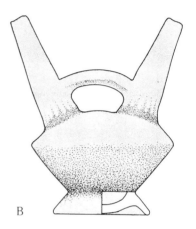

B

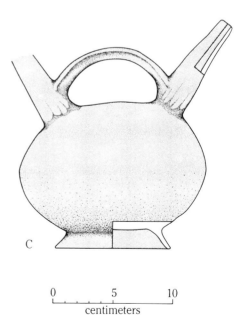

C

```
0        5        10
└────┴────┴────┴────┘
       centimeters
```

Figure 8. Reduction-fired double spout and bridge vessels. A and B from Burial Chamber 2, C from Burial Chamber 3.

---

3. Identical gourd rings were also found in the long north-south trench indicated in Figure 2. These may have been looted from Burial Chamber 2.
4. The term alpaca follows standard usage in recent reports on Andean textiles. However, since no precise identification has been made, it is possible that the fiber is from another type of camelid, such as the llama (Mauersberger 1947:638,639; Harris 1954:72,76).

Figure 9. Carved wooden finial from Burial Chamber 2. 18 cm.

chunks of adobe bricks, and loose earth and sand.

Two clusters of disarticulated bones and a single mandible were encountered, representing at least two individuals, 12-14 years in age (sex undetermined). Some of the bones and associated artifacts were set in hardened adobe, suggesting they were probably left exposed to moisture for some time after the chamber was looted.

Bone cluster 1 was located near the top edge of the chamber along the west perimeter. These remains probably represent one individual who was interred later than the individual(s) represented by bone cluster 2 and the single bone. The cluster included a left hand holding a strombus shell, two tibia, two fibulae, vertebrae, and other miscellaneous bones. An undecorated oxidation-fired bowl was associated with the skeletal material.

Bone cluster 2 was located 25-40 centimeters below the top edge of the chamber near its southeastern edge. Included were a cranium, cervical vertebrae, a mandible, two femora, one scapula, an ulna, several ribs, finger phalanges, and teeth. Some decomposed textile fibers and copper fragments were also associated.

The single mandible was located 24-45 centimeters below the top of the burial chamber near its northeastern perimeter. It was associated with two undecorated gourd bowls—20 centimeters in diameter, 5 centimeters in depth—and other undecorated gourd fragments.

One hundred fifteen oxidation-fired ofrendas and fragments of three oxidation-fired ollas were found in Burial Chamber 3 (Fig. 3). One complete reduction-fired double spout and bridge bottle (Fig. 8C) and fragments from several similar bottles were recovered. Also present were yarn fragments, one bobbin or spindle, one shell bead, and copper fragments. Neither miniature textiles nor other woven textile remains were found within the burial chamber, and thus it is considered an unlikely source for the looted miniature textiles.

Textiles

Approximately seven hundred textiles were recovered from the excavations of the Audiencia Room and the hallway outside its west wall. Other reports describe the textiles in greater detail (see Bruce, in press; Donnan, Elaborate Textile, this volume) and thus they will only be summarized here.

Many of the textiles are fragments of undeco-

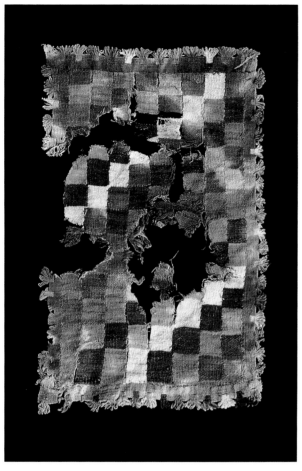

Figure 10. Small rectangle with slit tapestry checkerboard pattern in brightly dyed alpaca and cotton yarns, found along the perimeter walls of the courtyard. 35.5 cm.

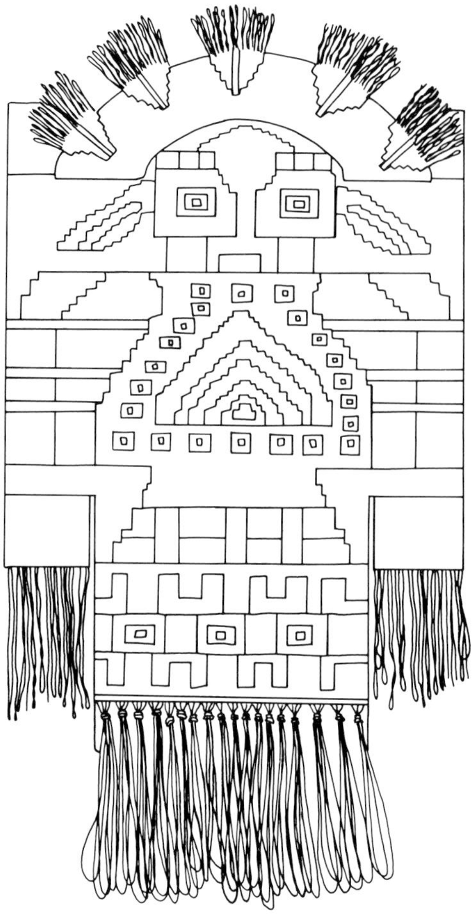

Figure 11. Drawing of slit tapestry patch with a double-headed bird motif, found near the U-shaped audiencia. This type of patch is used as an applique on large shirts. 18 cm.

rated or striped cotton plain weaves.[5] Others are slit tapestry rectangles with checked designs (Fig. 10), tassels, brightly colored decorative bands, and patches used as appliques on large tunics (Fig. 11).[6] Several spindles and/or bobbins (some with yarn), balls of yarn, tassels, feathers, and a large quantity of unravelled yarns were also found. One of the most elaborate textiles is a fragment of slit tapestry with complex iconography, possibly reflecting the ceremonial activities that took place

within the Major Quadrangle (Donnan, Elaborate Textile, this volume).

The ninety-three miniature textiles excavated include sleeveless tunics, ponchos, loincloths, rectangles, squares, crowns, bags, and a pillow.[7] They range in size from approximately 3 x 4 centimeters to approximately 10 x 10 centimeters, with most being small enough to fit in the palm of one's hand. The miniatures are usually woven with brightly dyed alpaca and cotton yarns in slit tapes-

---

5. The textile terminology follows that presented by Emery (1980).
6. Similar patches, used as appliques on large tunics, were recovered at Pacatnamu by Ubbelohde-Doering (1967:84, pl. 102) and were discussed by Keatinge (1978:36). Nearly identical patches were also found at Pachacamac on the Central Coast. Keatinge argues that these textiles and other archaeological evidence indicate a close relationship be-

tween Pacatnamu and Pachacamac (1978; 1982:219-221).
7. Miniature textiles were also recovered from a looted burial (H1M1 Burial 2) and from fill in mound H1M1 (Verano and Cordy-Collins, this volume), located in the southeastern corner of the Major Quadrangle, and from a looted cemetery northeast of Huaca 31 (Bruce, in press). The miniatures from these areas are very similar to and probably contemporary with those found in the Audiencia Room.

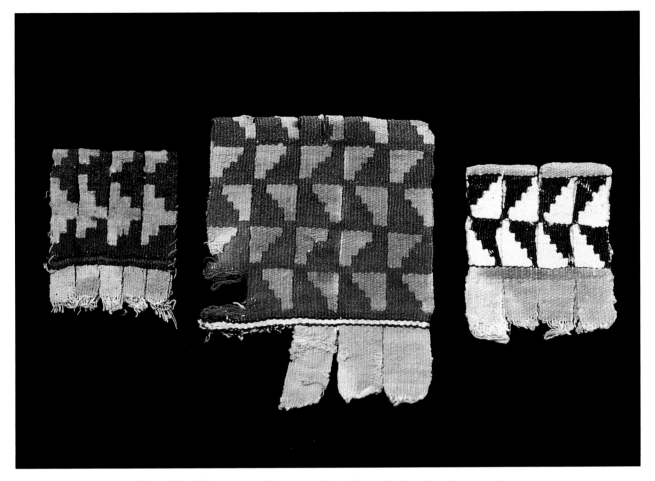

*Figure 12.   Slit tapestry miniature tunics with vertical neck and arm openings,
found along the perimeter walls of the courtyard. Largest 13 cm.*

try and weft faced plain weaves. Cotton plain weave fabrics are also used. Embellishments such as embroidery, weft loop pile, tassels, decorative bands, and fringe commonly supplement the basic fabric. Some of the miniatures were rolled and tied into small bundles (Figs. 4,5).

Thirty-seven of the miniatures are tunics, of which there are two styles. Thirty have a center vertical slit for the neck opening and vertical arm openings along the sides (Fig. 12). The remaining seven have horizontal neck and arm openings along the top transverse edge of the tunic (Fig. 13). Both styles are found in large-scale garments excavated from other areas of Pacatnamu.[8] The tunics with

horizontal neck and arm openings are particularly interesting since the only other previously reported examples, in miniature or large scale, were excavated from the Central Coast of Peru (O'Neale 1935; Emery and King 1957; Gayton 1955; Stumer and Gayton 1958; Van Stan 1961, 1967).

Among the miniatures are two ponchos, nine loincloths, and thirteen bags (Figs. 14-16). The basic fabric for these is a cotton plain weave, but decorative bands were sometimes added to the loincloths and bags.

Eleven of the miniatures are squares and twenty-four are rectangles (Figs. 17,18). Some of the squares have decorative bands and tassels added to

8. Three burials of adult females excavated at Pacatnamu contained large-scale horizontal neck slit tunics made from multiple panels of cotton plain weave. The tunics were either worn by the individual or were used as padding (see Stumer and Gayton 1958:fig. 1 for a reconstructed view of the tunic when worn). It is argued elsewhere that these horizontal neck slit tunics are a female garment type (Bruce, in press).

Figure 13.   Fragmentary miniature tunic with horizontal neck and arm openings along top edge, found along perimeter walls of the courtyard. 8 cm.

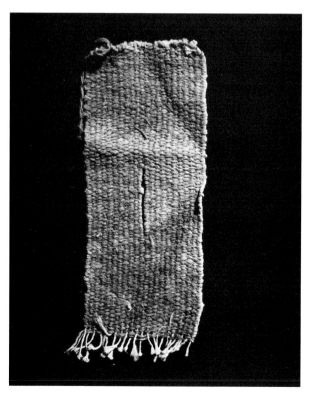

Figure 14.   Miniature poncho in cotton plain weave, found along the perimeter walls of the courtyard. 16.5 cm.

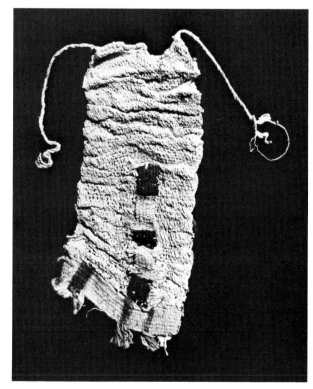

Figure 15.   Miniature loincloth in cotton plain weave with decorative bands on the front flap and yarn ties, found along the perimeter walls of the courtyard. 16.5 cm.

Figure 16. Miniature bags in cotton plain weave with decorative border bands, found along the perimeter walls of the courtyard. Left: 9.5 cm; right 8.7 cm.

the basic weft-striped fabric. It is not known if their forms imitate garments or other types of textiles.

A miniature crown (Fig. 19) was the only type of headgear found and is represented by one complete example and several fragments. The crown base is formed from a tapered cane cylinder with the vertical uprights held in place by three horizontal rows of cotton twining. A slit tapestry checkerboard fabric is attached to the outside and a wide cane band, painted black, covers the lower edge.

Conclusion

The Audiencia Room contained at least three looted burial chambers, each with one or more disturbed burials. Many artifacts recovered from the Audiencia Room are similar to those found in the burial chambers, and it is likely that many of these looted artifacts were originally a part of the grave goods. Burial chamber offerings included textile, ceramic, gourd, metal, shell, and wood artifacts. A large number of these artifacts were miniatures: textiles, gourd drums, and ofrendas. Of these, miniature textiles comprised a substantial part of the elaborate offerings, possibly substituting for large-scale fancy textiles (see Bruce, in press).

Although the damage to the area caused by looters and natural forces rendered it impossible to determine conclusively the chronological relationship of the burial chambers to the construction of the Audiencia Room, some, if not all of the burials were probably placed beneath its floor at the time of construction.

No specific date can yet be given for the construction of the audiencia or the burial chambers. However, we do know that the bricks used in the architecture are identified with the Chimu occupation of the site (approximately A.D. 1100-1400) and probably pertain to the early part of the Late Intermediate Period.

Figure 17. Miniature square with weft stripes, border bands, and tassels, found along the perimeter walls of the courtyard. 7.5 cm (incomplete).

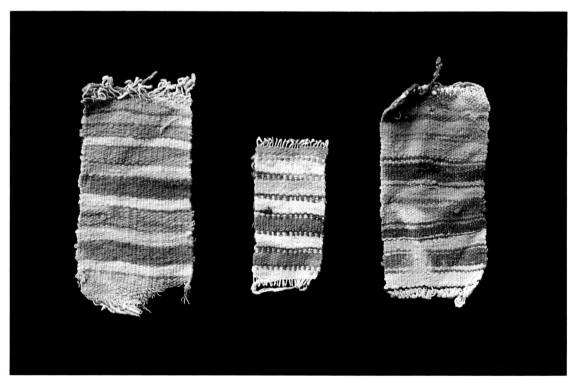

Figure 18. Weft-striped miniature rectangles with cut-warp fringe on both ends. Left and right from along the perimeter walls of the courtyard; center from the U-shaped audiencia. Left to right: 13 cm, 8 cm, 12 cm.

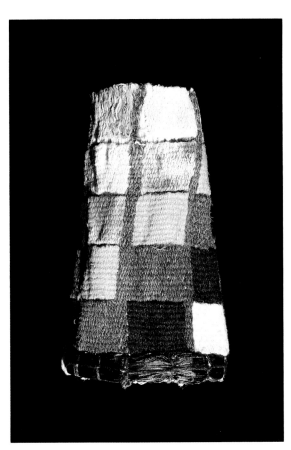

Figure 19. Miniature crown with slit tapestry checked fabric covering a cane frame, found along the perimeter walls of the courtyard. 10.4 cm.

RESUMEN:
El Recinto de la Audiencia en el Complejo de la Huaca 1

El recinto de la audiencia está ubicado en el Complejo A, cerca de la esquina sur-oeste del Cuadrángulo Mayor (Figs. 1 y 2). Se compone de un patio que mide 21 mts. norte-sur y 19 mts. este-oeste, y una porción recesada, que contiene la audiencia, que mide 6 mts. norte-sur y 7 mts. este-oeste (Fig. 2).

Aunque las paredes perimétricas del recinto se hallan erosionadas hasta casi el nivel del piso actual, se piensa que la altura original fue lo suficiente como para asegurar privacidad al recinto; por otro lado, restos de cañas, sogas y barro con impresiones de caña, sugieren que el recinto estuvo por lo menos parcialmente techado.

La audiencia está formada por una gruesa pared en la parte posterior y dos más delgadas a los lados, ocupando un área de aproximadamente 4 mts. cuadrados. Mucho del interior de la audiencia está destruido por huaqueo, incluyendo el posible poyo de la pared posterior.

Las excavaciones en el recinto mostraron evidencia de los niveles estratigráficos; el más profundo, encima del suelo estéril tiene 30 cms. de grueso y contuvo fragmentos de cerámica Moche, restos vegetales y un huso con hilo de algodón.

En el nivel superior se hallaron miniaturas textiles, fragmentos de tejidos, cerámica y mates; también, restos vegetales y restos humanos disturbados. Este material cultural pertenece al período de ocupación Chimú. El estado de este material fue considerablemente mejor que el del estrato Moche.

La evidencia sugiere que el recinto pasó por dos períodos de huaqueo:

1. *El primero está representado por los textiles recuperados cerca de las paredes perimétricas del recinto. La posición de ellos, relativos al piso, sugiere que las cámaras funerarias ubicadas en el recinto fueron huaqueadas poco después que éste se abandonase, por lo que, cuando las paredes comenzaron a desmoronarse, cubrieron estos tejidos, asegurando su preservación.*

2. *El segundo ocurrió mucho desqués, cuando el piso del recinto había sido erosionado por el viento y la lluvia. Los tejidos, y otro material cultural, fueron encontrados en el centro del patio, protegidos por*

un depósito de adobe derretido, tierra y arena.

Al momento de las excavaciones, la superficie del recinto aparecía plana y no disturbada, lo que sugiere que ambos episodios ocurrieron hace mucho tiempo.

Cámaras Funerarias

La primera se localizó en el centro de la estructura en U o audiencia; parece haber sido de forma circular y midió, aproximadamente, 1.50 mts. de diámetro por 50 cms. de profundidad (Fig. 2). El huaqueo había destruido la evidencia de la relación exacta entre la cámara y la arquitectura. Los huesos humanos recuperados corresponden a un individuo del sexo femenino, de 11 a 13 años de edad, así como restos de cuatro otros entre los 15 y 20 años, cuyo sexo no pudo ser determinado por estar incompletos los huesos. El tamaño y forma de la cámara sugiere que fueron deposita- dos en posición flexionada. Asociados a ellos se recuperaron fragmentos de tejidos simples adheri- dos a algunos huesos, una concha grande (Conus fergusoni) con una banda de tejido alrededor, adobes rotos, fragmentos de Spondylus, pedazos de cerámica, huesos de camélidos, restos vege- tales, fragmentos de mates, husos, hojas de cobre y conchas (Thais, Donax y Tegula atra). También, pequeñas vasijas (Fig. 3) que miden de 4 a 8 cms. de alto, dos de las cuales conservaban tapones de algodón.

Entre las miniaturas textiles, se recuperaron dos bolsas, dos taparrabos y tres túnicas, dos rec- tangulares y una cuadrada. Uno de los taparrabos estaba doblado y amarrado con un hilo (Fig. 4), lo mismo que otros tejidos (Fig. 5).

La Cámara Funeraria 2 estuvo a 4.5 mts. al frente de la pared sur del recinto; era de forma circular y midió 2 mts. de diámetro por 1.30 de profundidad. Contenía los restos incompletos de un individuo de 12 a 14 años de edad cuyo sexo no se pudo precisar.

No se pudo determinar la posición del entierro, pero el tamaño de la cámara podría haber conte- nido un cadáver flexionado o extendido. El relleno de la cámara contuvo 15 mates rotos, de 16 a 20 cms. de diámetro y de 6 a 8 cms. de altura. Otras piezas de lagenaria incluyeron anillos con dos perforaciones y restos de pintura blanca en el exterior, que midieron casi 6 cms. de diámetro (Fig. 6). Estos parecen haber sido tambores en miniatura, como se ve en la cerámica Moche (Fig. 7). También se recuperaron pequeñas ollas (Fig. 3), fragmentos de cerámica identificables como Moche, Lambayeque, y Chimú.

Fragmentos de ornamentos de cobre martilla- do, 4 cuentas de Spondylus y una imagen tallada en madera (Fig. 8) fueron también recuperados en esta cámara. No se pudo determinar si los frag- mentos de textiles eran parte de miniaturas, pero los tipos de fibra (algodón y lana), las técnicas y los colores de los tejidos son similares.

Aunque un fechado preciso parece ser difícil, el contexto sugeriría que se trata de una cámara del período Chimú, donde los restos Moche prov- endrían de una ocupación más temprana en el área.

La Cámara Funeraria 3 estuvo 1.50 mts. al frente de la audiencia; tenía forma circular midien- do 1.85 mts. de diámetro y una profundidad de 1.10 mts. desde el piso actual. Se hallaron tres grupos desarticulados de huesos que corresponden a dos individuos de 12 a 14 años de edad, cuyo sexo no pudo determinarse.

Entre los objetos recuperados se hallan 115 ollas pequeñas (Fig. 3), una vasija con doble pico y asa puente (Fig. 9C), fragmentos de otras botellas similares, trozos de hilo, un huso, fragmentos de cobre, una concha de Strombus, etc.

Textiles

Muchos de los tejidos son fragmentos de telas de algodón llanas, sin decoración o con listados. Otros son tapices rectangulares con diseño en damero (Fig. 10), bandas en brillantes colores y paneles para ser cosidos en túnicas (Fig. 11). Uno de los tejidos más elaborados es un tapiz con ico- nografía compleja, que posiblemente refleja las actividades llevadas a cabo en el Cuadrángulo Mayor (Donnan, este volumen).

Las 93 miniaturas excavadas incluyen túnicas sin mangas, ponchos, taparrabos, coronas, bolsas y una almohada. Varían en tamaño de 3 x 4 cms. a 10 x 10 cms. Son generalmente tapices hechos de algodón o lana y teñidos en colores brillantes.

Treinta y siete de las miniaturas son túnicas, que corresponden a dos estilos. En el primero hay 30 que poseen una abertura vertical y central para la cabeza y aberturas también verticales para los brazos (Fig. 12). Las otras siete pertenecen al otro estilo, y tienen aberturas horizontales para la cab- eza y los brazos (Fig. 13). También se cuentan 2 ponchos, 9 taparrabos y 13 bolsas (Figs. 14, 15 y 16).

Once de las miniaturas son cuadrados y 24 son rectángulos (Figs. 17 y 18). El único tocado de cabeza completo fue una corona en miniatura (Fig. 19).

An Elaborate Textile Fragment from the Major Quadrangle

Christopher B. Donnan

A remarkable textile fragment with complex iconography was uncovered in the process of excavating the Major Quadrangle south of Huaca 1. The textile depicts several individuals who appear to be engaged in ceremonial activities (Figs. 1,2). Since other archaeological material excavated inside the Major Quadrangle indicates that these kinds of activities actually took place there, this textile provides a fascinating glimpse of how the Quadrangle could have functioned, as seen through the eyes of the ancient people who lived there.[1]

The textile was found near the southwest corner of the Major Quadrangle, on the south side of the large open courtyard where the U-shaped audiencia is located (Fig. 3; Donnan, Huaca 1, this volume). It was found with many other textile fragments and miniature garments, which appear to have been looted from their original context and left scattered on the floor of the courtyard. This textile, and others found with it, were remarkably well preserved because they lay adjacent to a wall and had been covered with windblown sand and melted adobe as the wall subsequently eroded.[2]

The original location of the textiles is not known, but it is likely they came either from the circular pits in the floor of the courtyard in front of the U-shaped audiencia, or from beneath the audiencia itself (Fig. 3; Bruce, this volume). The fill in these areas contained numerous fragments of textiles, shells, gourds, and ceramic vessels. Of the more than one hundred textile fragments found in these areas and on the patio floor, the elaborate textile discussed here is unique in having complex iconography illustrating numerous figures involved in a variety of activities.

The textile is a slit tapestry with cotton warps and wool wefts. The long slits are sewn closed with an overcast stitch. The garments worn by some of

1. This textile was excavated by Mary E. Doyle and was cleaned, blocked, and mounted by Sharon Gordon Donnan. The drawing (Fig. 2) was made by Alana Cordy-Collins and Genaro Barr. Giesela and Wolfgang Hecker kindly showed me illustrations of the similar textile fragment that they found. They also made several helpful suggestions after reading a previous draft of this paper.
2. One small fragment of a textile nearly identical to this one was found at Pacatnamu by Giesela and Wolfgang Hecker in 1962. It came from the west side of Huaca 16, almost exactly 400 meters northwest of where this textile was found. It consists of a narrow strip of cloth, which appears to be a vertical piece of the same, or at least a very similar, textile. It does not appear to add any new iconographic details to those visible on this piece. Like this piece, it was found near the surface of the ground and appeared to have been looted. There were no clearly associated artifacts.

Figure 1. The elaborate textile fragment from the Major Quadrangle.

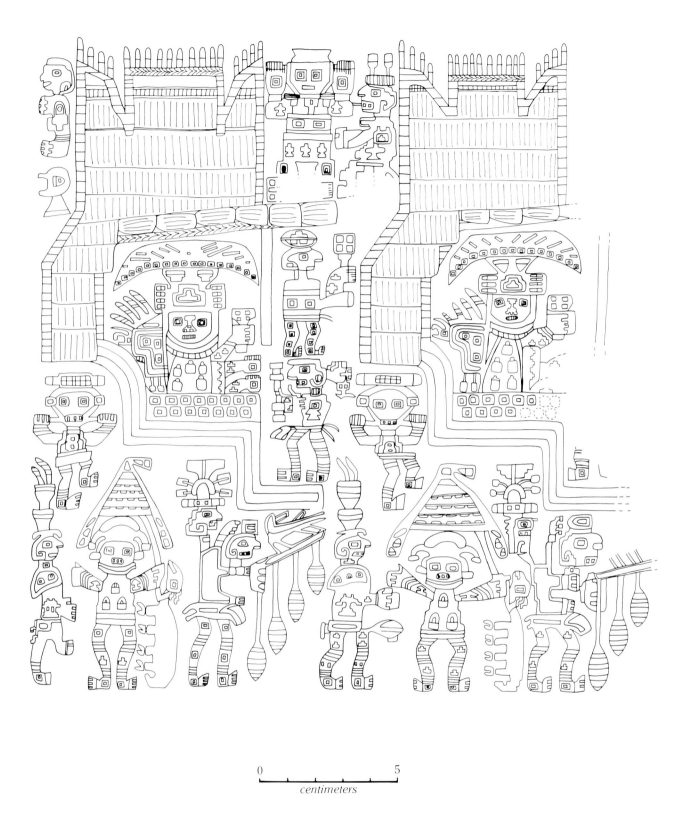

Figure 2.   Drawing of the design on the elaborate textile fragment shown in Figure 1.

Elevated Architecture

U-shaped Audiencia

Textile Excavated Here

Figure 3. Plan of the Major Quadrangle.

the individuals shown on the textile have a three-dimensional quality created by weft-looped pile. The thatch on the roofs of the two structures depicted has a similar effect, achieved by bands of wool fringe sewn onto the textile after it was woven.

The textile has original selvages along the bottom and left side, but the top and right side are torn. An elaborate border is sewn along the bottom of the piece, and several multistrand tassels extend below it. This border continues beyond the left selvage, suggesting that there was originally another panel of cloth extending the piece in this direction. Several loose threads and sewing holes along the left selvage provide further evidence of this.

The border with fringe along the bottom, and the evidence for at least one additional vertical panel suggest that the textile originally may have been part of an elaborate shirt. Sleeved shirts with elaborate tapestry weave central panels are known to come from the lower Jequetepeque Valley, and some are thought to have been looted from Pacatnamu (Bruce 1983).

Date

It is difficult to assign a precise date to the textile, but it clearly belongs to the Chimu occupation of Pacatnamu that occurred after A.D. 1100. Fragments of ceramics found in the looted pits and presumed to be associated with the textile include double spout and bridge bottles of reduction-fired blackware, a form generally associated with the Late Intermediate Period occupation of the North Coast. Also, the manner in which figures are depicted on this textile is similar to that found on other textiles from the Jequetepeque Valley thought to have been woven during the early part of the Late Intermediate Period. Thus, it is reasonable to suggest a date of between A.D. 1100 and 1300 for this textile; the reader must be cautioned, however, that this date is not based on good archaeological evidence. It is anticipated that a precise chronology for Pacatnamu will be developed during the next few years which will make it possible to date this textile with greater precision.

Figure 4.   Chimu ceramic bottle depicting a structure with a gabled roof. The two notches at the top of the roof are similar to those shown on the textile.

Activities

The predominant figures on the textile are the two, shown frontally, seated under tall thatched roofs. They wear large crescent headdresses and elaborate clothing, including a birdlike element that projects from their backs. Each holds a decorated goblet, raised as though proposing a toast. The stepped line patterns beneath the figures suggest raised platforms or elevated architecture on which the thatched roof structures were built. Symmetrical notches on top of the thatched roofs are identical to those on some architecture depicted on Chimu ceramics (Fig. 4).

Below and to the left of each of the seated major figures is an individual whose face, arms, hands, and torso are presented frontally and whose legs and feet are shown in profile. His hands are raised; one leg is extended with the foot on the ground, the second is elevated with the knee bent. The intent of the weaver may have been to imply movement, possibly dancing. They will henceforth

be referred to as "dancers."

Beneath and to the right of each dancer is an individual in frontal view, holding a white llama in his left hand.[3] The llama almost certainly has been or is soon to be sacrificed. It is suspended from a rope tied around its neck which extends upward to a large triangular element positioned above the head of the llama holder. To the left of each llama holder is what may be an attendant figure, shown in profile, who is helping with the llama sacrifice.

To the right of the llamas are weavers, shown standing and in profile. In front of each is a loom, indicated by a diagonal line extending upward from their hands, with a series of bobbins hanging vertically from it. The multiple bobbins suggest that tapestry is being woven. Each of the weavers has a human head projecting from the wrist nearest the loom. William Conklin has recorded another textile with a weaving scene, possibly from Pacatnamu, which shows infants adjacent to the weavers (pc: January 1985). Perhaps the heads emanating from the wrists of the weavers in this scene also represent infants.

The activities of the other figures depicted on this textile are more difficult to interpret. The figures in profile, standing one above the other between the major figures, may be attendants. The upper figure appears to be holding a goblet similar to those held by the major figures.

At the top of the textile, between the thatched roofs, are two figures, one of which is shown in frontal view with hands raised alongside his head. To the right, and facing him, is a standing figure in profile with his arm extending forward. A similar figure is shown in the upper left corner of the textile, with an enigmatic object beneath him.

Archaeological Correlations

Excavation in the Major Quadrangle provided striking correlations to the activities and objects depicted on the textile. The elevated architecture where the two principal figures are seated is analogous to the elevated architecture located near the entrance to the Quadrangle (Fig. 3; Donnan, Huaca 1, this volume). The summit of this architecture is approximately three meters above the floor of the Quadrangle, and can be reached only by two narrow ramps. It had at least eight rooms, including

---

3. The identification of this animal as a llama is based on the cloven hoofs, long head, relatively small ears, and a tail that curves down.

one with a series of niches along one side. The smaller rooms and portions of the large patio area were probably roofed. Some of the roofs may well have been gabled and covered with thatch, although no good evidence of roofing was uncovered. This elevated architecture clearly had limited access and probably served either as a residence for individuals of high status, or as an area for performance of ceremonies. In either case, it would have been an appropriate location for ceremonial drinking by high-status individuals, and as such, provides an interesting parallel to the analogous structure on the textile.

Assuming our identification of two of the individuals as dancers is correct, it is clear that their activity could well have taken place inside the Major Quadrangle, where there are numerous large rectangular plazas of varying sizes and forms (Fig. 3). These plazas are flat, with clean clay floors that would have been ideally suited for the performance of dance.

The depiction of two individuals sacrificing llamas is of particular interest because sacrificed llamas, carefully wrapped in textiles, were found ritually buried beneath the floors of two of the rooms inside the Quadrangle (Altamirano 1984). In each instance a single llama was found; its chest had been cut open but there was no other evidence of trauma. The llamas were less than one year of age; one had white fur, and the fur of the other was a light tan color.[4] It is possible that the ritual sacrifice of llamas within the Quadrangle took place in ceremonies similar to the one shown on the textile.

The two weavers depicted on this textile have particular significance because abundant weaving materials were found inside the Quadrangle. Many balls of yarn, bobbins, and spindles were uncovered, and the yarns they contained were identical in fiber, spin, thickness, and color to those used in the textiles found inside the Quadrangle. This indicates that at least some of the textiles were actually woven in this area. As noted above, the multiple bobbins hanging from the looms depicted on the textile suggest that tapestry is being woven. Most of the textiles found inside the Quadrangle are tapestries.

The activities of the other figures depicted on the textile cannot be identified, but there is nothing to suggest that what they are doing could not have taken place inside the Quadrangle.

Historic documents from the Early Colonial Period confirm that some of these activities were staged in monumental architecture at important sites on the North Coast of Peru. One of the most interesting of these documents was written by Pedro Cieza de Leon, who traveled in Peru in the late 1540s and visited the Jequetepeque Valley in September 1547. In reference to the curacas (lords) of Lambayeque and Jequetepeque, he states they were well served by women and men, were carried on litters, and had guards for their custody and the custody of their houses (Cieza 1984[1553]:Ch. LXVII,205; Cock, this volume). They had dancers, musicians, singers, the most beautiful women of the valley, big "houses" or palaces with matted roofing and adobe columns, big courtyards, columnates, and in the interior of the houses they had courtyards where they held their dances and festivities. At meal time, great numbers of people congregated with the lord, and they drank chica and had their meals together. The entrances were always protected by guards who controlled the people entering and leaving the lord's house (Cieza 1984[1553]:Ch. XI,191-192). Many other early documents allude to these and similar activities and imply the importance of elaborate palace and ceremonial complexes.[5]

In essence, everything depicted on this textile appears to be taking place in an urban setting, adjacent to elevated, high-status architecture. Individuals appear to be engaged in ceremonial activities, utilizing various types of appropriate paraphernalia. It is not clear whether the distinct activities are meant to be occurring simultaneously, sequentially, or in various combinations, but their juxtaposition suggests that all were enacted in relatively close proximity. The correlation between what is shown on the textile, what was excavated archaeologically, and the information contained in historical documents suggests that the staging of these ceremonial activities was a primary function of the quadrangle. Thus we can postulate that various individuals went inside the quadrangle to perform ritual activities, which included ceremonial drinking, dancing, llama sacrifice, and weaving. This remarkable textile allows us to view these activities through the eyes of the people who practiced them centuries before the arrival of Europeans.

---

4. The sacrificed llama with white fur was found carefully buried beneath a floor in the elevated architecture.

5. A discussion of these sources and the information they provide is available in Rostworowski 1975; Netherly 1977:ff. 231; Ramirez-Horton 1982; Cock 1985, and this volume.

RESUMEN:
Un Fragmento de un Textil Elaborado Proveniente del Cuadrángulo Mayor

En el proceso de excavación en el Cuadrángulo Mayor se descubrió un notable fragmento de tejido con iconografía compleja, la que muestra varios individuos que parecen estar realizando actividades ceremoniales (Figs. 1, 2). Desde que otras evidencias arqueológicas excavadas en el Cuadrángulo indican que las actividades ilustradas en el textil se desarrollaron en ese recinto, el tejido provee una visión fascinante de la función del cuadrángulo como visto por la gente que vivía allí.

Fue localizado en el sector sur-oeste del Cuadrángulo Mayor, dentro del Complejo A, en el lado sur del patio donde está la única audiencia del Cuadrángulo (Fig. 3; Donnan, Huaca 1, este volumen). Se hallaba revuelto con otros frgmentos y tejidos en miniatura. El tejido Corresponde al Período Intermedio Tardío, entre 1100 y 1300 DC.

Actividades

Los personajes predominantes son dos, mostrados frontalmente, sentados bajo estructuras techadas. Poseen tocados de cabeza y vestimentas elaboradas, mientras sostienen vasos ceremoniales en sus manos. Aparentan estar sobre una plataforma escalonada, con techos similares a los ilustrados en cerámica Chimú (Fig. 4).

Más abajo, a la izquierda de cada uno de estos personajes, hay un individuo que aparenta estar bailando, por lo que lo denominaremos bailarín. En el siguiente panel, bajo el lado derecho de cada bailarín, hay un individuo, acompañado por un ayudante, sosteniendo una llama blanca que ha sido sacrificada, o que está próxima a serlo. A la derecha de cada llama se pueden apreciar tejedores, con sus telares y bobinas, lo que sugiere que se hallan manufacturando tapices.

Las actividades de los otros personajes en el tapiz son más difíciles de interpretar: los dos de perfil, uno encima del otro, entre las dos figuras principales, parecen ser ayudantes; el de encima, parece estar sosteniendo un vaso similar al de las figuras principales.

En la parte superior, entre los techos, hay otras dos figuras paradas, una de frente, y la otra de perfil.

Correlación Arqueológica

La plataforma elevada es similar a una ubicada cerca de la entrada al Cuadrángulo (Fig. 3; Donnan, Huaca 1, este volumen), donde podrían desarrollarse actividades como las mostradas por los personajes principales.

En el Cuadrángulo Mayor existen ambientes propicios para la danza, por lo que los personajes identificados como bailarines podrían haber desarrollado su actividad allí.

Se han recuperado llamas sacrificadas, las que estaban cuidadosamente envueltas en tejidos, entre pisos de dos recintos del Cuadrángulo. Una llama fue blanca y la otra parda clara. Tenían un corte en el pecho, registrado también en las costillas. Es posible que hayan sido sacrificadas en un ritual similar al mostrado en el tejido.

El hallazgo de madejas y husos con fibra de la misma calidad, torción, grosor y color que el de los tijedos hallados en el Cuadrángulo indicaría que esta fue una actividad que se realizaba en su interior. El tejido que se comenta muestra la confección de un tapiz: un gran porcentaje de los hallazgos consisten de tapices.

La correlación entre lo que es mostrado en el tapiz, lo excavado en el Cuadrángulo y la información contenida en documentos históricos, muestra que estas actividades se realizaban allí. El tejido las muestra a través de los ojos de gente que vivió siglos antes del arribo de los Europeos.

A Mass Burial of Mutilated Individuals at Pacatnamu

John W. Verano

During the 1984 field season at Pacatnamu, the skeletal remains of fourteen young males were found buried in a deep defensive trench outside the entrance to the principal ceremonial complex of the city. The remains represent three groups of individuals who appear to have been ritually sacrificed and mutilated before being deposited in the trench. This paper presents the preliminary results of the excavation and analysis of this material.[1]

Location and Context

The mass burial was discovered just east of the primary entrance to the Huaca 1 Complex, in the bottom of the defensive trench that extends along the north side of the Inner Wall (Fig. 1; Donnan, City Walls, this volume). The skeletons were found while clearing the east face of the causeway that crosses the trench at this location. Today the trench is filled with sand, melted adobe, and wall collapse, capped by a layer of windblown sand that has banked up against the north side of the wall (Figs. 2,3). The fourteen human skeletons were found in three superimposed groups in the bottom of the trench in a matrix of sand, rubble, and refuse. The stratigraphic relationship of the skeletons suggests that individuals were placed in the trench on three separate occasions. For this reason they will be described below as Groups I, II, and III.

Group I

The uppermost group consists of four skeletons that lay approximately 2 meters below the present-day ground surface (Figs. 4-6). Associated with these skeletons was a fragmentary plain weave textile found under the pelvis of Individual 1 (possibly the remains of a loincloth) and several fragments of rope encircling the ankles of Individuals 1 and 2 (Figs. 7,8). The rope was poorly preserved, making it difficult to ascertain its original length or

1. This research was conducted under project support from the National Geographic Society and the National Endowment for the Humanities. Additional funding was provided by a research fellowship from the Organization of American States (OAS), the UCLA Friends of Archaeology, and a student research grant from the UCLA Department of Anthropology. I am very grateful to all of these sources. I would also like to thank Patricia Wade of UCLA and Nancy Porter of California State University, Northridge, for important information on ethnohistoric documents and depictions of prisoners and human sacrifice. My thanks also to the Instituto Nacional de Cultura, Departmental La Libertad, for permission to photograph the Dragon figures.

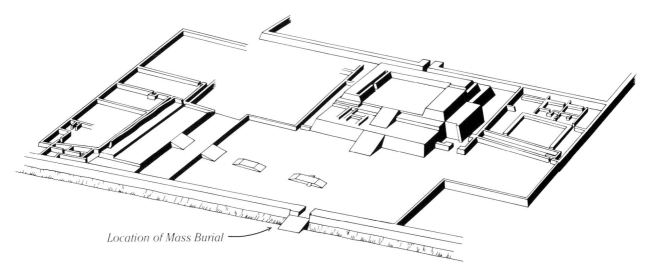

Figure 1. Isometric view of the northern portion of the Huaca 1 Complex
(looking southeast) showing the location of the mass burial.

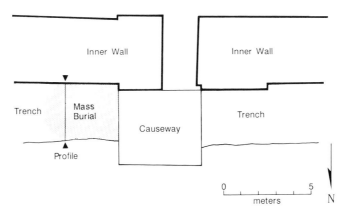

Figure 2. Plan of the northern entrance to the Huaca 1 Complex. The location
of the profile in Figure 3.

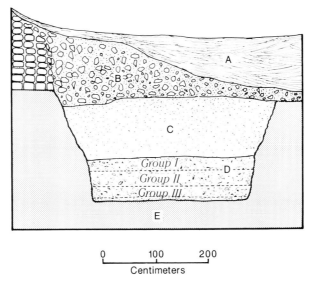

Figure 3. Profile of the trench approximately 2 meters east of
the causeway, indicating the stratigraphic position of the skeletons.

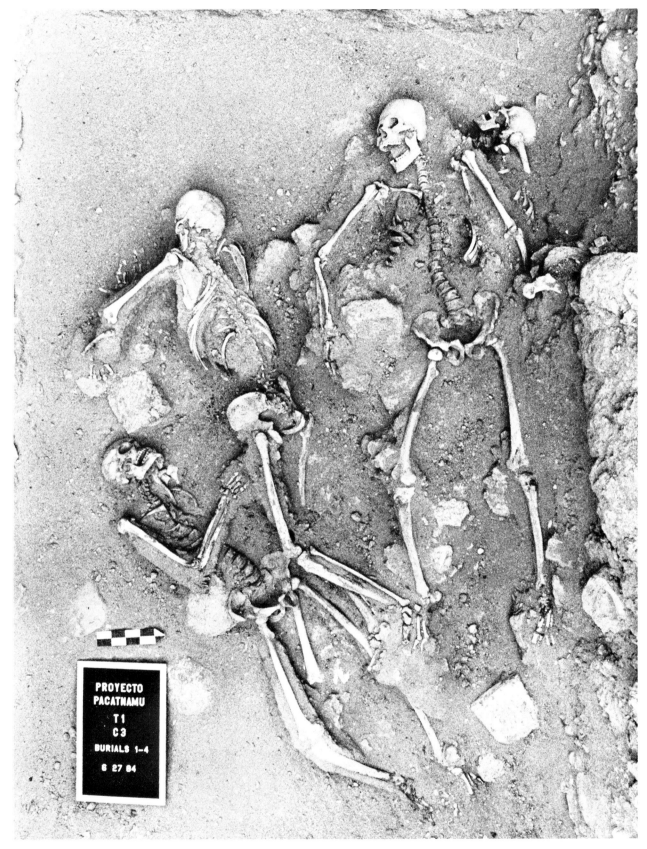

Figure 4. Photograph of part of Group I.

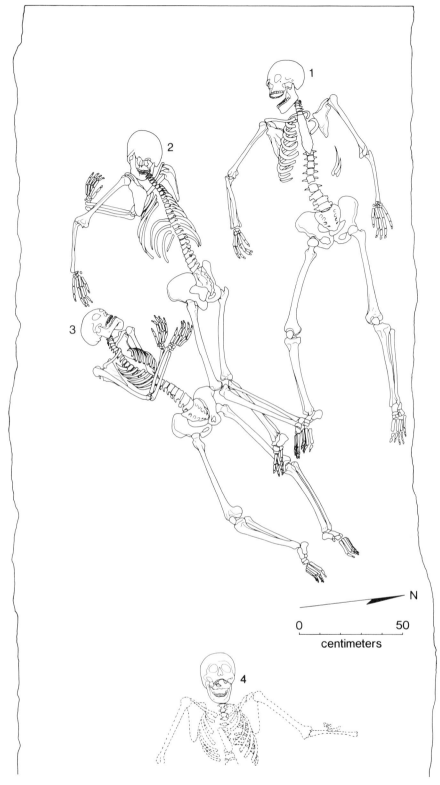

Figure 5. Group 1 (Individuals 1-4). The straight line at the top of the figure marks the eastern face of the causeway across the trench; the irregular vertical lines indicate the contour of the trench walls at the level at which the skeletons were found. The postcranial skeleton of Individual 4 is indicated by dotted lines because it extends beyond the original 2 x 3 meter excavation unit (see Fig. 6). Note the splayed position of the skeletons, and that all four individuals are missing the left radius.

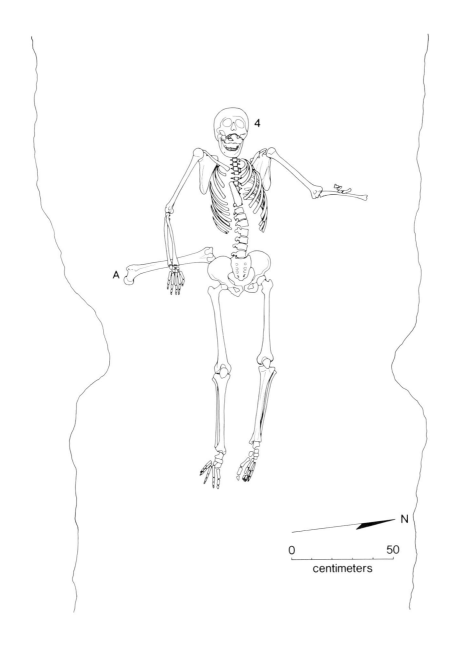

Figure 6.   Group 1, Individual 4, found furthest east from the walkway across the trench. An isolated human femur lies under the right forearm. Isolated bones that could not be associated confidently with any particular individual are indicated by letters in the illustrations. Note the absence of the left radius and the location of a cluster of bones from the left hand lying midway up the forearm.

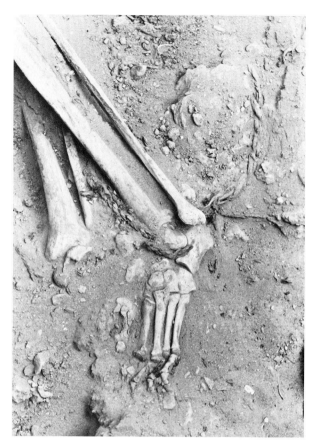

Figure 7. Fragments of rope passing around the left ankle of Individual 2. Note the surrounding matrix of sand and adobe rubble in which the skeletons were found.

Figure 9. Close-up views of penetrating wounds to the left 7th (above) and right 8th (below) ribs of Individual 3. Note the multiple radiating fracture lines and bending out of bone fragments—characteristic features of injuries to fresh bone.

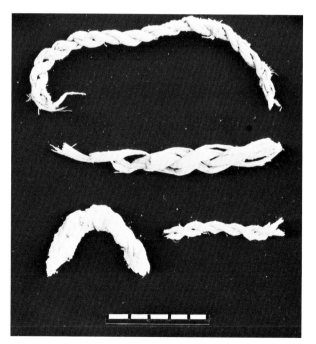

Figure 8. Examples of the four distinct rope types found around the ankles of Individuals 1 and 2. Scale is 5 cm.

the way it encircled the ankles. However, the position of the feet of Individuals 1 and 2 indicated that the rope did not bind the ankles tightly together (Fig. 5). Although the purpose and function of the rope is conjectural, it may have served to hobble the individuals or to restrict their movement in some way.

Each of the four skeletons in Group I shows evidence of multiple wounds. Numerous perimortem[2] fractures and punched-out lesions are present on the vertebrae and ribs, indicating that the individuals were stabbed repeatedly in the chest and abdominal region with a pointed object (Figs. 9,10). The number of stab wounds each individual re-

2. "Perimortem" refers to wounds that occurred at or around the time of death of an individual. With reference to injuries to bone, a perimortem wound is one that occurs while the bone is still fresh or "green."

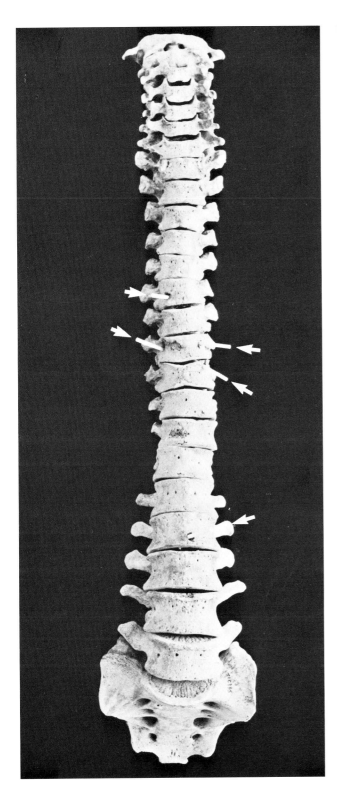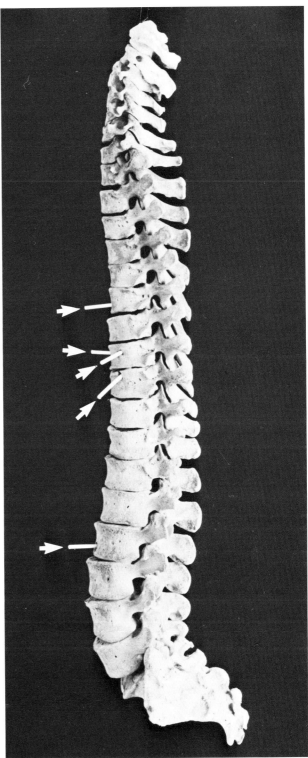

Figure 10.   Reassembled vertebral column of Individual 3. Pins are inserted in the punched-out lesions of the vertebrae to indicate the location and orientation of the wounds. In addition to five penetrating wounds, two glancing blows can be seen on the ventral aspect of vertebrae T8 and T11. Note the variety of angles of the entry wounds, suggesting that more than one individual was involved in stabbing the victim. Note also the cluster of wounds in the vertebral levels T6-T9. If the wounds were delivered by a spear or javelin, as is suggested in the text, considerable accuracy of delivery is indicated by such a tight grouping. Perhaps not coincidentally, the heart is located between vertebral levels T5 and T9.

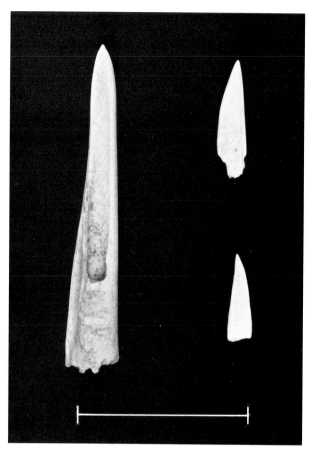

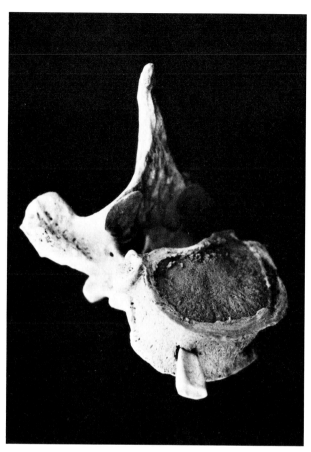

Figure 11.   Right: Two sharpened bone fragments found in direct association with the skeletons of Individuals 1 and 2. Left: A larger sharpened bone object found in another excavation unit at Pacatnamu. It may represent a more complete example of the type of object used to stab the victims. Scale is 5 cm.

Figure 12.   One of the sharpened bone fragments (Fig. 11, below right) inserted into a penetrating wound in a vertebra of one of the victims. Its size and cross-sectional shape closely match the wound.

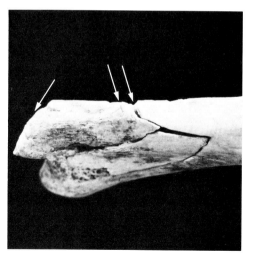

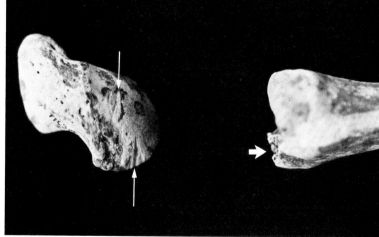

Figure 13.   Left: Distal end of the left ulna of Individual 2 showing multiple fractures, cut marks, and a styloid process that has been partially cut away (arrows).   Right: The scaphoid bone (left) and distal end of the left ulna (right) of Individual 1. The scaphoid bone shows numerous cut marks on its proximal articular surface (arrows). The styloid process of the ulna is broken away (arrow).

Figure 14. Photograph of part of Group II.

ceived can be conservatively estimated from thrusts that struck bone. Based on a count of individual lesions on the ribs and vertebrae, it is estimated that each of the four victims was stabbed a minimum of five to nineteen times (see Appendix).

The orientation of the fractures and penetrating lesions indicates that each individual was stabbed from several distinct angles in the front and sides of the chest and abdomen (Fig. 10). The large number of wounds and the variety in their orientation suggest that more than one person was involved in stabbing the victims. The wounds appear to have been delivered with great force; the location of the lesions indicates that the penetrating object frequently transversed the entire thoracic cavity before imbedding itself in bone on the opposite side of the body. This would suggest that the victims were not standing freely as they were repeatedly stabbed, since they would either have collapsed from the severity of the wounds or have been knocked down by the force of the blows. Presumably, the victims were stabbed while they were lying on the ground or fixed to some supporting object. Perhaps the ropes found around the ankles of Individuals 1 and 2 were used to tie the victims to a rack or post.[3]

Two sharpened and polished fragments of bone, each approximately 2 centimeters in length, were recovered from matrix directly beneath the skeletons of Individuals 1 and 2 (Fig. 11, on right). These appear to have been points from weapons used to stab the victims. Comparison of their size and cross-sectional shape with the punched-out lesions of the victims' vertebrae reveals a good match (Fig. 12). These bone fragments show a fractured edge at the end opposite the sharpened tip, suggesting that they were points broken from larger objects. One bone object found elsewhere at Pacatnamu (Fig. 11, on left) has a similar sharpened point and may represent a more complete example of the type of object used to inflict the stab wounds.

---

3. A number of depictions of individuals tied to racks are known from Moche ceramics. Several examples can be seen in Donnan 1978:figs. 137,147,148.

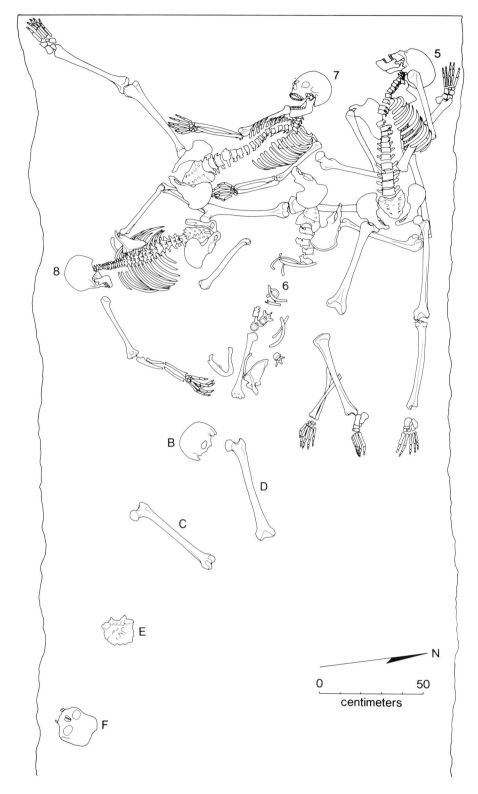

Figure 15. Group II, Level 1. Note that the left legs of Individuals 7 and 8 are missing, and that Individual 6 is disarticulated from the waist up. Note also the fractured left forearm of Individual 8 and the scattering of isolated bones and skull fragments (B-F) in the southeast quarter of the unit.

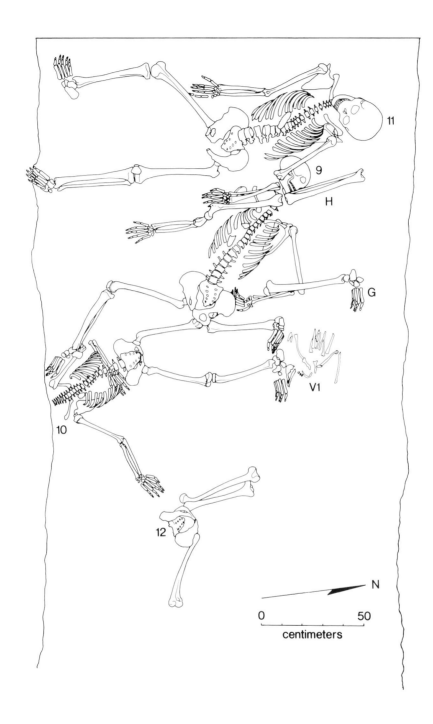

Figure 16. Group II, Level 2. Note the decapitated skeleton of Individual 10 and the two partial isolated legs (G and H). The left leg of Individual 9 is missing; Individual 12 consists of only an articulated sacrum, pelvis, and femora. Note the vulture skeleton (V1) at the feet of Individual 10.

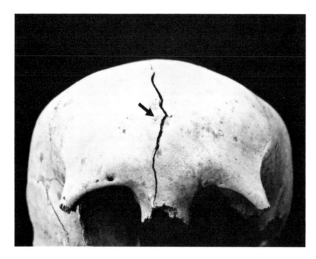

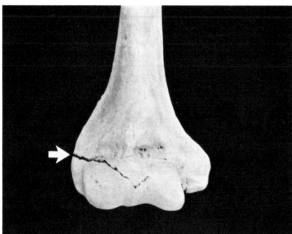

Figure 17. Examples of trauma from Group II. Above: Circular depressed area (arrow) and radiating fracture produced by a sharp blow to the forehead. Below: Fracture line extending medially across distal end of right humerus (arrow). This fracture may have been caused by forced hyperextension of the elbow. Scale is 10 cm.

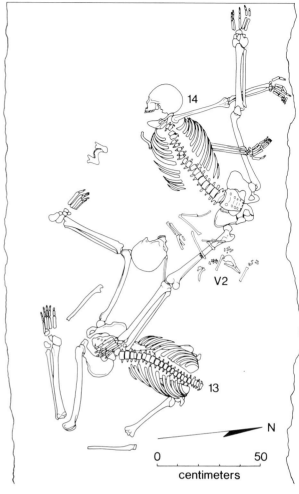

Figure 18. Group III. Note the decapitated skeleton of Individual 13, the splayed legs and arms of Individual 14, and the second vulture skeleton (V2).

Presumably, these bone points were originally hafted to a javelin or spear shaft; a bone point held in the hand could not have inflicted wounds of such depth.

In addition to multiple stab wounds, all four individuals in Group I have the radius missing from the left forearm (note in Figs. 5,6). Evidence of trauma is visible on the distal end of the left ulna of each individual, the styloid process having been fractured or cut off in each case. In Individual 2, the distal end of the bone is badly fractured and shows multiple cut marks (Fig. 13, on left). In Individual 1, cut marks can also be seen on the scaphoid bone where it articulated with the radius (Fig. 13, right). These fractures and cut marks indicate

that the radius was intentionally removed from each of the victims. In three of the four individuals, the hand bones were found in proper anatomical position, indicating that the radius had been removed without completely severing the hand. In the case of Individual 4, however, the bones of the left hand were found lying halfway up the forearm, as though the hand had been either partially or completely severed (Fig. 6).

Group II

Approximately 15 centimeters below the first four skeletons lay a second group of eight individuals (Fig. 14). Because many of the skeletons lay

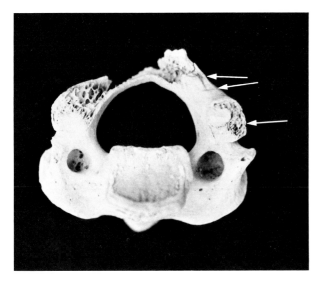

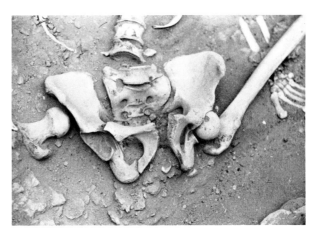

Figure 20. Pelvis of Individual 14. Group III, showing evidence of forcible disarticulation of the hip joints. Note that both femoral heads are out of proper articulation and that the right half of the pelvis is fractured through the acetabulum and midway along the ischio-pubic ramus.

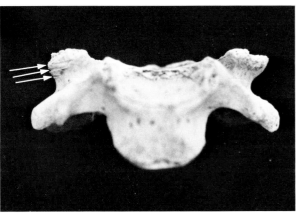

Figure 19. Cervical vertebrae C2 and C3 of Individual 13. Group III, showing evidence of decapitation with a sharp instrument. Above: C2, inferior view, showing fractured spinous process, cut marks (arrows), and damage to inferior articular facets. Below: C3, ventral view, showing multiple cut marks below right superior articular facet.

Group III

Two more skeletons lay approximately 15 centimeters below Group II, and 10 centimeters above the floor of the trench. They rested on a thin deposit of sand and scattered cultural debris (Fig. 18). One of these individuals was decapitated (Fig. 19), and both appear to have had their legs forcibly pulled apart and their hips disarticulated (Fig. 20). The position of the arms of Individual 14 suggests that the shoulders were disarticulated as well. A second vulture skeleton was found in this level, lying over the right leg of Individual 14 (Fig. 18; Rea, this volume).

There are several similarities in the types of injuries seen in Groups II and III. One of the most distinctive is a pattern of injuries to the chest. This is seen in Individuals 5, 6, and 7 in Group II, and in both members of Group III. In all five of these individuals, the manubrium is bisected by an oblique cut extending from the jugular notch infero-laterally to the region of the left first intercostal space (Fig. 21). Associated with the bisected manubrium is a distinctive pattern of rib fractures. In each case many of the ribs show complete fractures at the neck. While fractured ribs were also found in Individuals 9 and 10 of Group II, the fractures were located in the midshaft region or at the sternal end of the rib rather than at the neck. Moreover, the manubria of Individuals 9 and 10 were not bisected.

The association of multiple cervical fractures of the ribs with a bisected manubrium in five different individuals suggests a relationship between

directly on top of one another, they were mapped in two levels (Figs. 15,16). The pattern of wounds in Group II is distinctive from that of Group I. There is no evidence of penetrating wounds of the type previously described, nor are the left radii missing. Instead, these individuals show evidence of a great variety of injuries, including fractures of the neck and limbs, deep slashes to the throat, and blows to the head (Fig. 17). One individual was decapitated, the left leg is missing from three, and two are largely disarticulated and the bones scattered (Figs. 15,16; Appendix). In addition to the human bones, the articulated skeleton of a black vulture lay near the right foot of Individual 10 (Rea, this volume).

 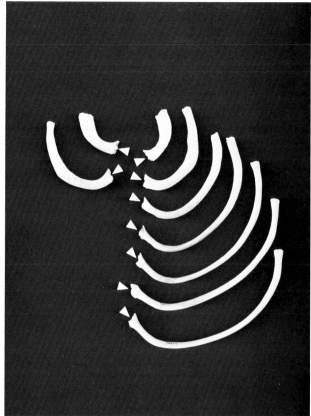

Figure 21. Pattern of chest injuries seen in five individuals in Groups II and III. Left: Bisected manubria. Right: Ribs with cervical fractures (arrows).

the two injuries. An incision deep enough to bisect the manubrium would almost certainly tear the underlying pleura, creating an opening into the chest cavity. Multiple fractures of the ribs at their vertebral articulations suggest that the rib cage was forcibly spread apart after an incision was made through the anterior wall of the chest.

Figure 22 illustrates the pattern of trauma observed in these skeletons and a hypothetical reconstruction of what this pattern may represent. According to the reconstruction, an incision was made at the jugular notch and extended downward and laterally, cutting through the spongy bone of the manubrium and avoiding the denser bone of the clavicle. The incision was then continued down the left side of the anterior aspect of the chest, severing the costal cartilages. Once the incision was complete, it would have been possible to grasp the opposing sides of the wound and pry the chest cavity open. The action of prying open the chest would put particular stress on the vertebral articulations of the ribs and could be expected to produce multiple cervical fractures. This means of opening an

individual's chest would have been swift and relatively easy.[4]

Temporal Relationships

The division of the fourteen individuals into three groups is based on the stratigraphic position of the skeletons and additional evidence that indicates temporal separation between different levels of the deposit. The skeletons of individuals in Groups I and II were separated by 10-15 centimeters of sand and rubble. In addition, the mandible of Individual 7 in the upper level of Group II and the ribs of adjacent Individual 8 show signs of bleaching and surface cracking, indicating that the bodies in Group II decomposed and lay exposed

---

4. In a recently published Dumbarton Oaks volume, Robicsek and Hales (1984) present a review of ritual human sacrifice in the Maya area, including a reconstruction of the Mayan surgical approach to the thoracic cavity and a discussion of the practical aspects of chest opening.

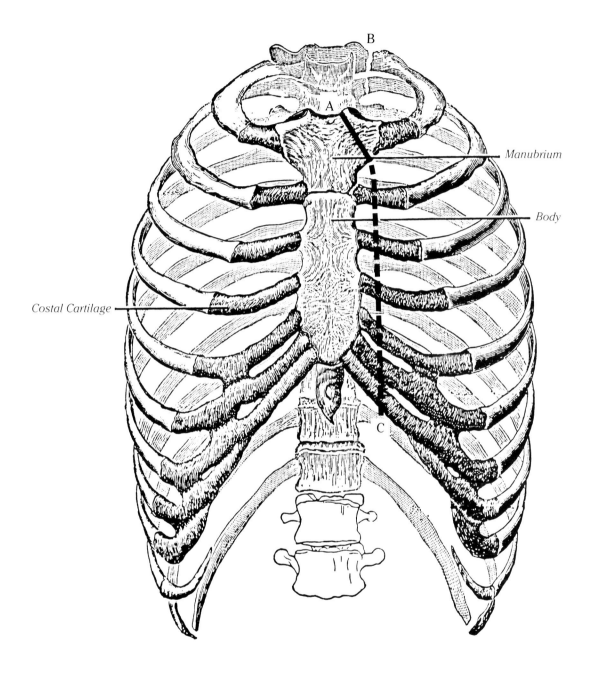

Figure 22.   The pattern of trauma observed in Individuals 5, 6, 7, 13, and 14.
A: Manubrium bisected by an incision extending from the sternal notch down to the first
intercostal space. B: Fractured ribs. C: Hypothesized extension of the incision through the
costal cartilages. An incision made in this manner would
allow swift and easy access to the organs of the thoracic cavity.

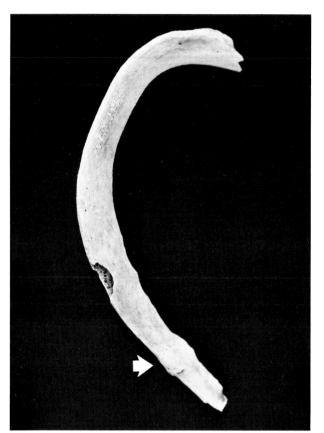 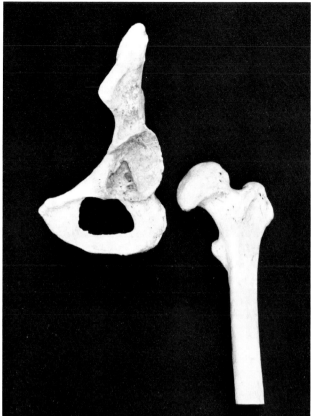

Figure 23. Healed injuries in the skeletons of the mass burial victims. Left: Right second rib of Individual 7 showing healed fracture (arrow). Right: Arthritic changes visible in the left innominate and femur of Individual 4 (enlargement and distortion of normal contours of acetabulum, enlargement of femoral head), which may be the result of an old injury to the hip.

on the surface for some period of time before being buried. How long these bodies lay exposed cannot be determined with certainty, but it is clear that some period of time (perhaps several months) elapsed between the deposition of the bodies in Groups I and II. The skeletons in Groups II and III were also separated by a thin deposit of rubble and sand. However, none of the bones in Group III show evidence of surface exposure.

Insect remains found in association with the skeletons provide additional information on the sequence of deposition of the three groups of victims. They were found in great numbers in the matrix surrounding the skeletons in all three groups, and represent scavenging insects that apparently entered the trench to feed upon the decomposing bodies. Analysis of the remains from the matrix around the skeletons of Groups II and III indicates that the bodies of these individuals were not buried immediately but were left exposed for a period of time estimated to have been between three weeks and several months (Faulkner, this volume).

Physical Characteristics

The fourteen individuals found in the trench constitute a homogeneous group in terms of age and sex, suggesting that they were not victims drawn at random from a mixed population. They are adolescent and young adult males, ranging in age from about 15 to 35 years, with an average age of approximately 21 years.[5] All appear to have been in good physical health, and many show strongly developed muscle markings and robust skeletal morphology. Notable, however, is a high frequency of healed injuries on the skeletons of these individuals: two have healed rib fractures, two have pronounced osteoarthritis of the hip joints which may be the result of old injuries, and one has a

5. Age determination is based on epiphyseal closure and morphology of the pubic symphysis. Sex determination in each case is based on pelvic morphology.

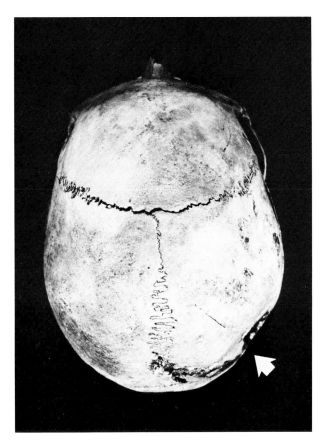

Figure 24. Healed depressed lesion on the right parietal of Individual 9 (arrow) that appears to represent an old blow to the head.

well-healed depressed skull fracture (Figs. 23,24). Such a high frequency of old injuries suggests that as a group these individuals had a particularly active and hazardous life-style. If the healed wounds on their skeletons can be interpreted as "occupational" injuries, one might hypothesize that these are the skeletons of soldiers who perhaps had been taken prisoners of war.

However, evidence that the bodies were deposited in the trench in three temporally distinct episodes suggests that there may be some differences among the groups. Of the three, Group I appears to show the most distinctive characteristics. It has the highest average age, with all individuals estimated to be older than 20 years. It also has the oldest member, Individual 4, age ca. 35 years. In its pattern of injuries (stab wounds and removal of the left radii), Group I is clearly distinct. Although Groups II and III do not show an identical set of injuries, they share many common features (e.g., decapitation, disarticulation of joints, and opening of the chest), which suggest similar treat-

ment of the victims. Morphological and metrical differences between the individuals in the three groups are difficult to evaluate, given such a small sample. There appear to be some differences in cranial morphology between Group I and Groups II and III, although at present this is only the subjective assessment of the author. Multivariate metrical comparison with cemetery populations from Pacatnamu may in the future provide some further information on group affinities of the victims.

Chronology

The approximate date of the deposit is based upon an assemblage of ceramic sherds recovered from around the skeletons and a radiocarbon determination on bone collagen from two of the individuals. Ceramics found associated with the skeletons include both Moche V and Chimu sherds. The latter indicate that the deposit corresponds to the Chimu occupation at Pacatnamu, after A.D. 1100. A combined sample of bone collagen from the femoral shafts of Individuals 2 and 4 from Group I yielded a radiocarbon determination of A.D. 1270 ± 110,[6] which is consistent with both the ceramic material and the relative date for the construction of the Inner Wall and trench (Donnan, City Walls, this volume; McClelland, this volume). In terms of presently accepted chronology for the North Coast of Peru, the deposit dates to the early part of the Late Intermediate Period.

Ethnohistoric and Iconographic Parallels

References to methods of torture, execution, and human sacrifice in the pre-contact Andean area are scattered throughout many of the sixteenth- and seventeenth-century Chronicles. While most writers refer to practices of the Inca, there are some references to pre-Inca peoples as well (Rowe 1946, 1948). References to human sacrifice are rare, but strangulation and cutting open the chest to remove the heart are two methods that have been described (Garcilaso de la Vega 1960[1614]: Book 1, Chap. 11; Rowe 1946:306).

A variety of punishments are known from the Inca Period for individuals accused of rebellion or other serious crimes against the state. These punishments include decapitation, dismemberment,

---

6. Beta 10740. Unadjusted date: 680 ± 110 B.P. If this date is isotopically adjusted for a delta [13]C = -12.45 0/00, it is 880 ± 110 B.P.

Figure 25. A Moche IV fineline drawing showing a variety of activities involving nude male figures presumed to be prisoners. The central scene shows individuals being brought in litters (note rope around neck of individual at far right) before an elaborately dressed figure seated atop ceremonial architecture. Surrounding scenes show splayed bodies, a decapitated head (bottom, right) and depictions of what appears to be the ritual sacrifice of these individuals. Associated with these scenes are anthropomorphized black birds, possibly vultures.

mutilation, and exposure of the corpse to scavengers (Basadre 1937:207-210; Cieza de Leon 1984[1553]:Chaps. 19,52,70; Guaman Poma de Ayala 1980[1614]:ff. 163,164,187,190,311,314; Santillan 1927[1563]:No. 15; Valcarcel 1971 I:636). Unfortunately, it is difficult to associate a particular form of punishment with a single situation or crime. There appears to have been considerable variability in the treatment of war captives and traitors during the Inca period, and this may have been true for pre-Inca cultures as well.

Rowe (1948) has reviewed and summarized the major ethnohistoric documents for the North Coast of Peru. Donnan (1978) and Cordy-Collins and McClelland (1983) have since presented evidence that certain North Coast cultural traditions described during the Colonial Period can be extended back in time. It could be argued in this context that one of the longest established traditions on the North Coast was the engagement in warfare and the taking of captives. Depictions of bound prisoners and scenes that appear to depict the ritual sacrifice and mutilation of prisoners can be seen in both Moche and Chimu iconography (Fig. 25). Examples that may be roughly contemporary with the mass burial at Pacatnamu include a group of painted textiles from the Viru Valley depicting bound, naked prisoners and decapitated and muti-

lated bodies (Lapiner 1976:279-282)[7] and wood figurines of bound captives from Huaca El Dragon in the Moche Valley (Fig. 26).

Desecration of corpses by exposure to vultures and other scavengers is mentioned in several Chronicles as a punishment for rebellion, treason, or other serious crimes (Basadre 1937:207-210; Cieza de Leon 1984[1553]:Chap. 70; Guaman Poma de Ayala 1980[1614]:ff. 187). With reference to the North Coast, exposure of the body to vultures was described by Calancha (1975–1982 [1638]) as part of the punishment for a curer who lost a patient through negligence. The two vulture skeletons found with the mass burial are particularly interesting in this context. Fresh wounds on the skeletons of both vultures indicate that they were intentionally killed—in the case of Vulture 2, by multiple penetrating wounds to the head (Rea, this volume). Whether these vultures played an active role in the mutilation of the human victims is a subject for speculation, but the iconographic and ethnohistoric data discussed above make such a scenario plausible.

7. The provenience of the "Prisoner Textile" illustrated in Lapiner is not certain. Lapiner attributes it to the Viru Valley.

Figure 26. Above: Three wood figurines found at the Huaca El Dragon in the Moche Valley that probably date to the Late Intermediate Period (ca. A.D. 1000-1470). The two figures on the left have their hands bound behind their backs; the cord binding the hands, feet and passing around the neck is still preserved on the first figure. The figure on the right does not have its hands bound, but is pierced by two holes, one in the upper left chest area and another in the back. The holes are painted red on their margins, suggesting that they were meant to depict wounds (see alternate views, below). All three figures wear only loincloths and their bodies are decorated with painted or tattooed designs. The bound figures appear to represent war captives, the third may be a sacrificial victim.

Concluding Remarks

Although the mass burial at Pacatnamu represents three temporally distinct events, common features shared by each of the groups of skeletons emphasize a single underlying pattern. The most obvious feature common to all is the location in which the bodies were deposited and the treatment the corpses received (i.e., exposure rather than prompt burial). The abandonment of the exposed corpses at the northern entrance to the Huaca 1 Complex suggests that the bodies were meant to be prominently displayed for some period of time. Another feature common to all three groups is some form of mutilation and dismemberment of the bodies. In Group I this takes the form of the removal of a particular bone; in Group II the left leg is frequently missing; in Group III the hips are disarticulated. No individual in any group appears to have been simply dispatched and tossed into the trench; all evidence suggests some form of ritual involving the execution and mutilation of the victims and desecration of the corpses.

There is presently no evidence to indicate where the killing and mutilation of the victims took place. It seems unlikely that it occurred either on the causeway or within the trench itself. It also seems unlikely that the victims were killed at some distant location and later carried to the trench. Since the bodies were deposited outside the northern doorway of the Huaca 1 Complex, it is quite possible that the execution and mutilation occurred close to this entrance. The northern courtyard of Huaca 1 with its two altars (Fig. 1) is an obvious possibility, but no physical evidence has yet been found to link the mass burial with the altars.

Although one can only speculate as to the identity of the fourteen individuals, their age distribution and sex, together with the evidence of numerous old injuries on their skeletons, makes it reasonable to assume they were war prisoners. Iconographic depictions of the ritual mutilation and sacrifice of war prisoners appear in both Moche and Chimu art. The mass burial at Pacatnamu may be the first actual evidence of such behavior found in a well-documented archaeological context.

APPENDIX:
Summary of Traumatic Lesions Observed on the Skeletons of the Victims

Group I

Individual 1: Two penetrating wounds to vertebrae (T8, T10: ventral aspect of centrum); single fractures and punched-out lesions on five ribs; three penetrating wounds through left scapula (entry from ventral aspect). Left radius missing; left ulna has fractured styloid process; left scaphoid has multiple cut marks on proximal surface.

Individual 2: Three penetrating wounds to vertebrae (T6, T7: ventral aspect of centrum; sacrum: right sacroiliac joint from dorsal aspect); penetrating wounds and single and multiple fractures on eight ribs; single penetrating wound through manubrium. Left radius missing, left ulna has multiple fractures of distal end.

Individual 3: Eight penetrating and glancing wounds to vertebrae (T6, T8, T9, T11, L2: all to ventral or lateral aspect of centrum); eleven ribs with fractures or penetrating wounds; single punched-out fracture through the left scapula (entry from ventral aspect). Left radius missing; left ulna has fractured styloid process and cut marks on head. Linear depressed fracture on dorsal surface of fifth metacarpal and proximal phalanx of left hand.

Individual 4: Eight penetrating wounds to vertebrae (T1, T3, T4, T7: all to ventral or lateral aspect of centrum); glancing blows to one rib; eight ribs show fractures at sternal end. Two penetrating wounds through right scapula (entry from ventral aspect). Left radius absent. Basal skull fracture, fractured nasals, cut mark on left malar.

Group II

Individual 5: All ribs except two (R1 and unidentified) absent on right side; two left ribs fractured. Manubrium sterni bisected. Neck vertebrae rotated to a degree suggesting forced disarticulation of intervertebral joints. Both arms missing, distal to humerus.

Individual 6: Torso and trunk largely disarticulated; skull not recovered with body. Multiple rib fractures; manubrium sterni bisected; multiple fractures of right scapula; right distal humerus fractured.

Individual 7: Multiple fractured ribs; manubrium sterni bisected; multiple cut marks on left transverse process of first thoracic vertebra and first rib; face heavily fractured; left leg missing.

Individual 8: Transverse cut mark across ventral aspect of body of sixth cervical vertebra; cut mark on superior surface of left clavicle at sternal end; left radius and ulna fractured at midshaft; left leg missing.

Individual 9: Multiple skull fractures; nine fractured ribs; multiple cut marks on sternal ends of both clavicles and on ventral aspect of manubrium; left leg missing.

Individual 10: Decapitated. Skull, mandible, first and second cervical vertebrae missing; third and fourth cervical vertebrae show fractured transverse and spinous processes; five ribs fractured.

Individual 11: Ten ribs (left 1-3, right 1-7) fractured at neck. Left first rib shows two cut marks lateral to fracture line on superior surface. Manubrium missing.

Individual 12: Most of skeleton missing. Present: pelvis, sacrum, and right femur (articulated); plus left femur and six vertebrae (T12, L1-5) found disarticulated but in association. Only visible pathology: multiple fractures of transverse and spinous processes of several of the vertebrae.

Group III

Individual 13: Decapitated (multiple cut marks on C3, C4); apparent blow to left cheek fracturing left malar, zygomatic process of left temporal, and left upper third molar at alveolus; nasals and nasal processes of maxillae fractured; manubrium bisected; multiple rib fractures; both femoral heads appear to have been disarticulated from acetabula.

Individual 14: Nasal bones and nasal processes of maxillae fractured; manubrium sterni bisected; multiple rib fractures; centra of T8 and L4 vertebrae fractured in half; fractured acromion process of left scapula; both femoral heads appear to have been disarticulated from acetabula; right innominate fractured through acetabulum and ischio-pubic ramus.

RESUMEN:
Un Entierro Masivo de Individuos Mutilados en Pacatnamú

En 1984, se encontraron los cuerpos de catorce adultos jóvenes enterrados en el foso de la Muralla Interior, al este de la entrada al Patio Norte de la Huaca 1 (Fig. 1). Los cadáveres se hallaban formando tres grupos y su relación estratigráfica sugiere que fueron depositados allí en tres ocasiones diferentes.

Grupo I

Consiste de cuatro esqueletos (Figs. 4–6) que muestran evidencias de múltiples heridas, incluyendo dos (individuos 1 y 2) que estaban amarrados por el tobillo (Figs. 7 y 8).

Los esqueletos indican que cada uno de ellos fue punzado de 5 a 19 veces, con un objeto puntiagudo (Figs. 9 y 10), desde distintos ángulos, tanto en el pecho como en el abdomen (Fig. 10). Esto implicaría que más de una persona se vió envuelta en la muerte de cada uno de estos individuos.

Dos puntas de hueso, pulidas y filudas, fueron recuperadas debajo de los individuos 1 y 2 (Fig. 11); de las comparaciones de estos objetos con las lesiones en los cadáveres, se desprende que estas pudieron ser las armas con las que fueron muertos (Fig. 12). Además, todos los miembros de este grupo carecían del radio del brazo izquierdo (ver Figs. 5 y 6), habiendo evidencias de corte para extraer este hueso (Fig. 13).

Grupo II

Ubicado 15 cms. debajo del primer grupo, reunió ocho individuos que fueron registrados en dos capas (Figs. 14–16). El tipo de heridas era diferente al Grupo I, mostrando una variedad que incluye decapitamiento, fracturas del cuello y desarticulación, entre otras (Figs. 15–17). También se ubicaron los huesos articulados de un gallinazo negro (Rea, este volumen).

Grupo III

Consistió en dos esqueletos ubicados 15 cms. debajo del Grupo II y 10 cms. encima del piso del foso (suelo estéril). Uno de los individuos estaba decapitado (Figs. 18, 19) y ambos tenían los muslos desarticulados (Fig. 20). Un segundo esqueleto de gallinazo negro apareció en este nivel (Fig. 18).

Los individuos 5, 6 y 7 del Grupo II y los dos del Grupo III muestran cortes en el pecho, a la altura del manubrium, que va desde la yugular hasta el primer espacio intercostal del lado izquierdo (Fig. 21). Asociado a este corte, hay fractura de costillas, que implica que luego del corte, el pecho fue abierto a la fuerza. La Figura 22 ilustra como se realizó este corte.

Los restos de insectos recuperados en asociación con estos cuerpos, proveen valiosa información sobre la secuencia de deposición y exposición de los cadáveres (Faulkner, este volumen), los que habrían quedado a la intemperie por un largo período de tiempo.

Características Físicas

Se trata de un grupo homogéneo en términos de edad y sexo, con un promedio de 21 años de edad y todos varones. Muestran buena salud, marcas de músculos fuertes y esqueletos robustos. Esto sugiere que no se trata de víctimas tomadas al azar.

Hay una alta frecuencia de heridas óseas curadas, como fracturas de costillas y golpes en el cráneo (Figs. 23 y 24). Si ellas pueden interpretarse como heridas "profesionales," entonces es probable que estos individuos fueron soldados, probablemente tomados como prisioneros de guerra.

Cronología

Una muestra de radiocarbono, da 1270 ± 110 DC, que correspondería con los fragmentos de cerámica recuperados en el foso, así como con el tipo de adobes y la construcción de la Muralla Interior (McClelland, este volumen; Donnan, Murallas, este volumen).

La iconografía Moche y Chimú, así como las fuentes etnohistóricas, contribuyen a pensar que estos individuos fueron prisioneros de guerra, y que ésta es, quizá, la primera evidencia proveniente de este tipo de personajes.

Black Vultures and Human Victims: Archaeological Evidence from Pacatnamu

Amadeo M. Rea

During the 1984 excavations at Pacatnamu, the mutilated remains of fourteen young adult males were found buried in a trench in front of Doorway 1 of the Inner Wall (Verano, this volume). The evidence suggests three separate episodes of deposition in which the bodies were left exposed above ground until final decomposition had taken place (see Verano, this volume and Faulkner, this volume). Two other vertebrates recovered from the burial were Black Vultures, *Coragyps atratus.*

Vulture Remains

The two vulture skeletons were superimposed; Vulture 1, associated with the bodies in Group II, lay immediately above Vulture 2, which was associated with the bodies in Group III (see Verano, this volume). The skeletal elements were brought to my laboratory in San Diego for analysis, together with photographs showing the skeletons in situ. The bones were in an excellent state of preservation, including such fine elements as the hyoid bones.

When excavated, Vulture 1 was found lying on its back. The skeleton shows indications of trauma that probably led to its death. These occurred in the "green" (perimortem) bone while the skeleton was still fleshed, and there is no evidence of healing. They include two small depressed fractures of the cranium (Fig. 1), a crumpled right scapula (Fig. 2), a right clavicle broken at the proximal end, a three-way fracture below the proximal end of the right humerus (Fig. 3), and a fracture near the base of the left humeral shaft. Damage to the hind part of the pelvis (ilium and ischium) may have been perimortem as well. There is no evidence of arthritic joints which would indicate an old or feeble vulture. Vulture 1 was probably killed by at least two blows to the skull, one to the right upper back, and perhaps another to the lower pelvic area.

The skeleton of Vulture 2, which was found lying on its belly, showed quite a different set of perimortem fractures. The head was pierced from different directions at least four times with a small pointed object. Two puncture wounds passed through the right eye orbit (Fig. 4), one through the left (Fig. 5), and a fourth from below passed through the mouth into the basitemporal plate of the cranial base. On the left wing, two adjacent bones of the hand region have fractures indicating twisting or bending of the "green" bone. The delicate keel of the sternum is badly fragmented, but there are indications of two wounds inflicted from

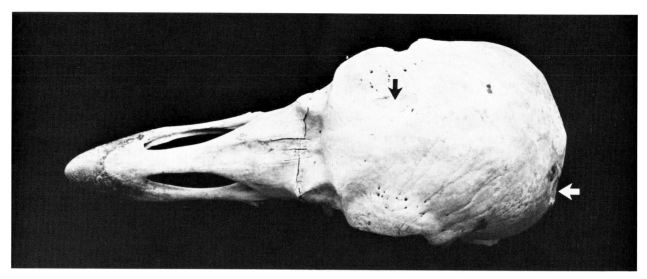

Figure 1. Cranium of Vulture 1 showing two depressed fractures (arrows).

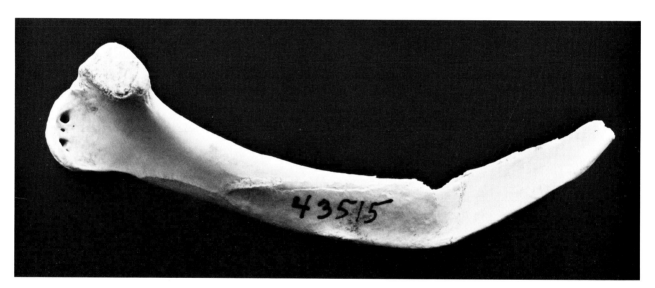

Figure 2. Right scapula of Vulture 1 showing fresh fracture.

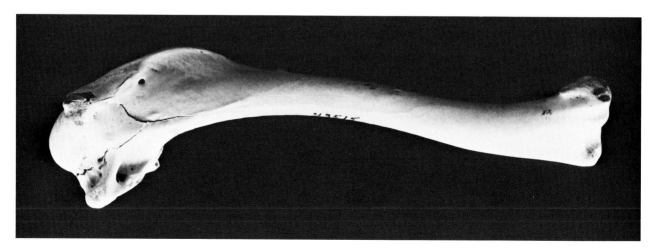

Figure 3. Right humerus of Vulture 1 showing a three-way fracture at the proximal end.

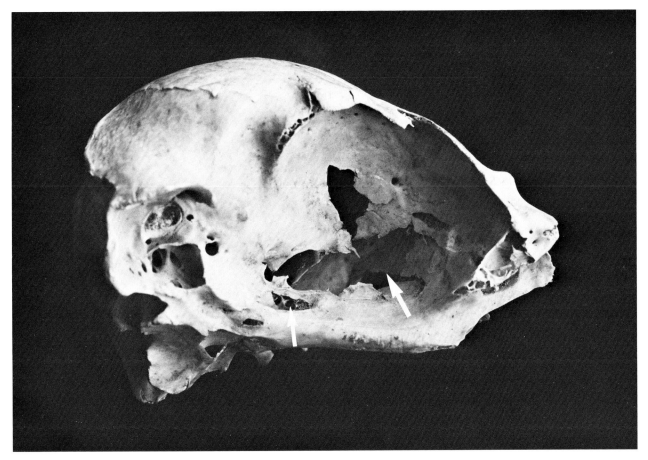

Figure 4. Right lateral view of the skull of Vulture 2 showing penetrating wounds through the orbit (arrows).

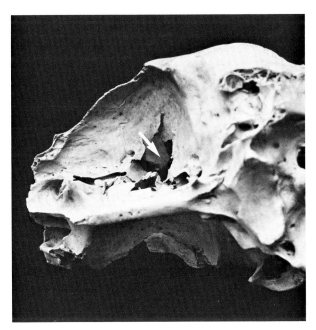

Figure 5. Oblique view of the base of the skull of Vulture 2 showing the penetrating wound through the left orbit (arrow).

opposite sides that would have passed laterally through the pectoral muscle mass.

Overview of Vultures

Of seven living species of New World vultures,[1] three occur in arid coastal Peru: the Andean Condor (*Vultur gryphus*), the Turkey Vulture (*Cathartes aura*), and the Black Vulture (*Coragyps atratus*). Vultures are more numerous and widespread than condors. Black Vultures and Turkey Vultures differ considerably from each other in behavior, even

---

1. Long classified in the order Accipitriformes (*Coniformes auctorum*), the New World Vultures, family Vulturidae (*Cathartidae auctorum*) are now considered by some taxonomists (Lignon 1967, Rea 1983, Olson 1985) to be members of the order Ciconiiformes, after that group has been rendered monophyletic by the exclusion of the Ardeidae and Phoenicopteridae (herons and flamingos). Old world vultures, a specialized scavenging subfamily of the family Accipitriadae, the hawks and eagles, are merely convergently similar to the New World vultures.

Figure 6. *Black Vulture* (Coragyps atratus). *San Diego Museum of Natural History specimen.*

Figure 7. *Turkey Vulture* (Cathartes aura). *San Diego Museum of Natural History specimen.*

though they may feed together on the same carcass. Turkey Vultures have well-developed olfactory abilities (Stager 1964) and generally forage singly or in pairs. They are essentially timid by nature and approach a suspected dead animal with caution. Turkey Vultures may ignore or avoid a carcass that even appears to move. Black Vultures, in contrast, are gregarious and aggressive, and have been known to prey on living animals (Hagopian 1947; Lovell 1947, 1952; McIlhenny 1939; Mrosovsky 1971). They have little or no olfactory ability and usually depend on visual cues while cruising known food sources such as beaches, rivers, and lake shores, as well as garbage dumps and slaughter houses. Black Vultures rarely forage opportunistically in open country. Though sometimes traveling in groups of a dozen or less, they are frequently found in tight social flocks of about a hundred. They show little fear of humans, and in many parts of Latin America today they are virtually urbicolous, completely at home in backyards, on housetops, and in open-air markets. Raymond Gilmore, who had extensive experience with the four smaller species of vultures in South America, wrote of the Black Vulture: "It seems to have developed semidomestic ... relations with man, which probably date far back into aboriginal times" (1950:395).

The Turkey Vulture and the Black Vulture are strikingly different in morphology. The Black Vulture is the smaller of the two (Fig. 6).[2] Its bill is long, slender, and relatively straight. Its wings and tail are short and broad, the tips of the toes extending beyond the tail edge in flight. Aloft, its appearance is almost batlike. The naked head and gular pouch of the adult Black Vulture is gray and copiously wrinkled and warted. The Turkey Vulture lacks this naked corrugated gular sac and has relatively smooth bright red skin on its bare head (Fig. 7). It has a rather short head and beak and very short legs. Its wings and tail are long and narrow.

Black Vultures follow a consistent sequence when feeding on a carcass. First, the contents of each eye orbit are plucked out and consumed. Next, the anus is attacked and the intestines pulled out through the opening. Often the genitals and tongue are probed for, making additional openings into the body. Even vultures hatched and raised in captivity without opportunity to learn from other vultures follow this sequence. When a group of vultures begins to feed on a carcass, the eyes, anus, genitals, and mouth are torn into simultaneously.

Presence of Vultures in the Trench

There are at least two possible explanations for the presence of Black Vultures in association with the human skeletons in the trench at Pacatnamu. Since these scavenging birds normally live in urban districts and are known to frequent food sources such as garbage dumps, it is reasonable to assume that vultures were living in the vicinity of Pacatnamu when it was inhabited, and that the exposed and decomposing bodies in the trench would have been a source of attraction for them. Given the aggressive nature of Black Vultures, it is

2. Black Vulture: length approximately 54 cm., wingspan approximately 132 cm. Turkey Vulture: length approximately 61 cm., wingspan approximately 176 cm (Robbins et al. 1982).

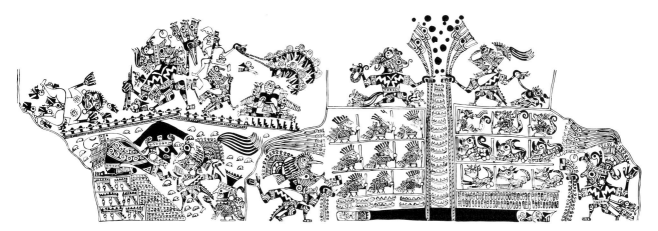

Figure 8. Rollout drawing of a Moche V bottle showing the Burial Theme (from Donnan and McClelland 1979).

likely that the birds would not have hesitated to enter the trench and feed. The set of injuries found on the skeleton of Vulture 1 could have been inflicted on an opportunistic scavenger that was surprised in the trench and killed by humans throwing objects down from above. On the other hand, the multiple penetrating wounds to the skull and the fractures on several bones of the wings of Vulture 2 suggest not only intentional stabbing but rough physical handling of the bird as well. It would be highly unlikely for such a set of injuries to be produced by pelting the bird in the bottom of the trench. It would appear that one or both vultures were involved in some way in the mutilation and killing of the human victims and were later dispatched and tossed into the trench along with them. The evidence of extensive perimortem injuries on the skeletons of both vultures further supports the latter hypothesis.

Black Vultures in Moche Art

Black Vultures are well known in Moche iconography, especially in fineline drawing where they are illustrated in connection with ritual sacrifice (Schaffer 1983). Of particular interest in terms of the mass burial at Pacatnamu is the role these vultures play in the Burial Theme, represented on Moche Phase V ceramic vessels (Fig. 8; Donnan and McClelland 1979). Black Vultures are always present in the upper left portion of these drawings. One of the participants in this part of the theme is a splayed nude female shown lying on her back, being mutilated by a flock of vultures. Her right eye has been gorged out and her genitals are being attacked by the birds. This represents the predictable behavior of Black Vultures, since these portions of the anatomy would be the initial target areas. Possibly the vultures had been kept in captivity and then freed to attack the bound victim. In this regard it is interesting to note the figure in this same scene who is holding a double strand of tethered vultures.

Vulture sacrifice and subsequent burial of vultures in a human grave is also suggested by this drawing. A splayed vulture is shown tied to two horizontal posts that represent a prisoner's rack. It is known that this form of sacrifice was practiced in Moche times since there are many examples in the iconography of warfare and the capture of prisoners showing humans tied to a rack (Donnan 1978:figs. 137,148). The presence of vultures ritually buried in a human grave is indicated in the lower right portion of the Burial Theme drawing, where two vultures are shown at the foot of a casket that has just been lowered with ropes into a grave pit. The vultures appear to be included among the other objects placed in the grave.

Conclusion

The two Black Vultures found associated with the mass burial victims at Pacatnamu show multiple perimortem injuries of the skeleton. Evidence suggests that at least one of these birds was physically manipulated and intentionally killed before being deposited in the trench along with the human victims. Depictions of Black Vultures involved with the ritual sacrifice and mutilation of human victims are known from Moche art. The vulture skeletons found in the mass burial at Pacatnamu constitute the first physical evidence of such activity to be documented in a firm archaeological context.

RESUMEN:
Gallinazos Negros y Victimas Humanas: Evidencia Arquelógica en Pacatnamú

Junto con los restos de los 14 cuerpos mutilados, hallados en el foso frente a la Puerta 1 de la Muralla Interior (Verano, este volumen; Faulkner, este volumen), se recuperaron los restos de 2 gallinazos negros, Coragyps atratus.

Los Restos de los Gallinazos

Los dos esqueletos estuvieron sobre-impuestos: el Gallinazo 1 estuvo asociado con los cuerpos del Grupo II, inmediatamente encima del Gallinazo 2, que estuvo asociado con los cuerpos del Grupo III (Verano, este volumen).

El Gallinazo 1 fue encontrado echado sobre su espalda. El esqueleto muestra signos de fracturas que, probablemente, ocasionaron su muerte. Entre ellas hay: dos fracturas en el cráneo (Fig. 1), una en la escápula derecha (Fig. 2), clavícula derecha rota, tres fracturas en el húmero derecho (Fig. 3) y una en el izquierdo. No hay evidencia de artritis en los huesos, por lo que no se trata de un espécimen viejo.

El Gallinazo 2, recuperado en posición ventral, muestra diferentes fracturas: la cabeza fue punzada, desde diferentes direcciones, por lo menos cuatro veces, con un objeto puntiagudo pequeño. Dos punciones pasaron a través de la órbita del ojo derecho, uno por el izquierdo, y la cuarta, a través del pico hacia la base del temporal en el cráneo (Figs. 4 y 5). En el extremo del ala izquierda, dos huesos adyacentes tienen fracturas que sugieren que el ala fue torcida cuando el animal estaba aun vivo; así mismo, el esternón muestra dos heridas, hechas desde lados opuestos, que habrían pasado lateralmente a través de la masa muscular del pecho.

Identificación de Gallinazos

De las siete especies que habitan en América, tres se presentan en la costa del Perú: el Cóndor Andino, Vultur gryphus, el Gallinazo Negro, Coragyps atratus, y el buitre. La determinación de la especie se hizo por diferencias en hábitos y las existentes en morfología (Figs. 6 y 7) entre los dos tipos comunes de gallinazos que habitan en la costa del Perú.

Presencia de los Gallinazos en el Foso

Desde que estas aves viven en áreas urbanas y frecuentan los basurales, es razonable asumir que vivían en Pacatnamú y que los cuerpos expuestos fueron una atracción inevitable.

Los traumatismos que muestra el Gallinazo 1 podrían haber sido ocasionados al ser sorprendido en el interior del foso, por personas que le arrojaron objetos desde arriba. Por el otro lado, las multiples fracturas y punciones en el cráneo del Gallinazo 2, sugieren que fueron infringidas de manera intencional, por lo que este pájaro habría estado envuelto, de alguna manera, en el proceso que resultó en la mutilación de las victimas humanas, siendo, después, arrojado al foso junto con ellas. Sin embargo, el tipo de traumatismos en los dos gallinazos, hace posible que ambos hayan pasado por el mismo proceso.

Gallinazos Negros en la Iconografía Moche

En la iconografía Moche hay representaciones del papel que los gallinazos jugaban en diversos contextos, especialmente en el "Tema del Entierro" (Fig. 8; Donnan y McClelland 1979). Allí, aparecen en la esquina izquierda del dibujo consumiendo el cadáver de una mujer. También se sugiere la matanza de gallinazos y su entierro en una tumba humana. Un gallinazo con las alas extendidas es representado atado a un marco, similar a los usados con prisioneros humanos (Donnan 1978: figs. 137 y 148). En la porción inferior derecha del dibujo, se puede apreciar dos gallinazos al pié de un ataúd, el que ha sido recién bajado a la sepultura, lo que sugiere que los gallinazos habrían estado entre las ofrendas depositadas en una tumba.

Conclusión

La evidencia sugiere que estas aves fueron físicamente manipuladas e intencionalmente muertas, antes de ser depositadas en el foso. Por otro lado, la evidencia proveniente de Pacatnamú pareciese ser la primera evidencia arqueológica que documenta este tipo de actividad.

The Mass Burial: An Entomological Perspective

Arthropods, especially insects, are a major factor contributing to the decomposition of dead plant and animal material. Sarcosaprophagous insects are attracted to a potential food source in successive waves, beginning with flies immediately following an animal's death and concluding with scavenging beetles, which take advantage of the desiccated remains. The collection and identification of these insects, or the evidence of their activities, as well as the presence or absence of other insects, can reveal information about the factors affecting the process of decomposition, such as the rate of degradation and the condition of a corpse during decay. Valuable clues can also be provided as to whether the remains were buried immediately or were exposed above ground during decomposition and the circumstances surrounding the individual's death.[1]

The insect remains analyzed in this paper were found associated with fourteen human skeletons and other vertebrate bones (Fig. 1) uncovered near Doorway 1 of the Inner Wall at Pacatnamu (Verano, this volume; Donnan, City Walls, this volume). The sample was taken from around the human skeletal remains of Group II at a depth of 2.75 meters.[2] Although the invertebrate remains are estimated to be about 800 years old, the material was well preserved, thus making it possible to identify the arthropod groups present. The major portion of the sample consisted of the empty puparia (pupal cases) of muscoid flies. Also present were a number of beetle elytra (the hardened forewings of beetles), and one entire beetle specimen. Following initial sorting and identification, a representative sample was forwarded to the insect identification services of the California Department of Agriculture in Sacramento for further evaluation.

It was determined that two different taxa of

1. The use of entomological observations as they relate to forensics was formalized in a treatise by Megnin (1894), a French entomologist. More recently, forensic entomology has been added to investigations throughout the world, with many of the cases summarized by Nuroteva (1977). Unfortunately, the forensic applications of entomology under normal conditions are most informative when restricted to the first month after death. Only a limited number of researchers have dealt with insects in relation to older human remains (Evans 1962; Ewing 1924).

   I am grateful to Fred Andrews and Eric Fisher of the California Department of Agriculture for their assistance in identifying portions of the insect sample as well as providing me with Scanning Electron Micrographs. I am also indebted to John Verano for allowing me to examine the invertebrate remains excavated by the Pacatnamu Project.
2. See Verano, this volume, for full description of burials.

Figure 1.   Photograph of Individual 13, Group III, during excavation. Dried muscoid puparia can be seen in and around exposed spinal column.

muscoid flies (order Diptera) were present. The larger of the two types were those of a group containing house flies (family Muscidae; Fig. 2). The smaller puparia represented another species that is still undetermined to the family level (Figs. 3,4). Both of these species are of primary importance in the initial stages of carrion degradation.

The beetle elytra (order Coleoptera) represented three different families. The first elytra were of a darkling ground beetle (family Tenebrionidae). Most likely this taxon was accidentally trapped in the open trench from which it could not escape, and it is not considered to have been involved in the decomposition of human remains. The second example, and only complete specimen, was a hister beetle (family Histeridae), and although not identified to genus, represents a group of beetles commonly associated with carrion as scavengers or as predators on other sarcosaprophagous insects (Fig. 5). The third type of elytra belong to the skin beetle Dermestes (family Dermestidae; Fig. 6). This genus of insect is an active decomposer of dried animal substances such as tissue and hair.

The first indicators relating directly to the decomposition of the remains were the large number of true fly puparia recovered from the excavation.

Muscoid flies require proteinaceous food sources for the adult diet and also for a substrate for oviposition and larval feeding (Nuroteva 1977). Since many species of muscoid flies will only deposit eggs directly on a larval food substrate or a fluid-saturated material covering the substrate, the large number of puparia indicate that oviposition sites were readily accessible. Sarcosaprophagous flies are among the first insects to arrive at an available carcass during the initial stages of decay and putrefaction. The larval stages (maggots) will feed progressively on the moister material for about 2-3 weeks, at which time they are gradually replaced by a succession of beetle groups as the nutritional value and moisture content of the host changes. It was observed that the anterior ends were missing from the puparia of both species of flies, indicating that in this sample all of the papae examined had emerged as adults. No dried larvae or underdeveloped adults were found.

Of minimal interest and importance as forensic indicators are the darkling ground beetles, since their occurrence is incidental to the decomposition of the corpses. The small, black oval hister beetle, on the other hand, is attracted to carrion, with both the adults and larvae of some species preying on

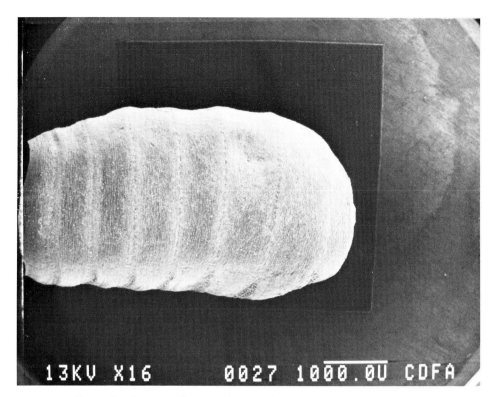

Figure 2. Scanning Electron Micrograph of larger dipteran puparium, family Muscidae (x 16). Scale (white line at lower right) is 1.0 mm.

Figure 3. Scanning Electron Micrograph of the smaller of the two species of muscoid puparia (x 26). Scale is 1.0 mm.

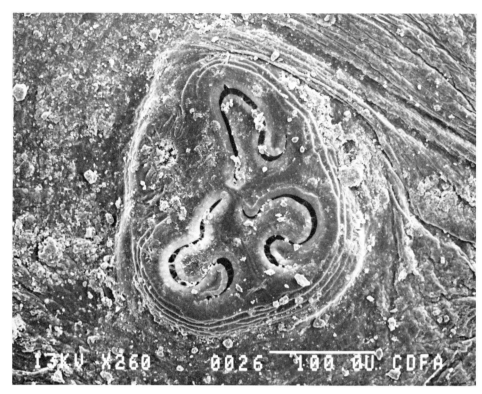

Figure 4. Scanning Electron Micrograph of the posterior spiracle (breathing structure) of the smaller muscoid puparium (x 260) indicating the fine structure of this character. Scale is 0.1 mm.

fly larvae and other insect scavengers. According to Megnin (1894), hister beetles are active on a corpse 4-8 months following death, at a time when the remains are beginning to dry. Although less abundant, adult beetles may still be present for even longer periods of time if insect prey are still available.

Of all the beetle remains identified, the presence of the *Dermestes* skin beetles is the most revealing. These obovate insects are scavengers that feed on dried animal or plant material of high protein content (Arnett 1968). They would not normally be expected to infest an exposed human corpse until at least two months following death (Johnston and Villeneuve 1897), and would most probably be in attendance during the final stages of decomposition.

From these observations it can be inferred that the human corpses had been exposed above ground and were buried much later, probably during or following the final stages of decomposition. The most compelling evidence supporting this opinion is the large number of muscoid fly puparia present, which is indicative of conditions favorable for larval exploitation of the entire corpse. Even the

spinal column was available to the larvae, which in an arid region would have normally been too dry for their use by the time they reached it. However, from all indications (Verano, this volume), the corpses were not normal; that is, the bodies were mutilated and thus a greater amount of substrate was exposed for fly larvae to feed on, resulting in an accelerated rate of decomposition. Due to this combination of a dry climate and the large amount of exposed substrate, there was a differential gradient in the way the tissues dried, allowing maggots to utilize the moist tissue while at the same time dermestid beetles and perhaps their larvae were actively feeding on the drier tissues. Instead of a gradual succession of insects using this resource, there was an overlap in the time of their arrival. The lack of dermestid remains other than adult elytra suggests that the bodies were not buried during the later stages of decomposition but after the resource had been fully exploited and was no longer attractive to these insects. Neither of these events could have taken place had the remains been buried within a few weeks following death, since burial would have resulted in incomplete decomposition (Payne 1965), and in an arid re-

*Figure 5.   Scanning Electron Micrograph of hister
beetle (x 36). Scale is 1.0 mm.*

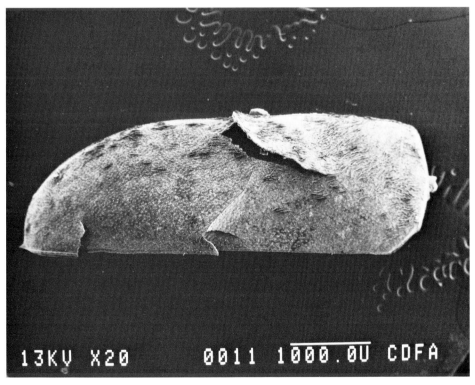

*Figure 6.   Scanning Electron Micrograph of elytron (hardened forewing)
of skin beetle, genus Dermestes (x 20). Scale is 1.0 mm.*

gion, would have most likely resulted in partial mummification.

The only insects that effectively excavate through the soil to reach a carcass are rove beetles (family Staphylinidae) and phorid flies (family Phoridae; Lundt 1964). Neither of these taxa were present in the sample, providing further confirmation that the bodies had decomposed prior to burial.

In correlating the above evidence, it appears that following the death of these individuals, the rate of decomposition initiated by fly activity was greatly accelerated by the condition of the corpses and that this first stage lasted only a month until the remains were too dry to attract flies. At the same time, and probably continuing for a few months more, dermestid and hister beetles continued their activities until the carcasses were picked clean.

It is clear from the insect remains that the mutilated victims at Pacatnamu were not buried until well after the final stages of decay had commenced. During the degradation process, the primary scavenging insects were muscoid fly larvae followed by hister and dermestid beetles, indicating that the bodies probably lay exposed for a minimum of several months following death.

RESUMEN:
El Entierro Masivo:
Una Perspectiva Entomológica

Los restos de insectos analizados aquí fueron encontrados asociados con 14 esqueletos humanos y 2 de otros vertebrados (Fig. 1), descubiertos a un lado de la Puerta 1 de la Muralla Interior de Pacatnamú (Verano, este volumen; Rea, este volumen). La muestra se tomó del Grupo II, 2do. nivel, a una profundidad de 2.75 mts.

Se determinó la presencia de dos diferentes tipos de moscas (order Diptera). Las más grandes fueron del tipo doméstico—familia Muscidae—(Fig. 2), mientras hubo una especie más pequeña que no se pudo identificar al nivel de la familia (Figs. 3 y 4). Ambas especies juegan un papel importante en las etapas iniciales de la degradación orgánica.

Los escarabajos (orden Coleoptera) estuvieron representados por tres diferentes familias. La primera, escarabajo tenebrionidos (familia Tenebrionidae) fue posiblemente atrapada de manera accidental en el foso. La segunda, único ejemplar completo, fue un hister beetle *(familia Histeridae), que representa un grupo comunmente asociado a la carroña (Fig. 5). La tercera, perteneció a los derméstidos (familia Dermestidae) (Fig. 6), que es un participante activo en la descomposición de materia animal seca, como tejidos y pelo.*

De la presencia de estos insectos y sus hábitos, se puede inferir que los restos humanos estuvieron expuestos, y sólo fueron enterrados durante o después de la última etapa de descomposición. La mejor evidencia de esto es el gran número de larvas de moscas domésticas, que indica que hubieron condiciones favorables para su reproducción durante un largo período, ya que llegaron, inclusive, a la espina dorsal.

Por otro lado, mientras las larvas de moscas se alimentaban de los tejidos húmedos, los escarabajos, y posiblemente sus larvas, se alimentaban de los tejidos secos. La ausencia de restos de derméstidos, que no sean especímenes adultos, sugiere que los cuerpos no fueron enterrados hasta que habían sido completamente aprovechados y ya no eran atracción para los insectos. También, hay que señalar que ninguna especie que excava el suelo para encontrar una carcaza estuvo presente, lo que confirma que la descomposición y degradación se produjo antes del entierro.

Todo esto lleva a la conclusión que los cuerpos estuvieron expuestos por varios meses después de la muerte de los individuos.

The Huaca 4 Complex

Richard W. Keatinge

The Huaca 4 Complex, located approximately 120 meters northeast of Huaca 1 (Map Insert), was excavated during a four-week period in August, 1985. It was chosen for excavation for several reasons. First, it is representative of a midsize huaca complex of which there are twenty-one at the site (Keatinge 1977). Second, it is one of two, or perhaps three huacas at the site that still exhibit the clear remains of a small three-sided structure on the summit (Keatinge 1977:239). Third, the rooms that constitute the eastern portion of the Huaca 4 Complex contain two small platform mounds similar to some sixty-nine other such mounds found in different contexts throughout Pacatnamu (Keatinge 1977:236). Therefore, it was anticipated that excavation of the Huaca 4 Complex would elucidate various architectural attributes that could be utilized for comparative purposes at Pacatnamu and at other archaeological sites on the North Coast.

General Architectural Data

The Huaca 4 Complex consists of two distinct parts. One is the huaca and its associated forecourt and rear compound, covering approximately 1,750 square meters, most of which was excavated. The other is the adjacent eastern room complex, covering at least four times this area, of which somewhat less than 25% was excavated.

With the exception of the basal section of the huaca platform, at least part of which was constructed with Standard Chimu bricks, virtually all the Huaca 4 Complex was constructed with Terminal Chimu bricks (McClelland, this volume).

Parts of the Huaca 4 Complex were built with case-and-fill construction—adobe casing walls were constructed to form the perimeter of what were to become mounds or platforms. The interiors were then filled with domestic refuse, presumably obtained from the immediately surrounding area, and the top was capped with bricks. The resulting structure would appear to be solid brick. Because fill material frequently eroded over floor surfaces, the identification of primary refuse deposits for use in dating by artifactual association or for interpretation of room function was extremely difficult, if not impossible.

The Huaca, Forecourt, and Rear Compound

Like most huacas at Pacatnamu, Huaca 4 is oriented toward the north and has its only access on the north side via a baffled entry and pilastered doorway, leading into the forecourt (Fig. 1). Such

Figure 1. Plan of Huaca 4 and associated eastern rooms.

Figure 2. U-shaped structure on top of platform, viewed looking east.

entries are a hallmark of Chimu architecture and are found at Chan Chan, Farfan, and at rural administrative centers in the Moche, Chicama, and Jequetepeque valleys (Keatinge 1974; Keatinge and Conrad 1983).

In the forecourt to the west of the doorway is a small rectangular altar, similar to those found in courtyards and rooms in other parts of the site. It measures 2.8 x 4.8 meters and is less than 50 centimeters high. Though partially destroyed by looting, it is clear that it was built with case-and-fill construction. This fill contained a wide variety of domestic refuse: shells, corn cobs, guanabana, donax shell, cane, chirimoya seeds, land snails, charcoal, fish bones, and plainware ceramics.

Just beyond the doorway, a ramp provides access to a bench, elevated slightly less than 1 meter above the floor of the forecourt. At the south side of the bench, and raised some 1.9 to 2.0 meters, is the platform of the huaca itself. Slightly east of the center of the bench there is a single row of bricks running about 7.2 meters in a north-south direction whose function is unknown. A series of benches abuts the front or north face of the platform, perhaps indicating the existence of several small rooms once located there. There are two post holes in the most westerly section of these benches, indicating that some of the rooms may originally have been roofed; however, no evidence of roofing material was encountered.

Access to the top of the platform was via an ascending ramp in the southwest corner of the bench. A portion of the ramp's base and the brick remains of its eastern side are still visible. The ramp was constructed by using the east ramp wall and the west building wall to hold in a core of fill, which was then plastered over and connected to the floor of the bench.

A test pit in the floor at the midpoint of the platform reached a depth of 1.2 meters before the base of the huaca was encountered. Thus the original height of the platform was probably slightly more than 3.0 meters. It appears that the floor of the forecourt extends underneath the bench and continues to the base of the platform, suggesting that the ramps, bench, and other associated features may have been later additions to the complex. The interior sides of the walls demarcating the bench on the east and west, which contain the fill underlying the bench floor, are covered with a well-preserved fine white plaster, suggesting that these walls were originally exposed.

The platform is 7 meters wide at its summit. Across its northern side is a low brick wall, 0.5 meters wide and 0.5 meters high. In the center of the platform are the remains of a small three-sided structure. This structure was presumably the focus of whatever activity took place on top of the hauca (Fig. 2). The wall along the north side of the platform dips 0.4 meters for a length of 1.85 meters in front of the three-sided structure. Presumably, this would have made it easier for anyone standing in the forecourt or on the bench to view the activity taking place there. Conversely, lowering the height of this wall would have made it easier for anyone sitting in the U-shaped structure to view the bench or forecourt areas.

Excavation of the three-sided structure revealed no evidence of roofing material, or holes in either the floor or the walls, and no artifactual material was uncovered. Some time after the structure was built, the east wall was extended 1.4 meters, apparently to limit access from the west side. Since this was accomplished by adding several adobes over a base of fill, it seems probable that it was a late addition and does not pertain to the original use. In the middle of the three-sided structure a 1.5 x 2.0 meter test pit was excavated to check for subfloor burials or chambers. Such features had been hypothesized in a 1974 survey of the building (Keatinge 1977). Nothing but fill, composed of Chimu sherds, pieces of plain weave textile, and food remains, was encountered.

On the south side of the platform is a rear compound. Its only access is via a 2.0 meter wide ramp descending from the northeast corner of the platform. A large (0.58 meter diameter) oxidation-fired urn was set into the middle of the ramp floor approximately 1.1 meters from the foot of the ramp (Fig. 3). The urn is complete and may have been placed there when the ramp was built, since the well-plastered floor does not appear to have been ripped out to accommodate it.

Inside the urn was a cooking olla with a flaring lip and a nondescript adorno on its body shoulder. It is oxidation fired and paddle stamped, with traces of sloppy white paint on the body. A piece of brick covered the lip of the olla, which was empty except for a small bit of dirt at the bottom. The earth in the urn surrounding the olla contained a large amount of charcoal, domestic refuse, and pieces of brick. The surrounding floor and the pieces of brick in the urn show no evidence of burning or reddening, which would indicate fire. Although the purpose of this feature is unknown, some sort of ritual may have been performed as one passed by, going to and from the platform.

The open compound to the rear of the platform is entirely enclosed by walls, with the only entrance via the previously described ramps on the north and south sides of the platform. It appears that there were no internal divisions in what was once a large open room. Trenches along the walls

Figure 3. Large urn containing cooking olla located in ramp.

of the compound revealed virtually no refuse, and no post holes or roofing material were encountered.

The Eastern Rooms

East of the huaca is an extensive area of rooms and open plazas that appear from surface survey to be directly associated with Huaca 4. Only the section immediately next to Huaca 4 was excavated. This area consisted of a series of small rooms, some of which may have originally been roofed, and others which may have been open patios or courts. Several of the rooms contained benches with well-preserved plastered floors. There was little floor-contact refuse, and what was encountered appeared to be above the floor in secondary context.[1]

Due to melting caused by standing water and what appears to have been deliberate dismantling, the large north-south wall separating the eastern rooms from the huaca could not be traced with

---

1. In one case, a shallow firepit had been gouged into the floor of one of the rooms, but it appears to have been the result of a secondary or squatter settlement.

Figure 4.   General view, niched room in southeastern corner of excavated area.

Figure 5.   Close-up view of niched wall. Note well-preserved plaster on wall below niches.

Figure 6. Northernmost platform structure, looking west.

Figure 7. Well-preserved woven cane matting found on bench of platform structure.

certainty. This wall may once have demarcated the eastern side of the huaca area and later been removed to allow access to the room section. The base is still visible below the surface, but the wall seems to have been taken down to the current floor level along its entire length.

There are three areas of particular interest in the excavated portion of the rooms: the room with niches in the southeastern portion, and the two small platform mounds with parallel benches to their immediate north.

The room in the southeastern portion of the excavated area has three niches in its east wall (Figs. 4,5). Two of the niches measure approximately 0.96 meters north-south x 0.82 meters east-west. The southernmost niche is partially destroyed, but clearly was once about this size. The floors of the niches are still reasonably well preserved and are covered with a thin layer of smooth plaster. This same plaster covers the west face of the wall in front of the niches (Fig. 5).

The clean fill in the room in front of the niches appears to have been intentionally deposited in level courses to the height of the niches (ca. 0.88 m). On the floor of the room was a large Lambayeque style paddle-stamped body sherd, oxidation fired

Figure 8. Southernmost platform structure showing ramp and two parallel benches, looking north.

and showing traces of sloppy white paint. Immediately next to the corridor are two smaller rooms, one with a raised bench accessed by a small, short ramp. No artifacts indicating the function of the room or the niches were encountered.

The two small platform mounds with parallel benches to their immediate north represent a type of structure originally identified in a surface survey of Pacatnamu in 1974. At that time it was called a "C-complex," the smallest type of repetitive building pattern at the site (Keatinge 1977:236). Survey identified at least sixty-nine such structures, occurring as isolated units, in groups, or, in this case, as integral parts of compounds.

The northernmost structure is characterized by a 0.6 meter thick east-west wall, to the south of which is a 6.2 x 3.2 meter platform, ca. 0.9 meters high. The platform is accessed by a ramp on the east side, 1.2 meters wide (Figs. 1,6).

On the north side is a narrow (0.4 meter wide) bench that slopes gradually to the floor of the court. To the west, this bench is connected to a much wider (3.8 meter wide) bench that appears to have been constructed as an addition, since its southernmost portion was built over the well-preserved western section of the bench that runs in

front of the platform. Along the sloping bench north of the platform is considerable evidence of reed matting and charcoal (Fig. 7). Since no post holes were encountered in the floors or walls to suggest that the area was roofed, the matting may have been used as floor covering. The floors are well plastered and show no evidence of burning.

To the north of the platform are poorly-preserved remains of what appear to be two parallel benches. These benches seem to have been defined by two rows of beach cobbles used to confine fill containing domestic refuse, which raised the bench floor about 0.1 meters above the floor of the room. No post holes or remains were encountered in these two benches to indicate their function.

The second platform mound, south of the first, is the same type (Fig. 8). This platform measures 3.0 x 4.0 x 1.3 meters and has a ramp on the west side that provides access to its top. Along the north side is a bench (ca. 0.9 m wide) running from the front of the platform to the west wall of the room. A reddish-brown liquid spilled in several places on this bench appears to be identical to that encountered in thick layers on the altars in front of Huaca 1 and Huaca 23a (Donnan, Huaca 1 and Huaca 23a, this volume).

Figure 9. Southernmost platform looking south, showing two parallel benches.

Figure 10. Flexed burial of young adult female found in top of southernmost platform structure.

In the court in front of the platform are two well-defined, low parallel benches measuring about 7.0 x 0.9 x 0.33 meters (Fig. 9). Six post holes were encountered in the floor of the room; there were none in the benches. Two of these post holes were quite large, 0.28 and 0.31 meters. Buildings with similar low parallel benches located in courts in front of platforms have been previously reported at Farfan and Talambo (Keatinge and Conrad 1983). However, the precise function of these benches is unknown. Day (1974) reports a similar kind of structure in the large entry courts at Chan Chan. He argues that the much larger benches there formed the base for a colonnaded structure.

A test pit (2.5 x 0.5 meters) was excavated in the top of the platform. A flexed burial of a young adult female was encountered approximately 0.4 meters below the surface (Fig. 10). The flexed position is typical of Chimu interments. The burial was set on a base of bricks and appeared to have been covered with rubble or broken adobes. No domestic refuse was encountered. The skeleton, a female approximately 20 years old, was oriented east-west and wrapped in a plain weave textile, now badly deteriorated. Other than the textile, no grave goods were associated with the burial. After removal of the skeleton, the test pit was excavated to a depth of 1.0 meter where bedrock was encountered. There were no additional features or artifacts.

Surface examination of similar structures at the site (Keatinge 1977:239) suggests that there may be other buildings containing similar burials. However, the absence of a burial in the other platform mound at Huaca 4 indicates that they are not found in all buildings of this type.

Conclusions

The Huaca 4 Complex was built almost entirely of Terminal Chimu bricks, and thus was one of the late constructions at Pacatnamu. It contains baffled entries, pilastered doorways, platforms overlooking courts, and low parallel benches in courtyards and plazas, typical of Chimu architecture generally. Although probably utilized for a relatively short period of time, many parts of the structure and the associated rooms were partially remodeled. The function of the huaca has not been clearly elucidated, but the activity associated with the three-sided structure on top of the platform presumably was the focus of whatever ceremony took place when the building was in use. The function of the walled compound on the south side of the platform, obscured from the view of anyone on the north side, is unknown. The same is true of the large urn in the ramp providing access from the top of the platform to the compound.

The eastern rooms associated with Huaca 4 may have had a domestic function. However, these rooms are relatively free of refuse in primary context, and the location of the two platform mounds in close proximity to each other raises questions regarding the activities that took place in this area. Small platform mounds exist in considerable numbers at Pacatnamu but are unknown at other sites on the North Coast. The ramp providing access to the top of each platform indicates that the slight elevation was important to whatever activity was associated with these structures. Elucidation of function awaits future excavation.

The excavations undertaken at Huaca 4 and its associated eastern rooms serve to amplify the present knowledge of building construction at Pacatnamu by elucidating a number of architectural patterns at the site. This information provides a base for comparisons with other archaeological sites and suggests a direction for future research at Pacatnamu.

RESUMEN:
Excavaciones en el Complejo de la Huaca 4

El Complejo de la Huaca 4 está ubicado a 120 mts. al nor-este de la Huaca 1. En 1985 se realizaron investigaciones en la pirámide principal y en los recintos al este de ella.

Con la excepción de la base de la huaca, que por lo menos en parte fue construida con adobes Chimú Standard, practicamente todo el complejo ha sido edificado usando adobes Chimú Terminal (McClelland, este volumen).

Arquitectura

La estructura muestra evidencia de haber sido remodelada continuamente. Como la gran mayoria de estas construcciones, está orientada hacia el norte, con una rampa en su parte frontal (Fig. 1); el acceso al conjunto es por el mismo lado, a través de una típica entrada Chimú. Al oeste de ella, hay un altar similar a los que se encuentran en otras pirámides del sitio.

Dirigiéndose hacia el sur, subiendo la rampa, hay una banquina y, a continuación, la plataforma de la huaca. En la parte este de la banquina y al norte de la plataforma hay una serie de paredes y poyos destruidos que sugieren la existencia de pequeñas habitaciones, que quizá estuvieron situadas al frente de la plataforma. El hallazgo de 2 postes indicaría que estuvieron techadas, pero no se halló evidencia de techos.

El acceso a la cima de la estructura es a través de una rampa ubicada en el lado sur-oeste de la banquina, pero sólo un pedazo de la base de esta rampa subsiste. En el centro de la cima de la plataforma hay una estructura en U (Fig. 2), que debe haber sido el centro de cualquier actividad que se haya llevado a cabo en esta huaca. Un pozo de prueba de 1.50 x 2.00 x 1.75 mts. de profundidad, en esta estructura, arrojó un relleno conteniendo fragmentos de cerámica Chimú y restos de alimentos, pero no un entierro dedicatorio, como se había pensado en 1974.

En una rampa que desciende desde la parte este de la plataforma, hasta el sur de la huaca, se ubicó un ceramio (58 cms. de diámetro) que sobresaliendo del piso de la rampa (Fig. 3), se hallaba incrustado en el enlucido original de la misma. Dentro, había una vasija doméstica cubierta con un adobe, rodeada de ceniza, basura doméstica y pedazos de adobe. El contenido de esta olla no fue visualmente reconocible.

El recinto abierto a espaldas de la plataforma está completamente cerrado por paredes, por lo que su acceso fue a través de la plataforma descrita.

Recintos Este

Hacia el Este de la Huaca hay una extensa área de recintos y patios que aparecen conectados a la Huaca 4. Hay una serie de pequeños recintos, algunos de los cuales pueden haber estado techados, donde varios poseen poyos y enlucido bien conservado.

Una pared que pareciese haber dividido los recintos este y la huaca, parece haber sido desmantelada para permitir el acceso de una a otra sección.

Un recinto con nichos (Figs. 4, 5) en el sureste presenta uno de los enlucidos mejor preservados de Pacatnamú. El relleno del corredor frente a este recinto, pareciese haber sido intencionalmente depositado para cubrir la altura de los nichos (88 cms.); en el piso de este corredor, se recuperó un fragmento de cerámica Lambayeque, paleteada, con pintura blanca. Al costado del recinto con nichos hay dos mas pequeños, uno con una banquina y una rampa, en los que tampoco se halló material cultural que permitiese entender la función de estos recintos.

Estas dos estructuras asociadas con poyos paralelos, habían sido identificadas, en 1974, como estructuras C (Keatinge 1977:236), el más pequeño tipo de construcción repetitiva en Pacatnamú, del cual hay 69 ejemplos.

Al norte de estos recintos hay un área con banquinas desiguales, siendo la del lado oeste de mayores dimensiones y, quizá, una adición más tardía. Hay evidencia de la presencia de esteras (Fig. 7), pero no la hay de postes, por lo que estas podrían haber servido para cubrir el piso; así mismo, el carbón y cenizas localizado no se puede asociar a hogares, ya que no hay evidencia de su existencia.

Al frente de las banquinas se hallaron evidencias de postes, así como dos poyos paralelos de 7 mts. de largo por 1 mt. de ancho (Figs. 1, 9). Construcciones con características similares se han observado en Farfán y Talambo (Keatinge y Conrad 1983), así como a la entrada de las Ciudadelas en Chan Chan (Day 1974), aunque su función es desconocida.

Durante las excavaciones, se recuperó un entierro flexionado de una joven mujer (Fig. 10) de unos 20 años de edad. Estuvo en la plataforma, orientada hacia el este, sin ofrendas funerarias

cubierta de adobes rotos y envuelta en un tejido llano, muy deteriorado. La ausencia de un entierro similar en la otra plataforma del recinto este, indicaría que este tipo de hallazgo no necesariamente aparece siempre en estas estructuras.

Aunque las funciones del Complejo de la Huaca 4 no han sido completamente elucidadas, se puede afirmar que los recintos al este pareciesen estar asociados más con un tipo de habitación doméstica, mientras la huaca misma aparece más ligada a funciones ceremoniales. Debido a que las diversas áreas del complejo se hallaron relativamente limpias de material cultural en contexto primario, nuestra comprensión se vio limitada, pero ha proveído valiosa información para ser usada en comparaciones con otros complejos en Pacatnamú.

The Huaca 23a, 49, and 50 Complexes

Christopher B. Donnan

In the northern portion of Pacatnamu is an area of well-preserved architecture consisting of three distinct complexes—Huacas 23a, 49, and 50 (Map Insert, Fig. 1). On the basis of the bricks used in their construction, it was clear that all three were built during the Chimu occupation, but that certain portions predated others (McClelland, this volume). Thus the area provided an excellent opportunity to study the development of Chimu architecture through time. Of particular interest was the way formal and functional aspects of the architecture adjusted to the constraints imposed by the existing buildings, the availability of adequate space, and the irregularities in the natural terrain. To better understand this development, the architecture is divided into two sequential periods.[1]

First Period

In the first period the Huaca 49 and Huaca 50 complexes were constructed (Fig. 2). Huaca 50 may be slightly earlier than Huaca 49 (McClelland, this volume), but for our purposes they can be seen as contemporary. They are situated on a north-south axis—Huaca 50 to the south of Huaca 49—with an open area between the two. Each consists of one or more pyramid structures and courtyards, surrounded in part by large perimeter walls. Neither complex is well enough preserved to reconstruct a complete plan, and in both cases it is difficult to determine the relationship of their various architectural components. It is likely, however, that both complexes are variations of the basic architectural form exemplified by Huaca 4 (Keatinge, this volume). This form is defined by Keatinge (1982:212) as having the following characteristics:

1. An elevated mound high enough to require a ramp to access its upper level.
2. Often, but not always, a small mound, which we will refer to as an altar, located in the forecourt in front of the elevated mound.
3. Usually, a compound located to the rear of the elevated mound.
4. The absence of a flanking pyramid to the northeast of the elevated mound.

To varying degrees both the Huaca 49 and Huaca 50 complexes exhibit these characteristics.

1. The author wishes to express appreciation to Coreen Chiswell, who assisted with the excavation and mapping of the Huaca 23a, 49, and 50 complexes and provided valuable comments on an earlier version of this report.

Figure 1.   Air photo of the Huaca 23a, 49, and 50 complexes, looking northeast.

Their huacas are high along the south and part of the east and west sides; the central and northern portions are somewhat lower. The ramps giving access to the elevated lower levels appear to be on the east side, where there is a doorway through the side wall.

To the northwest of Huaca 49 is Huaca 24a, another pyramid that appears to be contemporary with, and part of, the Huaca 49 Complex.[2] It is similar in form to Huacas 49 and 50, but the ramp giving access to its lower level could not be identified.

There is some evidence that during this early period a third complex of essentially the same form existed west of Huaca 49 (Fig. 2). It consisted of a solid mound with a ramp near the center of its north side, one or more rooms on its south side, and a cluster of rooms located to the northeast. There was also an altar in front of the mound, near

2. Hecker and Hecker (1982, 1985) have designated this mound as Huaca 24a, but it clearly is not associated with Huaca 24, which is located almost 100 meters west of it.

its north ramp. These hypothetical reconstructions are based upon evidence of earlier architecture found inside or beneath the structures that now exist in these locations.

Second Period

In the second period, the Huaca 23a Complex was developed. While some existing structures were utilized, there was a deliberate attempt to transform them into a completely different architectural form. The objective was to create something similar to the Huaca 1 Complex (Donnan, Huaca 1, this volume), which possessed these essential features:

1. A large huaca, oriented north-south, with a ramp near the center of the north (front side) that leads to the summit.
2. A large courtyard in front of the huaca. This courtyard is roughly rectangular in form and has a central pilastered doorway near the center of its north wall, which serves as the primary entrance to the architectural complex.

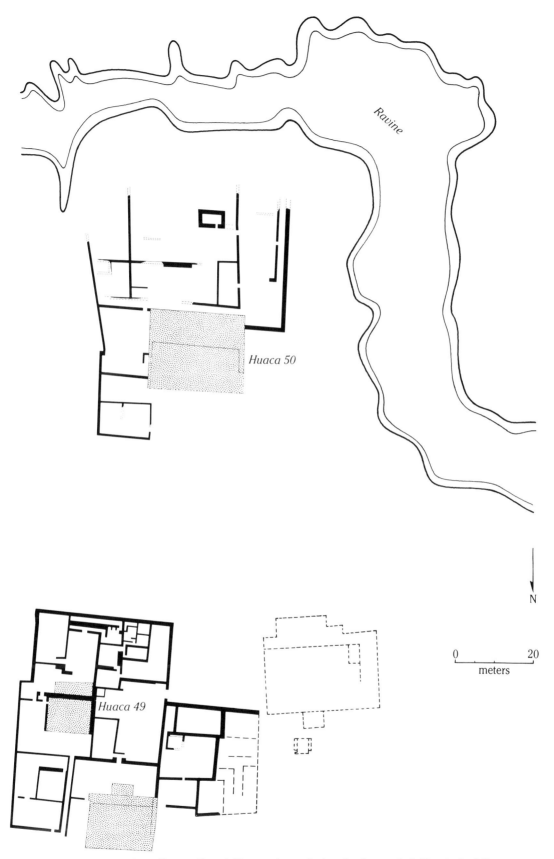

Figure 2.   Plan of the Huaca 49 and 50 complexes during the first period. The dashed lines indicate the location of later architecture that was probably in an incipient form at this time.

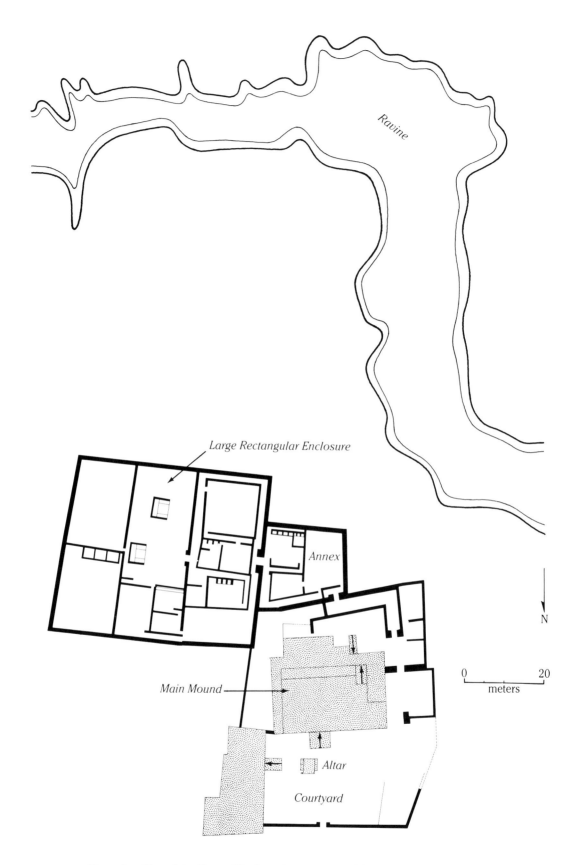

Figure 3.   Plan of the Huaca 23a Complex constructed during the second period.

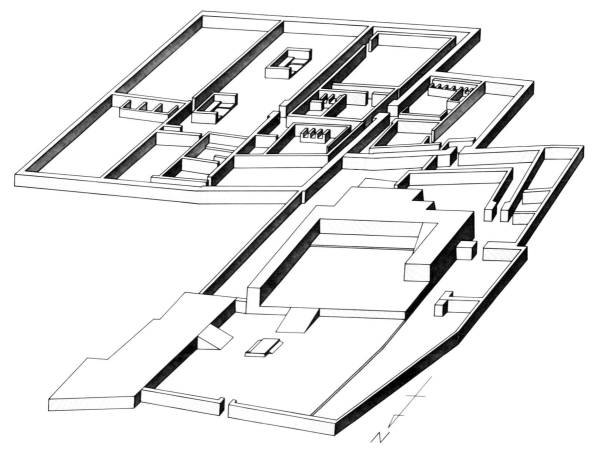

Figure 4.   Isometric view of the Huaca 23a Complex constructed during the second period.

3. A large flanking mound northeast of the large huaca. This mound has a ramp near the center of its west side, which provides access to the summit.

4. One or two altars near the center of the courtyard. These altars are often in alignment with the ramps of either the huaca, the flanking mound, or both.

5. An elaborate series of doorways and corridors along the west side of the hauca, which provide access to the area on its south (back) side.

6. A large rectangular enclosure at the south (back) side of the huaca. This enclosure has a single entry through a narrow, pilastered doorway, normally located near the center of its north side. The interior of the large rectangular enclosure is divided into courtyards, rooms, and corridors.

In order to create this type of architectural complex with all its essential components, the builders utilized some already existing structures. They created the large huaca with its north ramp by enlarging the huaca that had been built during the early period. The large courtyard on the north side was made by adding walls along the north and west sides, and the primary entrance was created by building a pilastered doorway near the center of the north wall (Figs. 3,4).

The flanking mound located along the east side of the courtyard was made by filling in several pre-existing small rooms.[3] The irregular form of its east side reflects the shapes of these rooms (Figs. 3,4). When the fill was complete, the upper surface of the mound was leveled and capped to form the summit, and a narrow ramp was built along its west side to provide access.

Normally, the ramp would have been situated near the center of the west side of the mound, in alignment with the altar in front of it. In this in-

---

3. Hecker and Hecker note that the flanking mound of the Huaca 23a Complex had internal walls, suggesting it was made by filling previously constructed rooms (1982:127-128, Abb. 11).

stance, however, a problem arose since the altar, which had been built during the early period, was not directly in front of the center portion of the mound. Presumably the builders had several choices. They could have destroyed the existing altar and rebuilt it several meters farther to the north, aligning it with the center of the mound. Alternatively, they could have kept the altar in its original position and built the ramp near the center of the mound where it would not be in alignment with the altar. Instead, they opted for a third possibility—leaving the altar in its original position and locating the ramp where it would align with the altar, even though it was not at the center of the mound. Apparently, the alignment of the ramp with the altar was the most important consideration.

The original altar appears to have been in use for some time prior to the remodeling of the Huaca 23a Complex (Fig. 5). Its central part was nearly square, measuring approximately 3.70 meters north-south by 4.35 meters east-west, and was approximately 30 centimeters high. The north and south sides were nearly vertical, but wide ramps along both the east and west sides sloped from the top of the altar to the floor of the courtyard. There was a reddish-brown residue on the top of the altar that appeared to be spilled liquid, which in some places had run down the sloping ramps. This appears to be similar to the residue on the altars of Huaca 1 (Donnan, Huaca 1, this volume) and Huaca 4 (Keatinge, this volume).

During the second period, the height of the square central portion of the altar was increased on two occasions. Each time the summit was raised about 15 centimeters and capped with a clay floor. The ramps on the east and west sides were not elevated, however, and thus a step was created at the top of the ramps. Liquid residue similar to that found on top of the original altar was found on both of the new floor surfaces. Unfortunately, the composition of the reddish-brown residue has not yet been identified, but it is assumed that its presence on the altar results from the ceremonial activities performed there. The fact that it was found on each of the superimposed floors implies that the ceremonial activities of the first period continued during the second period.

An elaborate series of doorways, corridors, and rooms was added along the west side of the large huaca to provide access from its front to the area on its south side. By turning left at the southwest corner of the huaca it was possible to enter the area adjacent to the south side. There a steep ramp provided a secondary access to the summit.

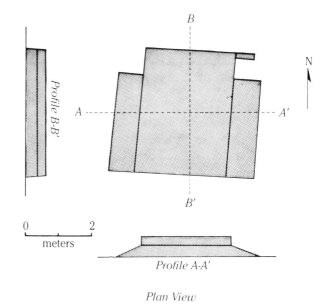

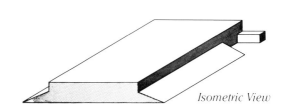

Figure 5. Altar in the Huaca 23a Complex.

Alternatively, one could proceed west along the back of the huaca, through a narrow door, and gain access to a long narrow room that extended along the entire east side of the huaca (Figs. 3,4).

In order to complete the architectural complex, a large rectangular enclosure had to be constructed near the back (south) side of the huaca. Normally, this would have been oriented north-south, with a single entry near the center of its north wall. However, in this instance, a deep ravine south of the main mound left insufficient space for this structure (Figs. 1,3). Rather than reduce the size of the enclosure to fit the space available, the builders chose to construct it in the vacant area between Huacas 49 and 50, thus turning it 90 degrees and orienting it east-west.

Because of its eastward displacement, the entrance is located near the center of the west wall. A trapezoidal-shaped annex was constructed in front of this doorway, providing access from the south side of the main mound to the entrance of the large enclosure. After entering this annex through an elaborately baffled doorway at its northwest corner,

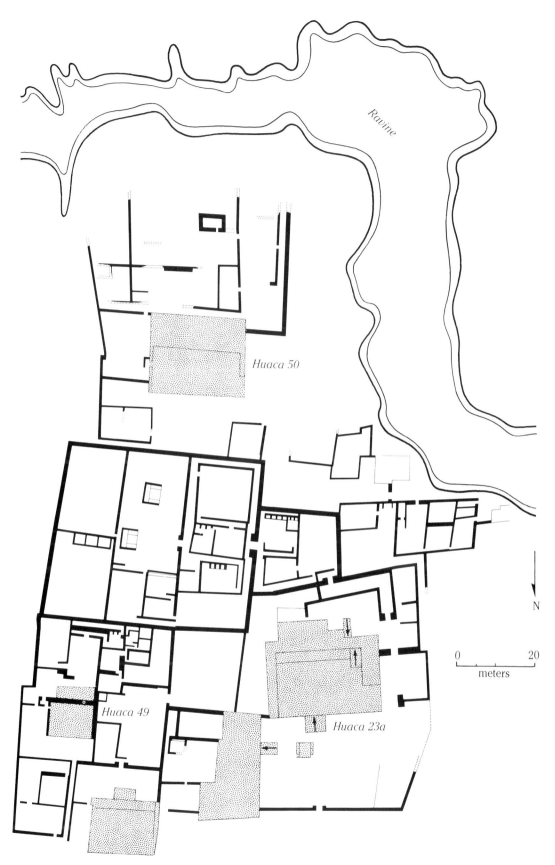

Figure 6. Plan of the 23a, 49, and 50 complexes showing their final form and position.

one proceeds through a series of rooms that divide the interior space. One of these rooms, located along the south side of the annex, has a series of binlike structures along one wall. Four of the bins are approximately the same size; the fifth is larger and its interior is divided (Figs. 3,4). Excavation of these bins yielded only rubble mixed with some redeposited refuse. Although their original function is not known, it is assumed that they were used for storage.

The large rectangular enclosure on the east side of the annex is approximately 44 meters north-south by 50 meters east-west. Its perimeter walls still stand in some places to a height of 2.5 meters and may have originally been as high as 3.5 meters. There is a single entrance near the center of the west wall, with large flanking pilasters underscoring its importance.

The interior space of the large quadrangle is divided into three sectors of almost equal size—the first sector is on the west side, the second in the center, and the third on the east. Entering the first sector through the pilastered doorway, one may turn either to the right or left and follow corridors that lead along the perimeter walls. Turning to the left, one proceeds along a narrow corridor to reach a large open room. At the northeast corner of this room is an opening that provides access to the second sector. Alternatively, turning to the right one follows a much longer and more circuitous corridor that ultimately provides access to a series of rooms occupying the major portion of this first sector. Some of these rooms have niches similar to those in the Huaca 1 Complex (Donnan, Huaca 1, this volume). The route to the right also provides access to the second sector, through what appears to be its primary entrance.

The primary entrance to the second sector is a pilastered doorway that provides access to a large room containing two audiencias. Both audiencias face west—one is opposite the pilastered doorway and the other is further to the south.

The room with audiencias has a small, unpilastered doorway leading to a series of rooms along the north side of the second sector—the same rooms that could be accessed by turning left at the front entrance. These rooms may well have had a domestic or secondary role relative to that of the audiencia room.

An east-west wall divides the third sector into two large rooms of approximately equal size. Access to one of these rooms is through a small, unpilastered doorway behind one of the audiencias. The entry to the second room was not located. It may

be that its entrance had been closed with mortared bricks, or it may have had an unusually high threshold with one or more courses of brick. Along much of the west side of the room the walls were eroded to only one brick in height, and the doorway may have been located in one of these areas.

The second room has three large bins built against one wall. These are heavily eroded, but careful excavation suggests they were without doors and would have been accessed from above. They contained nothing that would indicate their original function but presumably they were used for storage.

Comparisons with Chan Chan

Although most parts of the Huaca 23a Complex have very little resemblance to the architecture of Chan Chan, the southern portion, including the annex and the large rectangular enclosure, have certain features that are remarkably similar to Chan Chan's ciudadela architecture.

Perhaps the most striking similarity is the general form and internal division of the large rectangular enclosure. Like the ciudadelas at Chan Chan, it has a small doorway with pilasters providing the only entrance. Also like Chan Chan it is divided into three sectors that lead from the front to the rear of the enclosure.

The annex is another feature that is reminiscent of Chan Chan, where the ciudadelas normally have an annex attached to the exterior of their perimeter walls, in front of the entrance. These annexes vary in size and are not as formally planned as the divisions within the ciudadelas (Day 1982:61).

A third feature is the distinctive form of baffled doorway leading into the annex. This doorway, with thick pilasters, has an L-shaped wall on its interior side that directs the flow of incoming traffic to the right. It also creates a small alcove to the left of the doorway. This form of baffled doorway is common at Chan Chan and has been identified at provincial Chimu sites thought to have been directly linked to Chan Chan (Keatinge and Conrad 1983). Its occurrence in the annex of the Huaca 23a Complex is the only instance yet identified at Pacatnamu.

There are, on the other hand, significant differences between the ciudadelas at Chan Chan and the Huaca 23a Complex. The audiencias differ in form and in the fact that they are not associated with major storage facilities. Moreover, the rectangular enclosure of Huaca 23a does not have a burial platform—a feature characteristic of the ciudadelas at Chan Chan. It should be noted that the late influence from Chan Chan did not result in the construction of ciudadelas, but merely lent new features to an architectural form that has clear antecedents at Pacatnamu and probably was of local origin.

Nevertheless, there are more typical Chan Chan features in the Huaca 23a Complex than have been found elsewhere at Pacatnamu. The fact that the Huaca 23a Complex is one of the latest structures built at the site suggests that influence from Chan Chan was more pronounced during the late occupation of Pacatnamu than it had been earlier.

RESUMEN:
Los Complejos de las Huacas 23a, 49 y 50

Uno de los objetivos de la temporada de trabajo 1985 fue el de estudiar como la arquitectura Chimú se desarrolló en el tiempo, ajustando sus características formales y funcionales a las restricciones impuestas por las estructuras existentes, espacio adecuado e irregularidades del terreno; por ello se escogió el sector donde están las Huacas 23a, 49 y 50 (Fig. 1). Ellas pertenecen a la ocupación Chimú, pero ciertas estructuras anteceden a las otras.

Primer Período

Durante él se construyeron las Huacas 49 y 50; no es posible determinar, por ahora, si se construyeron al mismo tiempo, pero para nuestro propósito actual, se pueden considerar contemporáneas.

Están orientadas de norte a sur, estando la Huaca 50 al sur de la 49, con un espacio abierto entre las dos (Fig. 2). Por su deterioro, ninguno de estos complejos permitió reconstruir su plano completo o las relaciones entre sus componentes estructurales, pero ambos parecen ser variantes de la forma arquitectónica básica ejemplificada por la Huaca 4 (Keatinge, este volumen).

Hay evidencia que un tercer complejo, de la misma forma básica, existió durante este período al oeste de la Huaca 49 (Fig. 2, dibujo con guiones).

Segundo Período

Durante él se construyó la Huaca 23a. Se utilizaron algunas estructuras preexistentes para crear algo similar al Complejo de la Huaca 1 (Donnan, este volumen). Para ello, se agrandó la huaca temprana; para crear un Patio Norte, se agregaron paredes en los lados norte y oeste, y se construyó un puerta cerca del centro de la pared Norte (Figs. 3, 4).

Se agregó una pirámide lateral (este) mediante el relleno de varias habitaciones pre-existentes. La rampa de este montículo no se centró, con el fin de alinearla con el altar más temprano que ya existía allí, al que se le añadieron 20 cms. de altura (Fig. 5).

Para proveer acceso desde el frente de la huaca a la parte sur, se construyeron una serie de elaboradas puertas y corredores, y, ante la dificultad de agregar un cuadrángulo adosado a la parte sur de la huaca, que estuviese orientado norte-sur, debido a la presencia de una quebrada, se construyó uno orientado este-oeste, en el espacio abierto entre las Huacas 49 y 50. (Figs. 2, 6). Por este desplazamiento, para llenar el espacio entre la parte sur de la huaca y el cuadrángulo, se construyó un anexo de forma trapezoidal, destinado a unir estas dos partes del complejo (Figs. 3, 4, 6).

El cuadrángulo al este del anexo mide 44 mts. norte-sur por 50 mts. este-oeste. Sus paredes perimétricas miden actualmente, en algunas partes, 2.50 mts., y podrían haber tenido originalmente unos 3.50 mts. El interior está dividido en tres secciones—la primera al oeste, la segunda al centro, y la tercera al este. El segundo sector, el central, posee dos audiencias, las cuales están orientadas hacia el oeste.

Comparaciones con Chan Chan

Aunque mucho del Complejo de la Huaca 23a tiene poco parecido con la arquitectura de Chan Chan, la porción sur, que incluye el anexo y el cuadrángulo, poseen ciertas características remarcablemente similares a las ciudadelas de Chan Chan. Entre ellas, la división tripartita del Cuadrángulo y la existencia del anexo, son quizá las más notables similitudes.

Entre las diferencias, está la falta de asociación de las audiencias de la Huaca 23a con depósitos y la ausencia de una plataforma funeraria, las que son características de las ciudadelas de Chan Chan.

De cualquier manera, hay más similitudes entre el Complejo de la Huaca 23a y Chan Chan, que las que pudiese tener cualquier otra estructura de Pacatnamú. El hecho que el Complejo de la Huaca 23a es una de las estructuras más tardías en el sitio sugeriría que la influencia de Chan Chan sobre Pacatnamú fue más fuerte durante la ocupación tardía, que en periodos más tempranos.

Power and Wealth in the Jequetepeque Valley during the Sixteenth Century

Guillermo A. Cock

To understand the basis and exercise of power in the Jequetepeque Valley during the pre-Hispanic and early Colonial periods, it is useful to examine the case of don Garcia Pilco Guaman, the lord or Curaca of Moro-Chepen, who ruled during the early part of the Colonial Period. He was the last powerful and relatively independent lord of that valley. The wealth and privilege that accompanied his position can be reconstructed in part from his will and testament, written in 1582,[1] and in part from the records of property that was disbursed by his successor, don Francisco Chepen. Since the property of these two individuals represents the essence of power of a major ruler in the Jequetepeque Valley, it provides valuable insights into the nature of pre-Hispanic and Colonial Period social organization.

Unfortunately, little is known about don Garcia Pilco Guaman. He was born between 1500 and 1520 and was probably a young adult when Spaniards appeared for the first time in the Jequetepeque Valley in 1533. In 1582, when he made his will, he did not know how to sign his name and asked don Francisco Chepen to sign for him (ADT, CO, Leg. 154, Exp. 204, ff 2v). This gives some indication of his possible age, because Curacas who were adolescents or younger in the 1530s usually knew how to sign their names, and many born during that decade learned to read and write. Alternatively, his inability to sign his name may have simply reflected an education and attitude that resisted all but the most necessary aspects of European acculturation and domination.

In his testament he asked to be buried near his mother in the Catholic church of Guadalupe, just outside the main chapel (doc. quoted ff 1r). This, however, does not necessarily imply acculturation, since the Colonial administration required Curacas to become Christians in order to serve as good ex-

---

1. This type of document is rarely encountered in the North Coast of Peru, a direct consequence of early and precipitous depopulation during the sixteenth century. Another factor that makes this document valuable is that the Curaca is mentioned in several other documents from the preceding two decades (1560s-1570s). The document is kept in the archive mentioned, in the Division: Judicial, Series: Corregimientos, Sub-Series: Ordinaria, Legajo 154, Expediente 204. It has 25 folios (50 pages), and is dated August 11, 1582 (from now on: ADT, CO, Leg. 154, Exp. 204). The document has two parts: the testament itself and the record of the auction of the Curaca's properties. Other Colonial manuscripts (from the 1560s and 1570s) and later ones (from the seventeenth and eighteenth centuries) that contain copies of sixteenth and early seventeenth century documents, provide supplementary information about the wealth and power of the Curaca of Moro-Chepen.

amples to their subjects (Cuenca 1977[1566]:141). Moreover, it was mandatory for Andean lords to be buried as Christians, either inside the church or in the courtyard just outside the entrance, depending on the prestige and economic status of the deceased.[2] Being buried inside the church, close to a main chapel or altar, was very prestigious, even though the lord's subjects might later take his body and rebury it in a pre-Hispanic cemetery, where a lord of his rank should be buried according to local tradition (Cieza 1984[1553]:Ch. LXI-LXIII, 191-198).

Pilco Guaman declared himself legitimately married to dona Juana Chumpi and the father of the only son from this marriage, don Juan (doc. quoted ff 2r). Apparently don Juan never became a lord of high rank, although it is possible he achieved the status of Principal, one of the lower-order lords who helped don Francisco Chepen administrate his chiefdom.[3]

Don Garcia Pilco Guaman's independence and power were based on prestige and economic strength, as well as his ability to deal with both Spaniards and natives in political, economic, and social arenas. Other local lords were forced to sell land to the Spaniards because they lacked the labor force necessary to cultivate it, a consequence of North Coast depopulation. Don Garcia Pilco Guaman was able to retain his landholdings, however, and avoided making big donations of land to the newly founded Augustinian monastery in the Jequetepeque Valley.

Prior to the Conquest, land, water, and irrigation ditches were considered the private property of the lords (Cuenca 1977[1566]:141-142). An individual or a community was granted the right to use the land and water in exchange for labor (RGI 1965[1586] II:43).[4] The lord's ability to grant these rights was not only the basis of his power but also the first step in the reciprocity system. It provided him with labor, the most valuable resource without which all other resources were worthless. With the agricultural surplus from his lands, the lord was able to maintain and control the non-food producers who served him, the most important of which

appear to have been the artisans and craftsmen. In this way, the lord controlled the production and circulation of prestigious goods, and subsequently was able to use these goods for access to more labor. This was a circular system, with the lords at the beginning and at the end.

Don Garcia Pilco Guaman died between June 20, 1582, when he made his will, and August of the same year, when documents pertaining to the liquidation of his properties were presented to the Colonial authorities in the city of Trujillo.

In the 1590s and early 1600s, don Garcia Pilco Guaman's successor, don Francisco Chepen, sold or gave away most of the Moro-Chepen landholdings in the Jequetepeque Valley (AGN Tierras de Comunidades, Leg. 5, Cuad. 38). As a result, by the 1620s, the Augustinian monastery had obtained possession of nearly all the valley's most valuable arable lands. This subsequently resulted in litigations between the monastery and the natives that lasted for centuries (approximately 1600-1800). The records of these litigations not only provide additional information about the landholdings of the Moro-Chepen polity, but also reveal its boundaries and its relationships with other chiefdoms in the valley. The evidence shows that boundaries were not clear: some portions of land given away by don Francisco Chepen were also claimed by the Cherrepe and Jequetepeque polities.[5]

Landholdings of the Curaca of Moro-Chepen

The landholdings listed below as belonging to the Moro-Chepen polity help to define the extent of the lord's influence over the widely scattered agriculturalist population living in the Jequetepeque Valley, as well as over those who depended on the products of these lands. In don Garcia Pilco Guaman's will, executed ten years after the Reducciones Toledanas, new towns were still called by their pre-Hispanic names.[6]

1. Namalo (ADT, CO, Leg.154, Exp. 204 ff lr); Namul, as Calancha called it; or Namur (Fig. 1). Namalo was the name of the hill

2. See Rostworowski 1977b:264-265,275 for comparative cases from Ica and Cajamarca.
3. Like the two sons of don Hernando Anicama, Paramount Lord in Lurin Ica (Rostworowski 1977b:263), don Juan did not especially benefit from the will of his father, a situation that is repeated in other lords' testaments.
4. This situation appears to be peculiar to the North Coast; in the highlands, land and water were considered communal property. Consequently, on the North Coast the lord's authority was reinforced by economic resources.

5. Disagreements regarding territoriality and boundaries are not peculiar to the North Coast but are a pan-Andean problem that has been reported in the highlands as well (Rostworowski 1972:39; 1977b:260; Cock 1976-1977:113-116; 1978:29-32).
6. This is very helpful for twentieth-century researchers, because in some cases the original names have been lost. With the help of don Luis Lostaunau, some of the names given by don Garcia Pilco Guaman have been identified.

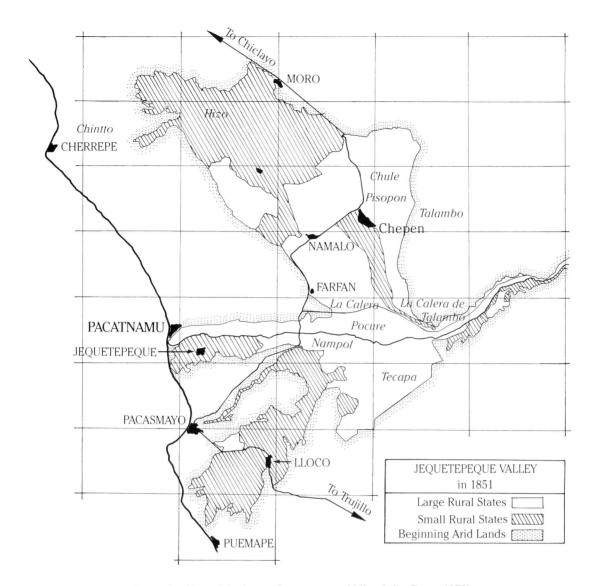

Figure 1. Map of the Lower Jequetepeque Valley (after Burga 1976).

and the pre-Hispanic settlement where the Augustinian monastery was built after it was moved from its first location in Cherrepe. It was also the site of the first town of Guadalupe, settled in 1572. It is one kilometer west of the central square of the present-day town of Guadalupe (see also Calancha 1975-1982[1638]:Book 3, Ch. 5, 1259). The documents indicate that these lands were donated to the Augustinian friars by don Francisco Chepen (AGN Tierras de Comunidades, Leg. 5, Cuad. 38, ff 64v-65r). However, the Augustinians had occupied them since the 1560s, in the belief that they belonged to the Cherrepe polity, which also claimed them. The people of Cherrepe called the place Cormot, and the agriculturalists of Cherrepe had lived there in pre-Hispanic times. The Augustinians called it Guadalupe, and in some Colonial documents it is referred to as Farfancillo. Cherrepe's prior ownership of these lands is further supported by the fact that the agriculturalists of this polity were congregated (reducidos) there in 1572 by the Visitador, Juan de Hoces, who identified them as living "next to the Nuestra Señora de Guadalupe Monastery," which had by then moved to Namalo (BNP, A 310, ff 31v-35r; see a partial translation of this document in Ramirez-Horton 1979:96-121).[7]

2. Chule (ADT, CO, Leg. 154, Exp. 204 ff lv); a pre-Hispanic settlement also known as Chulle, Chulle Melica, and Chulle Millea (Fig. 1). Today it is called Moro (different than the pre-Hispanic settlement of the same name below) or El Trust. According to Pilco Guaman's will, he kept 36 bulls and cows there (doc. quoted above). In 1596, don Francisco Chepen gave 500 fanegadas of these lands to the Augustinian monastery, including some corrals (corralones) and a pyramid (huaca) called Osno (Usno) by the Notary of the document. These lands were located in the Talambo area (AGN, Tierras de Comunidades, Leg. 5, Cuad. 38, ff 64r-64v).

3. Hizo (ADT, CO, Leg. 154, Exp. 204 ff 2r); a pre-Hispanic settlement also known as Izo, Izocoton, Socoton, Nocoton, and Coton (Fig. 1; also possibly the pyramid and associated buildings known today as Huaca Coton). It is located between the present-day towns of Pueblo Nuevo and Santa Rosa.[8] Pilco Guaman kept 860 goats and sheep there. If the identification of this settlement is correct, it is located inside the lands of the Cherrepe polity, within the lands farmed by its agriculturalists, and would constitute the second case of territorial problems (see Namalo, above).

4. Moro (ADT, CO, Leg. 154, Exp. 204 ff 1r); a pre-Hispanic settlement (Fig. 1). Pilco Guaman declared that he lived there. In pre-Hispanic times the name seems to have been restricted to the site, but today it refers to the surrounding area as well.

5. Pisopon (doc. quoted, ff 2v); a pre-Hispanic settlement that also could have been Chepen Viejo or pre-Hispanic Chepen (Fig. 1). Today it is included in Chulle Melica where there are a number of huacas associated with buildings (see Chule, above).

Don Garcia Pilco Guaman called Moro and Pisopon "asientos," which means settlements of an unspecified size. Like Chule and Hizo, they were places where he kept livestock.

The information in Pilco Guaman's testament regarding the polity's landholdings may be supplemented with records of the sales and donations of land by his successor, don Francisco Chepen, and his widow. Some of these lands, acquired by the Augustinian monastery, are listed below.

1. La Calera (Fig. 1). Six fanegadas (17.34 hectares) from "his part," was left to the Augustinian monastery in Chepen's will (AGN Tierras de Comunidades, Leg. 5, Cuad. 38, ff 64v-65r). The meaning of "his part" cannot be determined and will be analyzed below.

   It should be noted that the pre-Hispanic Chimu center of Farfan is located on these lands, but it is unclear if it was included in the six fanegadas donated by the lord or in the holdings mentioned below.[9]

   The presence of Chimu administrative centers on the land of the highest lord in the northern part of the Jequetepeque Valley poses some questions about the Chimu presence there: who were the administrators, and what was the relationship between the "foreign" (Chimu or Inca) state and the local power represented by the lords? Unfortunately, present data are insufficient to answer these questions. Nevertheless, Keatinge and Conrad's suggestion that La Calera de Talambo was "a strategic control point both for the Lower Valley irrigation networks and for up-and-

7. Ramirez-Horton and Netherly both failed to give the correct location of Cormot or Namalo. Later, Maria Rostworowski located Cormot more accurately, but she did not realize it was another name for Namalo. Here, we have the first case where land ownership, territoriality, and boundaries (Western-style) cannot be defined. This is either because the lands were "shared" between the Curacazgos, or because a Curacazgo had landholdings inside the holdings of another polity. The latter is possibly analagous to Murra's "islands" (see Murra 1975b).

8. It appears that this is the location of the town of Noquique. The information regarding its location is in the same document as the Cherrepe Visita and the Acta de Reduccion. In part of the document, the witnesses Fray Alonso Salguero (an Augustinian friar), Antonio de Corzo (majordomo of the encomendero Francisco Perez de Lescano), Pedro de Morales, Martyn Lescano (lower-ranking lord of the town of Guadalupe, Namalo or Cormot), don Benito Respen (Indian mayor or Mocupe), and don Francisco Cascala (Paramount Lord of Mocupe), all identify Noquique with Nocoton or Noquic (BNP A 310, ff 64v, 67r, 68v, 70v, 72r, 72v, respectively).

9. In 1978, Richard Keatinge and Geoffrey Conrad excavated at Farfan and at another site called La Calera de Talambo (Fig. 1), which was identified as a possible local center subordinate to the Chimu administrative center at Farfan (Keatinge and Conrad 1983:258).

down Valley trade or communication routes" (1983:278), is consistent with the power exercised by a high-ranking lord in the valley. Keatinge and Conrad "do not know whether this land [surrounding La Calera de Talambo] was owned by the state or by local kin-groups in Chimu times" (1983:282). Perhaps it belonged to the highest lord of Moro-Chepen.

Another piece of land in La Calera was bought by the Augustinian monastery at an auction after don Francisco Chepen's death. Because the amount of land was not stated, some years later the friars appropriated almost all the land in the area, claiming that they had purchased part of it and received the rest as a donation (AGN, Tierras de Comunidades, Leg. 5, Cuad. 38).

A third parcel of land, with a windmill on it, was auctioned to a Spaniard, Juan de Villegas, who later sold it to the monastery (doc. quoted ff 70r).

The land under the dominion of don Francisco Chepen in La Calera was at least 92 fanegadas (265.87 hectares). This is the amount that a Colonial decree, issued in 1596, recognized as his, and prohibited him from selling or donating during his lifetime (doc. quoted ff 70v).

2. Nampol (Fig. 1). In his will don Francisco Chepen stated: ". . . also, my part of the lands of Nampol" (doc. quoted, ff 65r). Nampol consisted of lands belonging to the local lords (Tierras Cacicales). It was shared by the Paramount Lord of the southern part of the Valley (Jequetepeque, Lloco, Puemape, and Tecapa), and the Paramount Lord of the northern part (Moro, Chepen, Cormot, and perhaps Cherrepe). This is the third instance of landholdings shared by at least two polities. After Chepen's donation, the Augustinians reinterpreted the will and took all the lands of Nampol, an action that resulted in long litigations between the lord of Jequetepeque and the monastery. Any interpretation of

"his part" in La Calera must include data on Nampol, since it is possible that La Calera lands were also Tierras Cacicales.[10]

Another piece of land measuring "3,500 varas" (approx. 3,300 meters) on the "border with the Pacasmayo [Jequetepeque] Valley" was donated by don Francisco Chepen to the Augustinian Monastery (doc. quoted ff 67r-67v). It is not clear if the measure is intended to be square varas or if it describes the length of one side. In any case, the ambiguity opened the way for claims and litigations for ownership. The exact location of this property is unclear, but its mention in the manuscript just after La Calera, suggests it was southeast of La Calera, on the north bank of the river, across from the Nampol lands.

3. Pocure (Fig. 1). After don Francisco Chepen's death, 20 fanegadas (57.8 hectares) of land in this area were sold at auction. Since these were mentioned with the third piece of land in La Calera, they were probably located nearby (doc. quoted ff 70).

Another piece of property measuring 3 fanegadas (8.67 hectares), which had a fruit and vegetable garden (huerta). It was sold to a Spaniard in 1609 after the death of don Francisco Chepen, who later (1623) sold it to the Augustinian monastery in Guadalupe (doc. quoted ff 71r-72r).

4. A vineyard, lands, houses, and Lagar (the meaning of which is unknown) were sold at auction after don Francisco Chepen's death and were bought by the Augustinian monastery in Talambo (doc. quoted ff 71r). The name of the property is not given, but the fact that it was purchased by the friars of Talambo suggests that it was close to the monastery. The price—699 pesos—gives an idea of the size of the property. Twenty fanegadas in La Calera were sold for 95 pesos. The amount paid for the property described here suggests it measured approximately 147 fanegadas (424.8 hectares).

---

10. Ramirez-Horton confused Nampol with Namalo located several kilometers away when she stated: "Lands called Namor [Namur, Namalo] served as open range on which to pasture livestock until the late seventeenth century, when they were cleared to become the hacienda Nampol" (1977:173).

Namalo or Namur was Cherrepe's town of Cormot and is located where the first town of Guadalupe was founded. Nampol, as already stated, consisted of Tierras Cacicales since pre-Hispanic times and was located south of the Jequetepeque River.

The total amount of land sold or donated by don Francisco Chepen amounted to well over 800 hectares, distributed in at least eight locations. It is impossible to determine exactly how much land was under his direct dominion because measurements were not given for some pieces, and because it is not known if all his lands were auctioned or given away. It should be noted that these lands appear to be under "his name," although the Cuenca (1977[1566]), and Toledo (1575) regulations abolished the lords' ownership of land and water and declared them communal property.

When a lord lost ownership of his land and water, under Colonial law he could reclaim the land as private property. While this was sometimes attempted, it was usually unsuccessful. Europeans were also interested in claiming the land, most of which was not being cultivated due to a lack of labor. Under Colonial law, uncultivated lands were declared vacant and subject to claim by Spaniards.

The lack of farm labor can be clearly illustrated: in 1572, when don Garcia Pilco Guaman was still alive, there were 189 tributaries in the Moro encomienda and 150 in the Chepen encomienda; in 1609, at the time of don Francisco Chepen's death, there were only 26 tributaries in Moro and 43 in Chepen (Cook 1982:80). Without workers to farm them, the lands became worthless. The lords lost their power and with it the ability to maintain a "court" and the non-agriculturalists who depended on agricultural products. They attempted to reestablish the reciprocity system by breeding European livestock but this was unsuccessful because the products were oriented to the European market. The venture provided money to pay salaries to their workers, but could not restore the traditional reciprocity based on agricultural labor.

Additional Property of the Curaca of Moro-Chepen

Don Garcia Pilco Guaman's will provides some information about the personal belongings of a high-ranking Curaca in the Jequetepeque Valley and the value of these belongings in the sixteenth century. However, it must be assumed that the personal properties of don Garcia Pilco Guaman were not necessarily typical of the possessions of every Curaca in Moro-Chepen. The will includes prestigious pre-Hispanic possessions as well as symbols of wealth and status introduced by the conquerors, which in some cases, replaced their pre-Hispanic counterparts.

The following description of his property is not complete, but includes his most valuable possessions—those that would be worth selling to pay debts and to provide just compensation to the people who served him during his lifetime. Based on known testaments of other Curacas (see Rostworowski 1982; Pease 1981), don Garcia Pilco Guaman would have been considered a "rich" man, although not the richest in the Andean area at that time.

Textiles and Clothing

The first items described were two chests containing European and Andean clothing and textiles. European clothing was not uncommon among Andean lords, who found it a new medium to symbolize their prestige and power.[11] The inventory included 29 different sets of clothing—a very large number for that time, especially considering that each set consisted of at least three garments.[12] Several sets of clothing allowed him to dress as a traditional high-ranking lord, while others permitted him to appear as a rich European in sixteenth-century Colonial Peru.

The Andean clothing included eight new sets made of polychrome tapestry, each with waist bands. One set was painted, two sets were of lion's color, two were red, one was "half" white, and there was a white anaco (shirt) made of cotton.

There were also two sets of women's clothing (in white), but it is unknown whether these were Andean or European.

There were three pairs of boots, two pairs of shoes, and three pairs of Andean sandals. Also listed were two black hats and a feather headdress—a combination of European elegance and a traditional Andean symbol of power. The feather headdress is significant because on the coast it was worn by a lord as a symbol of his rank (Cieza 1984[1553]:Ch. LXII, 195).

Also included were three pairs of gloves, two pairs of handkerchiefs, six pieces of fabric measuring 15 meters, and a number of "minor" pieces including hand towels, pillow and mattress cases, tablecloths, belts, and European jackets and pants.

---

11. For an example of a Curaca's clothing from Cajamarca, at the headwaters of the Jequetepeque River, see Rostworowski 1977b:277. Zevallos Quiñones (1975:126-127) provides several examples from the North Coast, which he sees as cultural degradation.
12. For the importance of clothes and textiles in the Andean society, see Murra 1975a:145-170. Valuable information about coastal clothing and the introduction of European garments among the natives can be found in Zevallos Quiñones 1975:107-127.

The detailed descriptions of the clothing and textiles demonstrate the high value and symbolic importance placed on them by the Andean population in general, and don Garcia Pilco Guaman in particular (Murra 1975a:145-170; Rostworowski 1977b:265-266; 1982:507-543).

Animals

A second important category in the will lists the animals that Pilco Guaman owned. There were four horses, three of which were mares. One mare was a foal and would not have been considered a horse in proper terms until it could be ridden (ADT CA, Leg, Exp. 204, ff 1v). It is interesting that the male horse had don Francisco Chepen's brand. The explanation for this could be that since high-ranking lords (Paramount Lords or Hatun Curacas) were forbidden to have more than two horses, and lower-ranking lords (Principales) were allowed to own one horse (Cuenca 1977[1566]:143; Rostworowski 1977c:122), Pilco Guaman transferred the ownership of one of his horses to Francisco Chepen.

Commoners were not permitted to own or ride horses, which were prestige symbols and helped to maintain the separation between lords and subjects. Riding a horse was equivalent to being carried in a litter, a prestige symbol that was prohibited by the Spaniards (Rostworowski 1977c:122). Obtaining a license to ride a horse was expensive: it cost two pesos, the price of a complete set of clothing or 1.2 hectares of land (based on the price paid for don Francisco Chepen's land). However, the cost was commensurate with the status conferred, as well as the power and authority implied. Although the Colonial tax on the right to ride a horse was intended to limit the Curacas' luxury, prestige, and wealth, as well as their political power, it only enhanced social distinctions and introduced new equivalents of traditional power symbols.

Pilco Guaman also claimed ownership of 36 cows and bulls and 860 sheep and goats. There is no mention of llamas or alpacas, but it is known that they existed in Moro in 1582 (Ramirez-Horton 1982:134, note 14). Moreover, at the auction, Pilco Guaman's sandals were described as made of llama wool (ADT, CO, Leg. 154, Exp. 204). The llamas may not have been listed because they belonged to the Curacazgo of Moro-Chepen, or they belonged to Pilco Guaman but were considered by the family too important to sell at the auction after his death. Refusing to sell camelids is not unusual—it can also be observed in the testament of don Alonso Caruatongo, Lord of the Guaranga of Guzmango, Cajamarca (Rostworowski 1977b).

Miscellaneous Items

Included in the will was an arcabuz, a firearm forbidden to lords and commoners (Cuenca 1977[1566]:148). Why Pilco Guaman had a firearm is not known. Perhaps it was simply a Spanish symbol of power, used to support pre-Hispanic ideology. Also mentioned are: two saddles (an appropriate number for the horses he was allowed to own legally), two candelabras, spare parts for his wagon, tools for shoeing horses, three cow-bells, three plows, one machete, and several other small tools and miscellaneous items.

Two trumpets from Mexico included in the will deserve special mention because trumpets were pre-Hispanic symbols of power and authority on the North Coast of Peru as well as in the highlands of Cajamarca (Rostworowski 1977b:269,273). Here, as in the case of horses that replaced litters, or the arcabuz, an "imported" object replaced its Andean counterpart, and thereby added to the Curaca's prestige and authority.

Obligations

The testament also contains a list of obligations that don Garcia Pilco Guaman owed to people that appear to have been his servants, a group of four women and ten men. Three of the male servants were shepherds, but it is not clear whether the animals they tended were European or Andean. Two of the women received tablecloths, and the other two women and all of the men were given from two to twenty pesos each. Additionally, he had an obligation to a low-ranking lord named Pucala and his "Indians," who received 25 fanegas (1,477.27 kilograms) of maize in compensation for damage to their fields by Pilco Guaman's oxen.

Don Francisco Chepen owed 50 fanegas (2,954.54 kilograms) of wheat to Pilco Guaman. Two Spaniards living in the valley, Juan Portugues and Hernan Garcia, owed him 9 pesos and one toston (the amount of which is not known), respectively.

The few obligations indicate that he was not engaged in the intense commercial exchange in which other lords participated, such as the one in Colan mentioned by Rostworowski (1982) or Moquegua, studied by Pease (1981:193-229, especially pages 209-221). This apparent lack of involvement in the European market affirms the evidence that he passively resisted integration into the Colonial system.

Conclusions

Judging in part from his will, and in part from the property disbursed by his successor, it appears that don Garcia Pilco Guaman, the Curaca of Moro-Chepen, was one of the highest-ranking lords in the Jequetepeque Valley. Extensive landholdings, many animals, and items symbolic of prestige and power constituted the properties of this lord.[13] In contrast, documents suggest that commoners in the Jequetepeque Valley owned only objects of little value— some small and medium-sized vessels which they used for their meals and drinks (AGN, Derecho Indigena y Encomienda, Leg. 2, Cuad. 26, 1580, ff 401r, 404v).

The pre-Hispanic basis of the lords' power in the Jequetepeque Valley was their ownership of all farmlands, water, and irrigation ditches. They distributed land and water to members of their communities in exchange for services, either agricultural labor or production of arts and crafts. This exchange was the basis of the reciprocal system. When the Spanish abolished the lords' ownership of lands and water and declared them to be communal property, a large part of their power base was destroyed.

The exercise of power implied the use of diverse symbols, including clothing, trumpets, litters, servants, and guards. Textiles and clothing appear to have been the most important symbols of power and wealth in the valley, as in other parts of the Andean area. The possession of large numbers of animals was another sign of wealth, both in pre-Hispanic and Colonial times. Following the Conquest, new symbols of power and prestige were introduced by the Spaniards. European clothing was added to traditional Andean attire, and the privilege of riding a horse became the equivalent of being carried in a litter.

A great deal more information must be compiled before the polities, chiefdoms or Curacazgos of the Jequetepeque Valley can be understood. Ideally, this will involve a combination of enthno-historic and archaeological research to determine the geographical location of settlements, the boundaries of political and economic units, and the activities that took place in different locations. But a true understanding of how the pre-Hispanic and early Colonial Period polities functioned, is impossible without an appreciation of the material and ideological basis of the lords' power. As this study has demonstrated, careful analysis of the power and wealth of specific lords can provide valuable data for reconstructing this aspect of Andean society.

---

13. It should be noted that at the time the documents used here registered the lords' valuables, most of the lords in the Andean area were already impoverished.

RESUMEN:
Poder y Riqueza en el Valle del Jequetepeque Durante el siglo XVI

Para entender las bases y el ejercicio del poder en el Valle del Jequetepeque durante la época pre-hispánica y los primeros años del periodo colonial, en este artículo se examinan los bienes que poseía un Hatun Curaca, don García Pilco Guamán, señor de Moro y Chepén, la más alta autoridad étnica en la parte norte del valle. Para ello se usa su testamento, encontrado en el Archivo Departamental de La Libertad, así como otros documentos sobre todo litigios entre los frailes Agustinos del Convento de Guadalupe con las comunidades del área.

Es posible que Pilco Guamán haya nacido entre 1500 y 1520, por lo que, cuando hizo su testamento, en 1582, no sabía firmar. El murió entre el 20 de junio y el 11 de agosto de dicho año, cuando sus bienes fueron rematados en pública almoneda. Fue sucedido en el Curacazgo por don Francisco Chepén, quién posteriormente hizo grandes donaciones de tierras al Convento Agustino del valle. Siendo éste el origen de disputas que duraron más de doscientos años.

La base de su poder estuvo en que, durante la época pre-hispánica, en la Costa Norte, todas las tierras y el agua pertenecían al Curaca Principal, quien las entregaba en usufructo a los miembros de la etnia, quienes, a su vez, se veían obligados a dar mano de obra como pago por este favor. La reciprocidad andina, de esta manera, tenía sus bases en principios ideológicos y factores socio-económicos.

La legislación colonial introdujo, desde muy temprano, modificaciones que alteraron el sistema, introduciendo, entre otros muchos cambios, la propiedad individual y la comunal, lo que afectó las bases del poder de los grandes Curacas del Valle del Jequetepeque.

Tierras bajo dominio del Curaca de Moro-Chepén

Esta es la primera vez que, en la Costa Norte, se pueden identificar tierras que estaban bajo dominio directo de un Hatun Curaca y que posiblemente lo estuviesen durante el período pre-hispánico. Ellas incluyeron (Fig. 1):

1. *Namalo, Namul o Namur. El cerro y el asentamiento pre-hispánico donde se erigió el primer Convento de Guadalupe y el primer pueblo con dicho nombre, conocido también como Farfancillo. Los habitantes de Chérrepe lo llamaban Cormot y allí tenían residencia los agricultores de dicho señorio. Pareciese ser, que en la época pre-hispánica, vivía allí gente de Moro-Chepén y de Chérrepe, Curacazgo que a su vez habría sido dependiente politicamente, durante el periodo pre-hispánico, del Hatun Curaca de Moro-Chepén.*

2. *Chule, asentamiento pre-hispánico conocido también como Chulle, Chulle Melica, o Chulle Millea. Hoy se le conoce como El Trust o Moro, en el área de Talambo (ésta, así como varias otras identificaciones, se han hecho con la generosa colaboración de Luis Lostaunau R.).*

3. *Hizo, asentamiento pre-hispánico conocido como Izo, Izocotón, Socotón, Ñocotón o Cotón. Es probablemente la Huaca Coton y el Ñoquique de Chérrepe.*

4. *Moro, asentamiento pre-hispánico donde vivía Pilco Guamán.*

5. *Pisopón, asentamiento pre-hispánico que podría ser el Chepén viejo.*

En todos estos lugares Pilco Guamán declaró tener ganado y chacras.

Por las donaciones hechas por don Francisco Chepén al Convento Agustino, se sabe que también pertenecían al Hatun Curaca de Moro-Chepén:

1. *La Calera, donde está Farfán, era el centro administrativo Chimú en el valle.*
   La Calera, fue otro sector con el mismo nombre.
   Un tercer sector, en la misma área, vendido a un español. Los tres pedazos sumaban 285.88 hectáreas.

2. *Ñampol, que eran Tierras Cacicales, compartidas con el Hatun Curaca de la parte sur del valle, el señor de Jequetepeque, Puémape, Lloco y Tecapa.*

3. *Dos chacras llamadas Pocure, una de 57.8 y la otra de 8.67 hectáreas.*

4. *Un viñedo, tierras y casas en Talambo.*

El total de tierras donadas por don Francisco Chepén fue de más de 800 hectáreas, de dominio directo del señor de Moro-Chepén, donde probablemente se producía para su sustento y el del mantenimiento de la red de reciprocidad inherente a su cargo.

Otras Propiedades del Curaca de Moro-Chepén

En el testamento de Pilco Guamán se incluyen:

Tejidos y Ropa

Dos baúles conteniendo 29 trajes completos (tanto europeos como andinos) compuestos cada uno de varias piezas, tres pares de botas, dos de zapatos y tres de ojotas, dos sombreros negros y un tocado de plumas, tres pares de guantes y dos de pañuelos. Entre las piezas menores: toallas, fundas de almohadas y colchones, manteles, cinturones y casacas europeas, así como varios cortes de tela. El grado de detalle denota la importancia que los tejidos tuvieron para la población andina.

Animales

Un caballo y tres yeguas, 36 vacas y 860 cabras y ovejas. No se mencionan camélidos aunque, por otras referencias, se sabe que los tuvo.

Miscelánea

Un Arcabuz, riendas para sus caballos, herraduras, clavos, piezas para carretas, 2 candelabros, herramientas de herrero, tres campanillas para sus vacas, un machete, dos trompetas Mejicanas, así como una diversidad de otros objetos.

Obligaciones

Tenía 14 sirvientes (yanacuna?), cuatro mujeres y diez hombres a los que les dejó tejidos y dinero. Así mismo, a un principal llamado Pucala le debía casi una tonelada y media de maíz.

Don Francisco Chepén le debía a Pilco Guamán casi tres toneladas de trigo, y los europeos Juan Portugués y Hernan García le debían dinero.

Conclusión

El prestigio y el poder del Hatun Curaca en el Valle del Jequetepeque estaba basado en la propiedad de tierras y agua, así como el ejercicio de dominio directo de grandes extensiones de tierra, las que eran cultivadas por sus súbditos. También, la posesión de gran número de animales y el uso de numerosos símbolos de poder (vestido, literas, caballos, adornos, etc), no sólo constituían parte de su riqueza, sino que formaban parte del recubrimiento ideológico que permitía la existencia organizada de la sociedad.

En contraste, los miembros de las comunidades eran descritos como propietarios de vasijas pequeñas y medianas, usadas para preparar y consumir sus alimentos y su chicha.

Es en estas diferencias, donde se puede evaluar las dimensiones del poder y la riqueza de los Hatun Curaca, así como las relaciones entre los señores y sus súbditos.

Bibliography

Altamirano, Alfredo
    1984   *Sacrificios de Camelidos en Pacatnamú*. Programa
         Academico de Arqueología. Lima: Universidad Nacional
         Mayor San Marcos. Unpublished manuscript.

Arnett, R.H.
    1968   *The Beetles of the United States*. Ann Arbor: American
         Entomological Institute.

Basadre, Jorge
    1937   *Historia del Derecho Peruano*. Biblioteca Peruana de
         Ciencias Juridicas y Sociales. Lima: Editorial Antena.

Bawden, Garth
    1977   Galindo and the Nature of the Middle Horizon in
         Northern Coastal Peru. Ph.D. dissertation, Department
         of Anthropology, Harvard University.
    1982   "Galindo: A Study in Cultural Transition during the
         Middle Horizon." In *Chan Chan: Andean Desert City*.
         Michael E. Moseley and Kent C. Day (eds.).
         Albuquerque: University of New Mexico Press.

Bonavia, Duccio
    1958   "Lostaunau y la Arqueología Peruana." *El Comercio*,
         Suplemento Dominical. 6 de julio:2-5.
    1974   *Ricchata Quellcani: Pinturas Murales Prehispánicas*.
         Lima: Fondo del Libro del Banco Industrial del Perú.
    1985   *Mural Painting in Ancient Peru*. Patricia J. Lyon (trans).
         Bloomington: Indiana University Press.

Bruce, Susan Lee
    In press   "Textile Miniatures from Pacatnamu." *The Junius B.
         Bird Andean Textile Conference 1984*. Washington, D.C.:
         The Textile Museum.
    1982   Adobe Seriation: The Site Reconstruction of Chotuna-
         Chornancap, Peru. M.A. thesis, Department of
         Anthropology, University of California, Los Angeles.
    1983   Textiles from the North Coast of Peru, A.D. 600-1600.
         Unpublished manuscript.

Burga, Manuel
    1976   *De la Encomienda a la Hacienda Capitalista: El Valle
         del Jequetepeque del Siglo XVI al XX*. Estudios de la
         Sociedad Rural 4. Lima: Instituto de Estudios Peruanos.

Calancha, Fray Antonio de la
    1975-1982 [1638]   *Coronica Moralizada del Orden de San
         Agustin en el Perú, con Sucesos Egemplares en esta
         Monarquia*. Ignacio Prado Pastor (ed.). Cronicas del
         Perú. Vols. 4-9. Lima.

Cieza de Leon, Pedro de
    1959   *The Incas*. Harriet de Onis (trans.), Wolfgang von
         Hagen (ed.). The Civilization of the American Indian
         Series. Vol 53. Norman: University of Oklahoma Press.
    1984[1553]   *La Cronica del Perú*. Vol. 1. Lima: Fondo
         Editorial Pontificia Universidad Catolica del Perú-
         Academia Nacional de la Historia.

Cock, Guillermo A.
    1976-1977   "Los Kurakas de las Collaguas: Poder Politico y
         Poder Economico." *Historia y Cultura* 10:95-118. Lima:
         Museo Nacional de Historia.
    1978   "Ayllu, Territorio y Frontera en los Collaguas." In
         Etnohistoria y Antropologia Andina. Marcia Koth de
         Paredes and Amalia Castelli (eds.). Lima: Primera
         Jornada del Museo Nacional de Historia.
    1981   "El Ayllu en la Sociedad Andina: Alcances y
         Perspectivas." In *Etnohistoria y Antropologia Andina*.
         Amalia Castelli, Marcia Koth de Paredes, and Mariana
         Mould de Pease (eds.). Lima: Segunda Jornada del
         Museo Nacional de Historia.
    1985   From the Powerful to the Powerless: The Jequetepeque
         Valley Lords in the 16th Century, Peru. M.A. thesis,
         Archaeology Program, University of California, Los
         Angeles.

Conrad, Geoffrey W.
    1974   Burial Platforms and Related Structures on the North
            Coast of Peru: Some Social and Political Implications.
            Ph.D. dissertation, Harvard University.
    1982   "The Burial Platforms of Chan Chan: Some Social and
            Political Implications." In *Chan Chan: Andean Desert
            City.* Michael E. Moseley and Kent C. Day (eds.).
            Albuquerque: University of New Mexico Press.

Cook, Noble David
    1982   "Population Data for Indian Peru: Sixteenth and
            Seventeenth Centuries." *Hispanic American Historical
            Review* 62(1):73-120. Durham: Duke University Press.

Cordy-Collins, Alana and Donna McClelland
    1983   "Upstreaming along the Peruvian North Coast."
            Proceedings 44th International Congress of
            Americanists. *Test and Image in Pre-Columbian Art.*
            Janet C. Berlo (ed.). Oxford: BAR International Series
            180.

Cuenca, Gregorio Gonzalez de
    1977[1566]   "Ordenanzas de los Indios." (Paleographical
            version by P. Ortiz de Zevallos and G. Cock.) *Historia
            y Cultura* 9:126-154. Lima: Museo Nacional de Historia.

Day, Kent C.
    1974   "Walk-in Wells and Water Management at Chan Chan,
            Peru." In *The Rise and Fall of Civilizations: Modern
            Archaeological Approaches to Ancient Cultures.*
            Compiled by C.C. Lamberg-Karlovsky and J.A. Sabloff.
            Menlo Park: Cummings Publishing Company.
    1982   "Ciudadelas: Their Form and Function." In *Chan Chan:
            Andean Desert City.* Michael E. Moseley and Kent C. Day
            (eds.). Albuquerque: New Mexico Press.

Disselhoff, Hans Dietrich
    1958   "Tumbas de San Jose de Moro (Provincia de Paca Mayo
            Peru)." In Proc. 32nd Inter. Cong. of Americanists.
            364–367. Copenhagen.

Donnan, Christopher B.
    1978   *Moche Art of Peru.* Los Angeles: Museum of Cultural
            History, University of California.

Donnan, Christopher B. and Donna McClelland
    1979   *The Burial Theme in Moche Iconography.* Studies in
            Pre-Columbian Art and Archaeology No. 21. Washington,
            D.C.: Dumbarton Oaks.

Emery, Irene
    1980   *The Primary Structure of Fabrics.* Washington, D.C.: The
            Textile Museum.

Emery, Irene and Mary Elizabeth King
    1957   "Additional Examples of an Unusual Peruvian Shirt
            Type." *American Antiquity* 23(1):71-4.

Evans, E.G.
    1962   "The Mummy Case 1. The Pathological Investigation."
            Medical Science Law 2:33-47.

Ewing, H.E.
    1924   "Lice from Human Mummies." *Science* 60(1556):389-390.

Garcia Rosell, C.
    1942   *Los Monumentos Arqueologicos del Perú.* Lima.

Garcilaso de la Vega, El Inca
    1960[1614]   *Obras Completas del Inca Garcilaso de la Vega.*
            4 vols. Biblioteca de Autores Españoles. Vols 132-135.
            Madrid: Ediciones Atlas.

Gayton, Anna H.
    1955   "A New Type of Ancient Peruvian Shirt." *American
            Antiquity* 20(3):263-70.

Gilmore, Raymond M.
    1950   "Fauna and Ethnozoology of South America."
            Handbook of South American Indians. Vol. 6. J.H.
            Steward (ed.). Bureau of American Ethnology Bulletin
            143. Washington, D.C.: Smithsonian Institution.

Guaman Poma de Ayala, Felipe
  1980[1614] *El Primer Nueva Coronica y Buen Gobierno.*
        3 vols. John V. Murra and Rolena Adorno (eds.).
        Mexico: Siglo XXI.

Hagopian, Ralph V.
  1947 "Black Vultures and Live Prey." *Auk* 64:132.

Harris, Milton (ed.)
  1954 *Handbook of Textile Fibers.* Washington, D.C.

Hastings, C. Mansfield and M. Edward Moseley
  1975 "The Adobes of Huaca del Sol and Huaca de la Luna."
        American Antiquity 40(2):196-203.

Hecker, Giesela and Wolfgang Hecker
  1977 *Archaologische Untersuchungan in Pacatnamu,
        Nord-Peru.* Indiana, Beihheft 9. Berlin: Mann.
  1982 *Pacatnamu: Vorspanische Stadt in Nord-peru.* Munich:
        Verlag C.H. Beck.
  1985 *Pacatnamu y sus Construcciones.* Frankfurt: Verlag
        Klaus Dieter Vervuert.

Hutchinson, Thomas J.
  1873 *Two years in Peru with Exploration of Its Antiquities.*
        London: S. Low, Marston, Low and Searle.

Ishida, Eiichiro et al.
  1960 *Andes 1: Report of the University of Tokyo Scientific
        Expedition to the Andes in 1958.* Tokyo: Kadokawa
        Publishing Co.

Johnston, W. and G. Villeneuve
  1897 "On the Medico-legal Application of Entomology."
        Montreal Medical Journal 26:81-90.

Keatinge, Richard W.
  1974 "Chimu Rural Administrative Centres in the Moche
        Valley, Peru." *World Archaeology* 6:66-82.
  1977 "Religious Forms and Secular Functions: The
        Expansion of State Bureaucracies as Reflected in the
        Prehistoric Architecture on the Peruvian North Coast."
        Annals of the New York Academy of Science
        293:229-245.
  1978 "The Pacatnamu Textiles." *Archaeology* 31:30-41.
  1982 "The Chimu Empire in a Regional Perspective: Cultural
        Continuities." In *Chan Chan: Andean Desert City.*
        Michael E. Moseley and Kent C. Day (eds.).
        Albuquerque: University of New Mexico Press.

Keatinge, Richard W. and Geoffrey W. Conrad
  1983 "Imperialist Expansion in Peruvian Prehistory: Chimu
        Administration of a Conquered Territory." *Journal of
        Field Archaeology* 10(3):255-283.

Keatinge, Richard W. et al.
  1975 "From the Sacred to the Secular: First Report on a
        Prehistoric Architectural Transition on the Peruvian
        North Coast." *Archaeology* 28:128-129.

Kolata, Alan Louis
  1978 Chan Chan: The Form of the City in Time. Ph.D.
        dissertation, Department of Anthropology, Harvard
        University.
  1982 "Chronology and Settlement Growth at Chan Chan." In
        Chan Chan: Andean Desert City. Michael E. Moseley
        and Kent C. Day (eds.). Albuquerque: University of New
        Mexico Press.

Kosok, Paul
  1965 *Life, Land and Water in Ancient Peru.* New York: Long
        Island University Press.

Kroeber, Alfred L.
  1930 "Archaeological Explorations in Peru, Part II: The
        Northern Coast." *Anthropology Memoirs* 2(2). Chicago:
        Field Museum of Natural History.

Lapiner, Alan
  1976 *Pre-Columbian Art of South America.* New York: Harry N.
        Abrams, Inc.

Ligon, J. David
    1967   "Relationships of the Cathartid Vultures." *Occasional
            Papers of the Museum of Zoology* 165. Ann Arbor:
            University of Michigan.

Lovell, Harvey B.
    1947   "Black Vultures Kill Young Pigs." *Auk* 64:131-132.
    1952   "Black Vulture Depredations at Kentucky Woodlands."
            Wilson Bulletin 64:48-49.

Lundt, H.
    1964   "Ecological Observations about the Invasion of Insects
            in Carcasses Buried in Soils." *Pedobiologia* 4:158.

Mauersberger, Herbert R. (ed.)
    1947   *Matthews' Textile Fibers: Their Physical, Microscopical,
            and Chemical Properties.* 5th ed. New York: Wiley &
            Sons, Inc.

McIlhenny, E.A.
    1939   "Feeding Habits of Black Vultures." *Auk* 88:672-673.

McKern, Thomas W. and T.D. Stewart
    1957   "Skeletal Age Changes in Young American Males,
            Analyzed from the Standpoint of Identification."
            Technical Report EP-45. Natick, Mass.: Headquarters
            Quartermaster Research and Development Command.

Medina, Felipe de
    1904[1650]   "Relacion del . . . Visitador General de las
            Idolatrias . . . Que se han descubierto en el pueblo de
            Huacho, donde ha comenzado a visitar desde 19 de
            febrero hasta 23 de marzo de 1650." In *La Imprenta en
            Lima (1584-1824), Tomo I (1584-1650)*:215-221. Jose
            Toribio Medina (ed.). Santiago de Chile: Fondo
            Editorial Jose Toribio Medina.

Megnin, P.
    1894   "La Faune des Cadavres: Application de L'entomologie
            a la Médecine Légale." *Encyclopédie Scientifique des
            Aides Mémoire.* Paris: Masson.

Middendorf, E.W.
    1894   "Das Kustenlan von Peru." *Peru.* Vol. 2. Berlin: Robert
            Oppenheim.

Moseley, M. Edward
    1975   "Prehistoric Principles of Labor Organization in the
            Moche Valley, Peru." *American Antiquity* 40(2):191-196.

Mrosovsky, N.
    1971   "Black Vultures Attack Live Turtle Hatchlings." *Auk*
            88:672-673.

Murra, John V.
    1975a   "La Funcion del Tejido en varios Contextos Sociales y
            Politicos." In *Formaciones Economicas y Politicas del
            Mundo Andino.* John V. Murra (ed.). Lima: Instituto de
            Estudios Peruanos.
    1975b   "El control Vertical de un Maximo de Pisos Ecologicos
            en la Economía de las Sociedades Andinas." In
            *Formaciones Economicas y Politicas del Mundo
            Andino.* John V. Murra (ed.). Lima: Instituto de Estudios
            Peruanos.

Netherly, Patricia Joan
    1977   Local Level Lords on the North Coast of Peru. Ph.D.
            dissertation, Department of Anthropology, Cornell
            University, Ithaca, New York.

Nuroteva, P.
    1977   "Sarcosaprophagous Insects as Forensic Indicators." In
            Forensic Medicine. C.D. Tedeschi, W.G. Eckert, and L.G.
            Tedeschi (eds.). Philadelphia/London/Toronto:
            Saunder.

Olson, Storrs L.
    1985   "The Fossil History of Birds." In *Avian Biology.* D.S.
            Farner, J.R. King, and K.C. Parkes (eds.). Orlando,
            Florida: Academic Press.

O'Neale, Lila
    1935   "Peque Prendas Ceremoniales de Paracas." *Revista del Museo Nacional* 4(2):245-266. Lima: Museo Nacional.

Pease, Franklin
    1981   "Las Relaciones entre las Tierras Altas y la Costa del Sur del Perú." In *Estudios Monograficos del Perú Meridional*. Shozo Masuda (ed.). Tokyo: University of Tokyo Press.

Payne, J.A.
    1965   "A Summer Carrion Study of the Baby Pig Sus Scrofa Linnaeus." *Ecology* 46:592.

Pozorski, Thomas G.
    1971   Survey and Excavation of Burial Platforms at Chan Chan. B.A. Honors Paper, Department of Anthropology, Harvard University.

Ramirez-Horton, Susan
    1977   Land Tenure and the Economics of Colonial Peru. Ph.D. dissertation, Department of History, University of Wisconsin, Madison.
    1979   "Cherrepe en 1572: Un Análisis de la Visita General del Virrey Francisco de Toledo." *Historia y Cultura* 11:79-121. Lima: Museo Nacional de Historia.
    1981   "La Organizacion Economica de la Costa Norte: Un Análisis Preliminar del Período Prehispánico Tardio." In *Etnohistoria y Antropologia Andina*. Amalia Castelli, Marcia Koth de Paredes, and Mariana Mould de Pease (eds.). Lima: Segunda Jornada del Museo Nacional de Historia.
    1982   "Retainers of the Lord or Merchants: A Case of Mistaken Identity." In *El Hombre y su Ambiente en los Andes Centrales*. Luis Millones and Hiroyasu Tomoeda (eds.). Senri Ethnological Studies 10. Osaka: National Museum of Ethnology.

Rea, Amadeo M.
    1983   "Cathartidae Affinities: A Brief Overview." In *The Biology and Management of Vultures of the World*. S.R. Wilbur and J.A. Jackson (eds.). Berkeley: University of California Press.

RGI
    1965   *Relaciones Geograficas de Indias*. Marcos Jimenes de la Espada (ed.). 3 vols. Madrid: Biblioteca de Autores Españoles.

Robbins, Chandler S. et al.
    1982   *Birds of North America: A Guide to Field Identification*. New York: Golden Press.

Robicsek, Francis and Donald Hales
    1984   "Maya Heart Sacrifice: Cultural Perspective and Surgical Technique." In *Ritual Human Sacrifice in Mesoamerica*. Elizabeth H. Boone (ed.). Washington, D.C.: Dumbarton Oaks.

Rostworowski de Diez Canseco, Maria
    1972   "Las Etnias del Valle del Chillon." *Revista del Museo Nacional* 38:250-314. Lima: Museo de la Cultura Peruana.
    1975   "Pescadores, Astesanos y Mercaderes Costeños en el Perú Prehispánico." *Revista del Museo Nacional* 1:311-349. Lima: Museo de la Cultura Peruana.
    1977a *Etnia y Sociedad, Costa Peruana Prehispánica*. Lima: Instituto de Estudios Peruanos.
    1977b "La Estatificacion Social y el Hatun Curaca en el Mundo Andino." *Historica* 1(2):249-285. Lima.
    1977c "Algunos Comentarios Hechos a las Ordenanzas del Doctor Cuenca." *Historia y Cultura* 9:119-125. Lima: Museo Nacional de Historia.
    1981   *Recursos Naturales Renovables y Pesca, Siglos XVI y XVII*. Historia Andina 8. Lima: Instituto de Estudios Peruanos.

1982   "Testamento de don Luis de Colan: Curaca en 1622."
      Revista del Museo Nacional 46:507-543. Lima: Museo
      del la Cultura Peruana.

Rowe, John Howland
1946   "Inca Culture at the Time of the Spanish Conquest." In
      Handbook of South American Indians. Vol. 2. Julian H.
      Steward (ed.). Bureau of American Ethnology Bulletin
      143. Washington, D.C.: Smithsonian Institution.
1948   "The Kingdom of Chimor." *Acta Americana* 6(1-2):26-59.

Santillan, Fernando de
1927[1563]   "Relacion." In *Historia de los Incas y Relacion de
      su Gobierno.* Coleci"n de Libros y Documentos
      Referentes a la Historia, Segunda Serie, no. 9. Lima:
      Imprenta y Libreria Sanmarti.

Schaedel, Richard P.
1951   "Major Ceremonial and Population Centers in Northern
      Peru." In *The Civilizations of Ancient America, Selected
      Papers of the 29th International Congress of
      Americanists.* Sol Tax (ed.). Chicago: University of
      Chicago Press.

Schaffer, Anne-Louise
1983   "Cathartidae in Moche Art and Culture." Proceedings
      44th International Congress of Americanists. *Flora and
      Fauna Imagery in Precolumbian Cultures: Iconography
      and Function.* Jeanette F. Peterson (ed.). Oxford: BAR
      International Series 171.

Shimada, Izumi
1976   Socioeconomic Organization at Moche V Pampa
      Grande, Peru: Prelude to a Major Transformation to
      Come. Ph.D. dissertation, Department of Anthropology,
      University of Arizona.

Stager, Kenneth E.
1964   "The Role of Olfaction in Food Location by the Turkey
      Vulture (*Cathartes aura*)." Los Angeles County Museum
      Contribution. *Science* 81.

Stumer, Louis M. and Anna H. Gayton
1958   "A Horizontal-Necked Shirt from Marques, Peru."
      American Antiquity 13(2):181-182.

Topic, John R. and Theresa Lange Topic
1978   The Archaeological Investigation of Andean Militarism:
      Some Cautionary Observations. Department of
      Anthropology, Trent University, Ontario. Unpublished
      manuscript.

Ubbelohde-Doering, Heinrich
1959   "Bericht über archäologishe Feldarbeitein in Peru." Vol.
      2. *Ethnos* 1-2. Stockholm.
1960   "Bericht, überarchäologische Feldarbeiten in Perú."
      Vol. 2. *Ethnos* 3–4. Stockholm.
1967   *On the Royal Highways of the Inca.* New York: Frederick
      A. Praeger.

Valcarcel, Luis E.
1971   *Historia del Perú Antiguo.* 3 vols. Lima: Editorial Juan
      Mejia Baca.

Van Stan, Ina
1961   "Miniature Peruvian Shirts with Horizontal Neck
      Openings." *American Antiquity* 26(4):524-531
1967   *Textiles From Beneath the Temple of Pachacamac,
      Peru.* A part of the Uhle Collection of the University
      Museum, University of Pennsylvania, Philadelphia.

Weiss, Pedro
1961   *Ostelogia Cultural: Practicas Cefálicas.* Vol. 2. Lima:
      Universidad Nacional Mayor de San Marcos.

Zevallos Quiñones, Jorge
1975   "La Ropa de Tributo de las Encomiendas Trujillanas en
      el Siglo XVI." *Historia y Cultura* 7:107-127. Lima: Museo
      Nacional de Historica.

Credits

Design/Coordination	*Robert Woolard*
Editing	*Irina Averkieff*
Type	*American Typesetting, Inc.*
Printing	*Alan Lithograph*
Binding	*Roswell Bookbinding Co.*